STAR WARS
ORIGAMI

Library of Congress Cataloging-in-Publication Data is available.

ISBN 978-0-7611-7344-1

Design by Netta Rabin
Origami paper illustrations by Phil Conigliaro
Origami designs, diagrams, and text by Chris Alexander

Workman books are available at special discounts when
purchased in bulk for premiums and sales promotions as well
as for fund-raising or educational use. Special editions or
book excerpts can also be created to specification. For details,
contact the Special Sales Director at the address below, or send
an e-mail to specialmarkets@workman.com.

Workman Publishing Company, Inc.
225 Varick Street
New York, NY 10014-4381

workman.com
starwars.com

Printed in the United States of America
First printing July 2012

10 9 8 7 6 5 4 3 2

STAR WARS® ORIGAMI

6 Amazing Paper-folding Projects   **from a Galaxy Far, Far Away. . . .**

CHRIS ALEXANDER

WORKMAN PUBLISHING ✸ NEW YORK

FOR MY MOM, JAN

A truly luminous being

ACKNOWLEDGMENTS

I'd like to take this time to thank several people who have had a lot to do with this book becoming a reality: First and foremost, Jan Alexander, who started me down the origami path when I was just four years old. Colleen O'Rourke, Fran Siller, and Ira Nixon: Without their love, friendship, and support through the years I would have long ago given up any hope that the book would ever be published. Chris Colquhoun, who, fifteen years ago, planted the seed that was to become this book. Tom Purpus and the numerous volunteers who've joined me at *Star Wars* events to teach my origami to the public. Origami masters Robert Lang and Michael La Fosse, for their encouragement. Tom Angleberger and Troy Alders, for putting the buzz in the right ears.
The hardworking talent at Workman Publishing, especially Raquel Jaramillo, Krestyna Lypen, Phil Conigliaro, Netta Rabin, and Beth Levy, for taking that buzz and making it a reality.
And of course, Mr. George Lucas, without whom the galaxy far, far away would never have existed.

CONTENTS

FOREWORD

MY LIFE PRETTY MUCH REVOLVES around *Star Wars* origami. I love it. I love to fold it. I love to try to invent new models. But the truth is, I'm not that good at it. I'm just a Padawan. Chris Alexander is a Jedi Master. And, like Yoda, he has a lot to teach the rest of us. Take his *Millennium Falcon*: It's beautiful to look at, but to really appreciate it you have to fold it yourself. It's a masterpiece of traditional origami technique, a simple yet elegant design. And though it took a Jedi Master to create it, us Padawans will be able to fold it, too—if we follow his careful and easy-to-follow directions. That's why I'm so excited for this book to finally exist. I'm happy that everyone will now have access to this amazing teacher . . . especially me!

Now—since I've used up all my specially designed paper (shout-out to Phil Conigliaro!) to fold Yodas—it's time for me to learn how to fold Chris' Jabba the Hutt! It is so stooky!

—TOM ANGLEBERGER,
author of *The Strange Case of Origami Yoda, Darth Paper Strikes Back,* and *The Secret of the Fortune Wookiee*

A LONG TIME AGO IN A GALAXY FAR, FAR AWAY. . . .

WITH THESE WORDS, *STAR WARS,* A SAGA of epic proportions, was born. First appearing in movie theaters on May 25, 1977, it had all the elements of a timeless myth: heroes, villains, monsters, knights, a princess in distress, and a climactic battle of good and evil.

Of course, the *Star Wars* universe also captivated audiences with its extraordinary aliens, droids, creatures, vehicles, and starships. Their distinctive shapes from long ago and far away are perfectly suited for re-creation in the present through the ancient art of origami. And so, a little bit of time ago, in a town in California that is not so far away, the concept for this book was born.

Origami can be defined as the Japanese art of sculpting by folding a piece of paper. Its exact origins are unknown, but it probably dates back to A.D. 600, when a Buddhist priest introduced Chinese papermaking methods to Japan. The Japanese saw the potential for shapes and forms in the paper. Throughout the ensuing centuries, the Japanese learned how to re-create the birds and animals around them, turning paper folding into an art form.

The purest form of origami starts with a single square of paper. Tearing the sheet, taping pieces together, or using tools to help the folding process are not allowed. Some artists, however, believe that as long as the paper is folded it can begin as any shape; you can cut the paper, glue it, or even combine multiple pieces of paper. My opinion is somewhere in the middle. I prefer not to glue the paper, but the number of pieces and starting shape are irrelevant, as long as it's within reason. As you explore this ancient art form and encounter the incredible variety of figures that can be made from a simple piece of paper, you can make your own decisions.

This book contains instructions for re-creating thirty-six objects, creatures, and characters from the *Star Wars* universe with just a simple piece of paper (or two). Though you can do the projects in any order you choose, there are four levels of difficulty: Youngling, Padawan, Jedi Knight, and Jedi Master. Unless you're already an origami guru, you might want to start with the Youngling or Padawan models first.

The diagrams in this book are designed to help you visualize the steps, and because of this, some of the edges are offset. Do not take these literally. By making all of your creases as accurate as possible, your model will be easier to fold and look neater when finished.

For example, in the center diagram to the right, the edges do not meet in the middle. But when properly folded there will be a sharp point at the top, and the edges will line up perfectly.

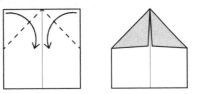

A typical diagram   *What your paper should look like*

When making a fold, glance ahead to the next step to see what it should look like when completed. It is very important to line up each fold as accurately as you can, especially in the earlier stages of the model. Try to start the crease right at a corner or point, and line up the edges along another edge or crease. Once you have the fold lined up, be sure to crease the paper sharply by running your fingernail along it a few times. This makes the crease more accurate, and the next step easier.

One last note: While origami is an art form, it is a simple and inexpensive art form. Any type of paper can be used, and it can be done anywhere. Like anything else, practice makes perfect. If in the beginning your models are not coming out the way they should, don't worry. Crumple it up, tell everyone it's a piece of the exploded Death Star, and try again.

Happy folding!

PART ONE
THE BASICS

ORIGAMI DEFINITIONS, SYMBOLS, AND BASIC FOLDS

Origami figures are made with just two folds, the valley fold and the mountain fold. All of the following folds are just combinations of these. As you study the diagrams, pay attention to the type of line used to represent each crease. This will indicate whether it should be a mountain or valley fold.

SIDE ONE

Side one of the origami paper is represented by the white side of the diagram.

SIDE TWO

Side two of the origami paper is represented by the colored side of the diagram.

START ARROW

This symbol, printed on the origami paper in the back of the book, tells you which way to orient the paper. The arrow should always point straight up.

VALLEY FOLD - - - - - - - - - - - - - - -

The valley fold, represented by a dashed line, is the most common fold. The paper is creased along the line as one side is folded toward you. A "valley" is formed in the process.

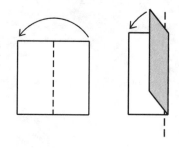

MOUNTAIN FOLD · — ·· — ·· — ·· — ··· —

The mountain fold is represented by a dashed and dotted line. The paper is creased along the line as one side is folded away from you. A "mountain" is formed as the paper is folded.

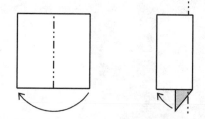

MARK FOLD

The mark fold is used to make a crease that will be used as a reference in a later step. Lightly fold on the line as indicated and then unfold. Ideally, the crease will not be visible when the model is finished.

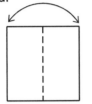

EXISTING CREASE

A thin line represents a crease formed in a previous step and is used for orientation or as a reference in the current step.

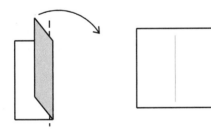

X-RAY LINES

The dotted line serves two purposes. In most cases it represents a fold or edge underneath another layer of paper. It is also used to represent an imaginary extension of an existing line.

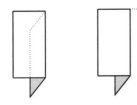

TURN OVER

This symbol means turn the model over to the other side.

ROTATE

This symbol means rotate the figure to a new position.

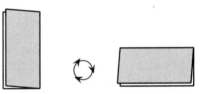

CUT

This symbol means you should cut the paper along the indicated solid line.

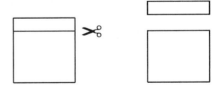

REVERSE FOLD

To make a reverse fold (sometimes called an inside reverse fold) put your finger inside the pocket to spread it open. Then, push down on the spine of the section to be reversed until the section is folded inside itself along existing creases.

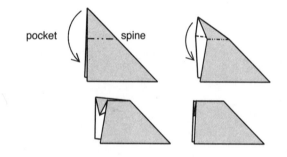

PIVOT FOLD

The pivot fold adjusts an existing point. The base of the figure is pinched while the point is swiveled into its new location and is re-creased. In this example, pinch point A, while pivoting point B upward.

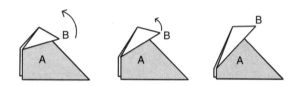

Start with an outside reverse fold.

OUTSIDE REVERSE FOLD

To make an outside reverse fold, open the pocket a bit and flip the point backward over the spine along existing creases. It's a little like peeling a banana.

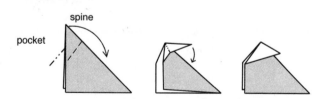

HOW TO MAKE A SQUARE

The only thing you will need to create an origami model is a square piece of paper. Specially designed origami paper is provided at the end of this book, and you can purchase origami paper in craft stores, online, and in some bookstores. But if you want to practice your techniques, this is a simple way to create your own origami paper! A square can be made out of any rectangle by following these steps.

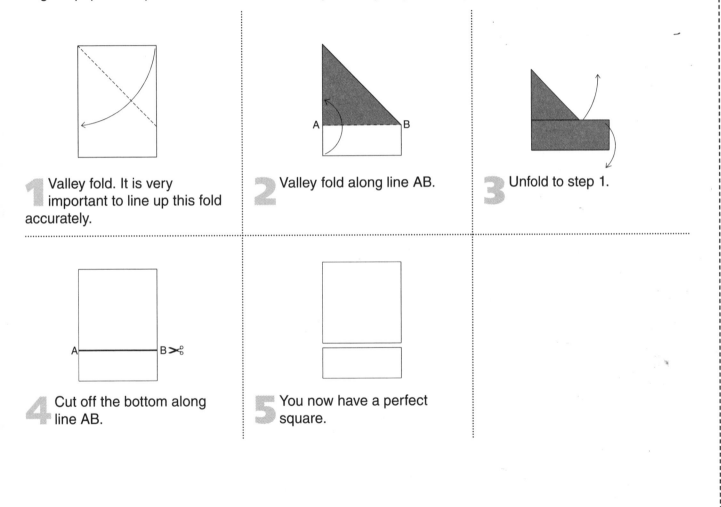

1 Valley fold. It is very important to line up this fold accurately.

2 Valley fold along line AB.

3 Unfold to step 1.

4 Cut off the bottom along line AB.

5 You now have a perfect square.

HOW TO MAKE AN EQUILATERAL TRIANGLE

An equilateral triangle has 60-degree angles at each of its corners, and has sides that are exactly the same length. Lucky for us, origami is based on geometric concepts. You won't need a protractor or ruler to map out the shape. This special triangle can be made from any rectangular or square piece of paper. Simply follow these steps.

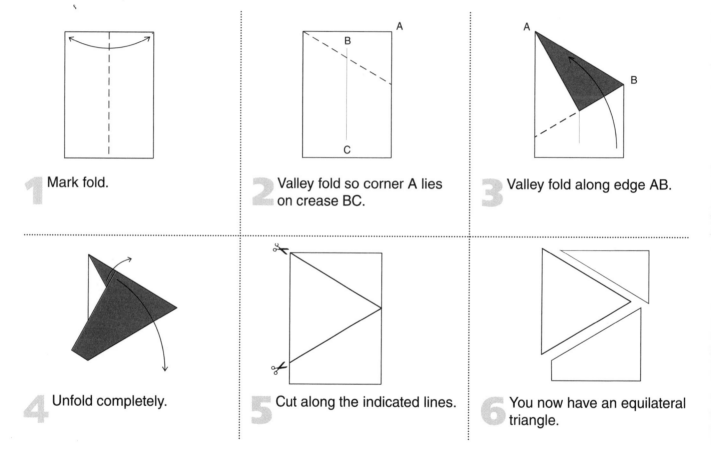

1 Mark fold.

2 Valley fold so corner A lies on crease BC.

3 Valley fold along edge AB.

4 Unfold completely.

5 Cut along the indicated lines.

6 You now have an equilateral triangle.

PLEAT FOLD

This fold resembles the pleat on a skirt when finished. You can think of it as two reverse folds.

This arrow indicates a pleat fold:

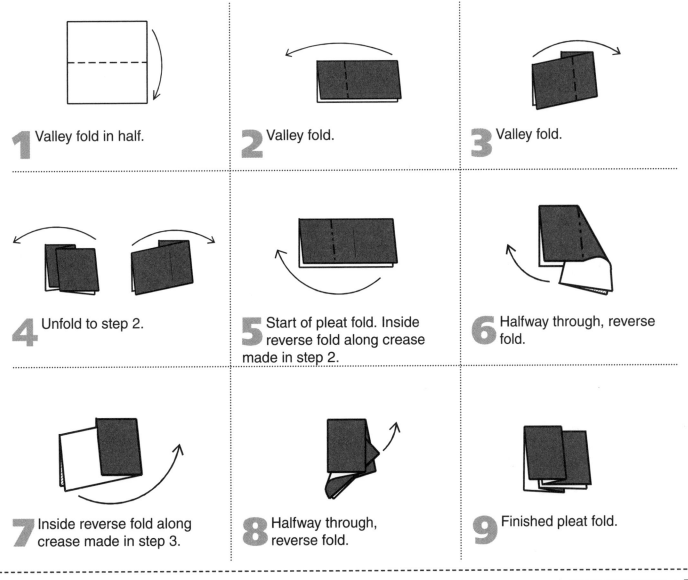

1 Valley fold in half.

2 Valley fold.

3 Valley fold.

4 Unfold to step 2.

5 Start of pleat fold. Inside reverse fold along crease made in step 2.

6 Halfway through, reverse fold.

7 Inside reverse fold along crease made in step 3.

8 Halfway through, reverse fold.

9 Finished pleat fold.

RABBIT EAR FOLD

This fold is used to narrow a point. In this example, the bottom half of the two existing creases are used, and two new creases are formed: the valley fold from the point to the center and the mountain fold from the center to the edge.

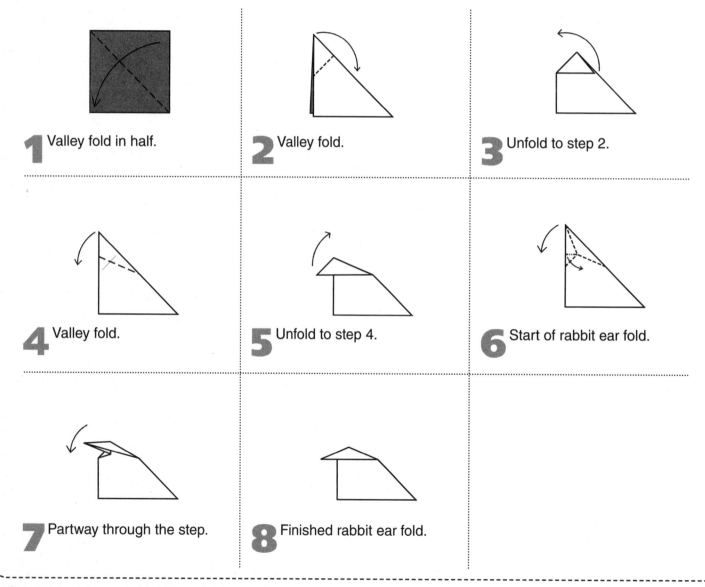

1 Valley fold in half.

2 Valley fold.

3 Unfold to step 2.

4 Valley fold.

5 Unfold to step 4.

6 Start of rabbit ear fold.

7 Partway through the step.

8 Finished rabbit ear fold.

SQUASH FOLD

A squash fold is formed by lifting one edge of a pocket and reforming it so the edge becomes a crease and an existing crease becomes a new edge.

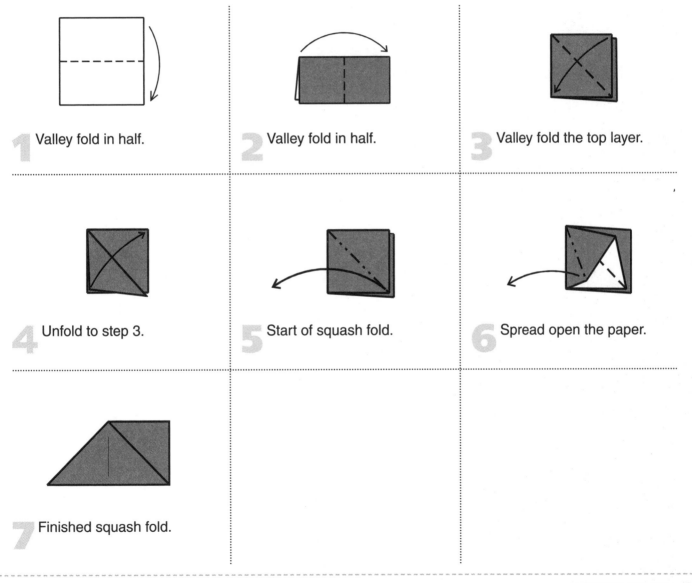

1 Valley fold in half.

2 Valley fold in half.

3 Valley fold the top layer.

4 Unfold to step 3.

5 Start of squash fold.

6 Spread open the paper.

7 Finished squash fold.

PETAL FOLD

Petal folds are used to isolate a point. This example starts with a waterbomb base (see p. 15). As the point is lifted, two new valley folds are added at the bottom.

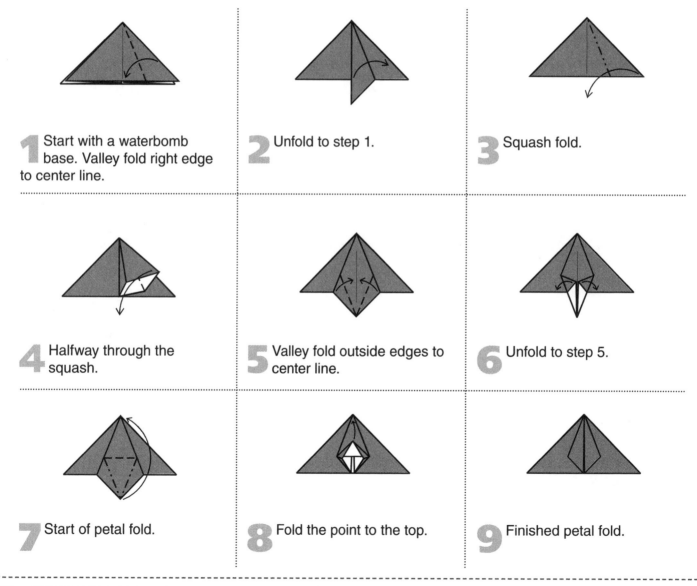

1 Start with a waterbomb base. Valley fold right edge to center line.

2 Unfold to step 1.

3 Squash fold.

4 Halfway through the squash.

5 Valley fold outside edges to center line.

6 Unfold to step 5.

7 Start of petal fold.

8 Fold the point to the top.

9 Finished petal fold.

SINK FOLD EXAMPLE 1

A sink fold requires unfolding a portion of the model. The section to be sunk is pushed inside-out along existing creases, and the model is then re-formed. No new creases are added. This arrow indicates a sink fold: ∨

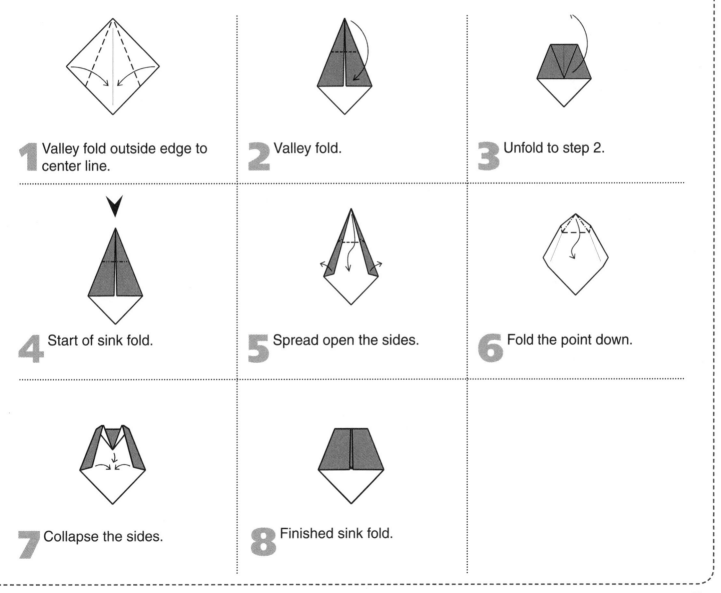

1 Valley fold outside edge to center line.

2 Valley fold.

3 Unfold to step 2.

4 Start of sink fold.

5 Spread open the sides.

6 Fold the point down.

7 Collapse the sides.

8 Finished sink fold.

SINK FOLD EXAMPLE 2

This example of a sink fold starts with a waterbomb base (see p. 15).

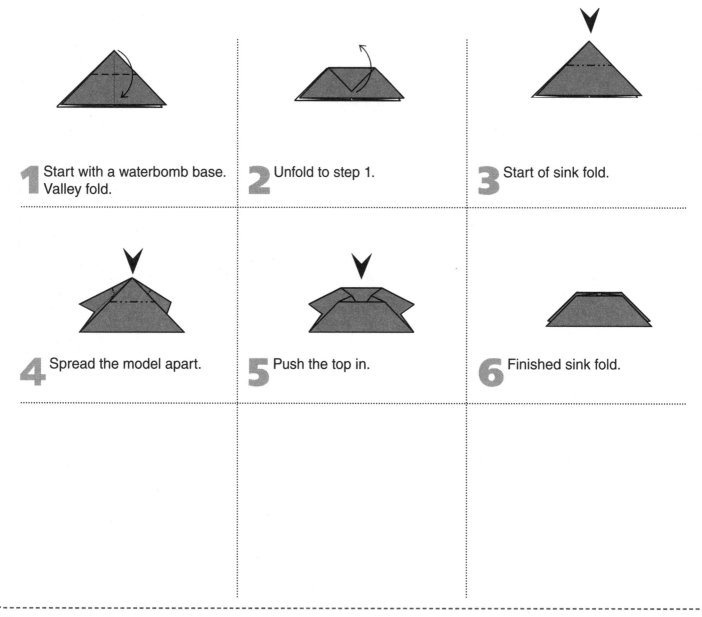

1 Start with a waterbomb base. Valley fold.

2 Unfold to step 1.

3 Start of sink fold.

4 Spread the model apart.

5 Push the top in.

6 Finished sink fold.

IMPORTANT ORIGAMI BASES

THE PRELIMINARY BASE

Bases are the building blocks of origami. The preliminary base is used as a starting point for many origami models.

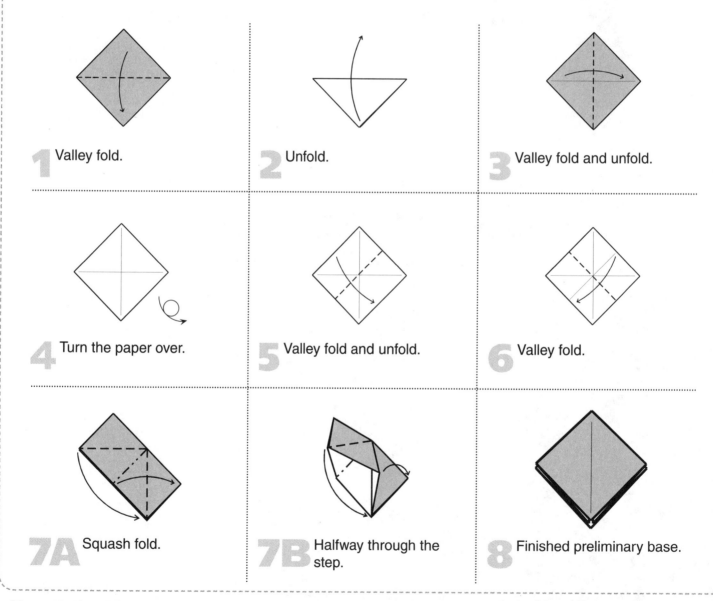

1 Valley fold.

2 Unfold.

3 Valley fold and unfold.

4 Turn the paper over.

5 Valley fold and unfold.

6 Valley fold.

7A Squash fold.

7B Halfway through the step.

8 Finished preliminary base.

THE WATERBOMB BASE

The waterbomb base is another common starting point for many origami models.

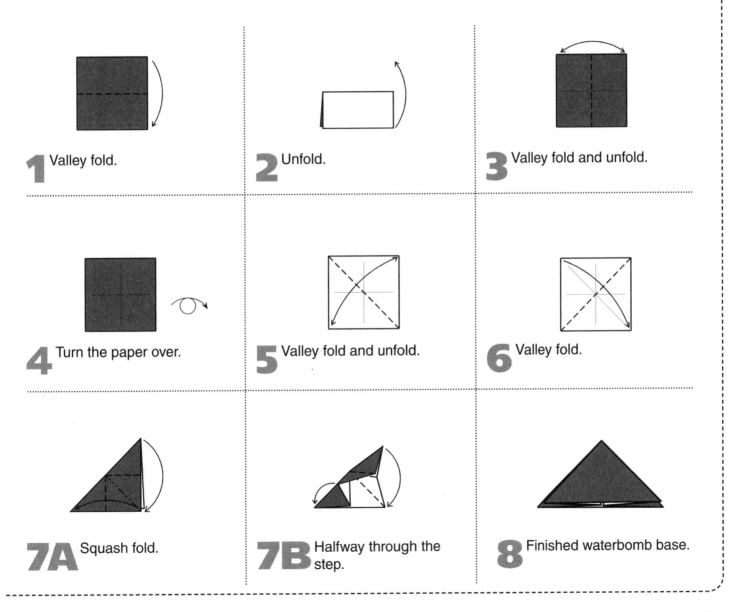

1 Valley fold.

2 Unfold.

3 Valley fold and unfold.

4 Turn the paper over.

5 Valley fold and unfold.

6 Valley fold.

7A Squash fold.

7B Halfway through the step.

8 Finished waterbomb base.

DISPLAY STAND

This little stand can be used to show off your origami models. Start with a piece of paper about a fourth of the size that you used for the model. Steps 9 through 13 can be adjusted to position the model to your liking.

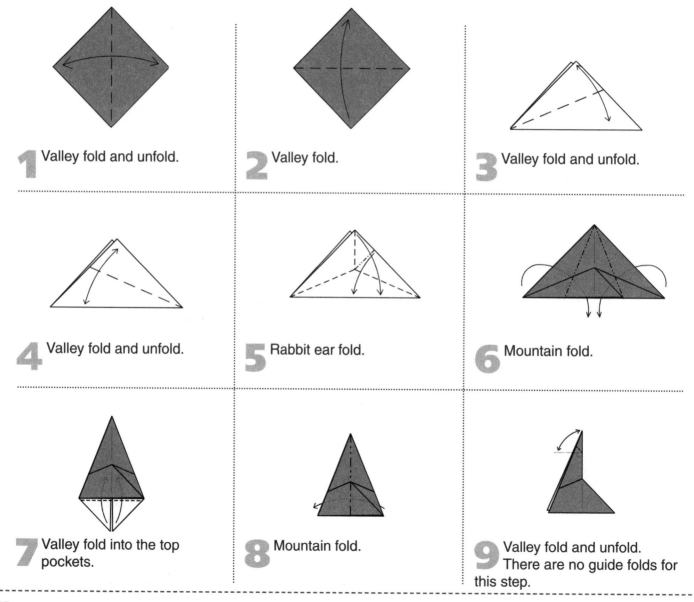

1 Valley fold and unfold.

2 Valley fold.

3 Valley fold and unfold.

4 Valley fold and unfold.

5 Rabbit ear fold.

6 Mountain fold.

7 Valley fold into the top pockets.

8 Mountain fold.

9 Valley fold and unfold. There are no guide folds for this step.

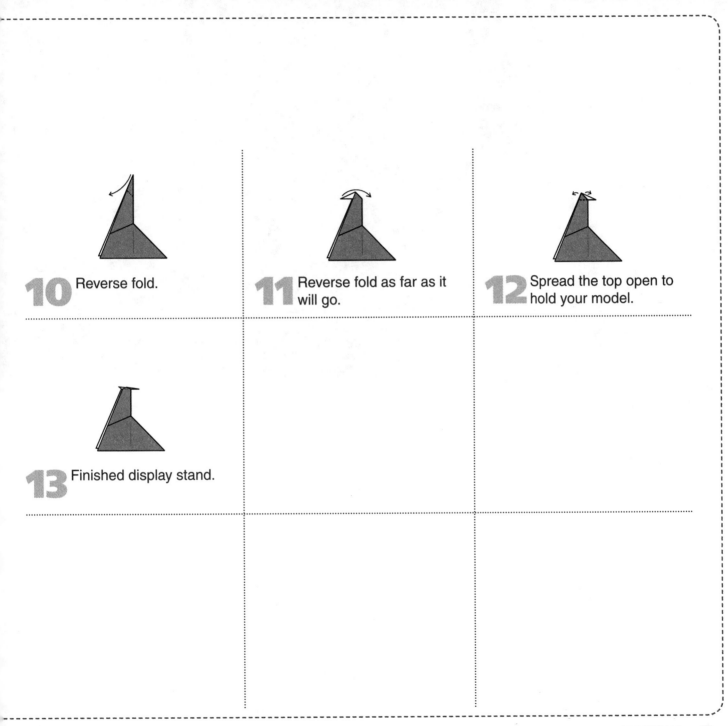

10 Reverse fold.

11 Reverse fold as far as it will go.

12 Spread the top open to hold your model.

13 Finished display stand.

PART TWO

THE PROJECTS

"An elegant weapon for a more civilized age."
—OBI-WAN KENOBI

LIGHTSABERS

The preferred weapons of both the Jedi Order and their Sith enemies, lightsabers were extremely powerful, but only in the hands of those trained to use them. With four-foot-long blades made of pure energy, they were capable of cutting through anything (except for another lightsaber) and were even able to deflect blaster fire. Jedi lightsabers were almost always blue- or green-bladed, while Sith lightsabers were always red-bladed.

Luke's lightsaber

Darth Maul's double-bladed lightsaber

Yoda's lightsaber

Darth Vader's lightsaber

Mace Windu's lightsaber

Count Dooku's lightsaber

HOW TO FOLD: A BASIC LIGHTSABER

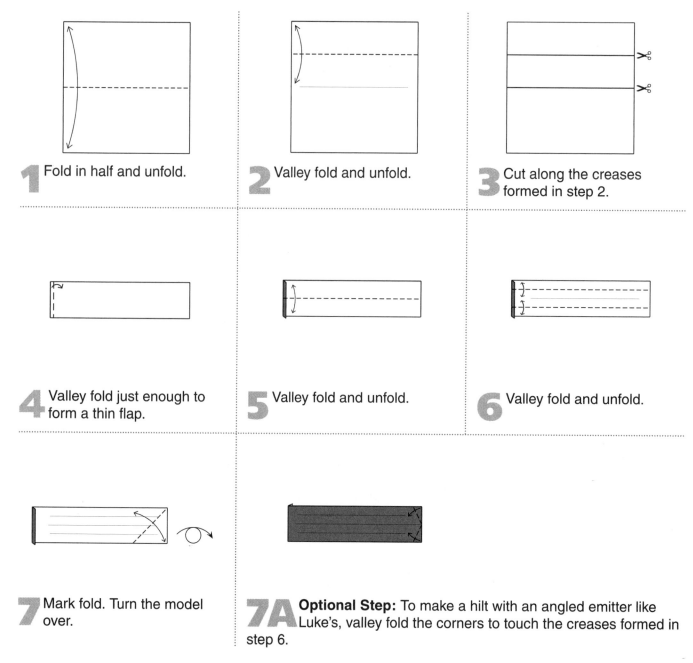

1 Fold in half and unfold.

2 Valley fold and unfold.

3 Cut along the creases formed in step 2.

4 Valley fold just enough to form a thin flap.

5 Valley fold and unfold.

6 Valley fold and unfold.

7 Mark fold. Turn the model over.

7A **Optional Step:** To make a hilt with an angled emitter like Luke's, valley fold the corners to touch the creases formed in step 6.

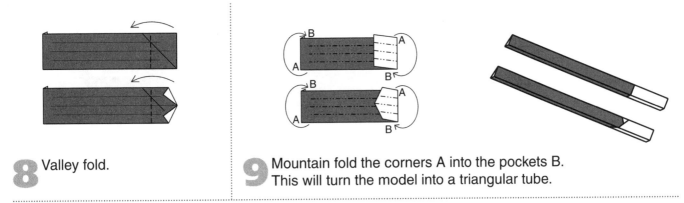

8 Valley fold.

9 Mountain fold the corners A into the pockets B. This will turn the model into a triangular tube.

HOW TO FOLD: DARTH MAUL'S LIGHTSABER

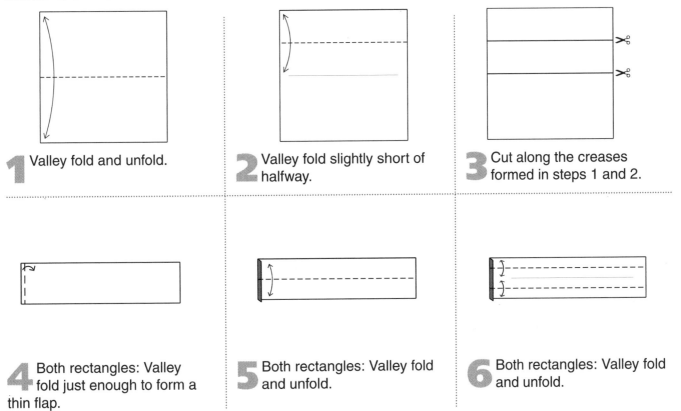

1 Valley fold and unfold.

2 Valley fold slightly short of halfway.

3 Cut along the creases formed in steps 1 and 2.

4 Both rectangles: Valley fold just enough to form a thin flap.

5 Both rectangles: Valley fold and unfold.

6 Both rectangles: Valley fold and unfold.

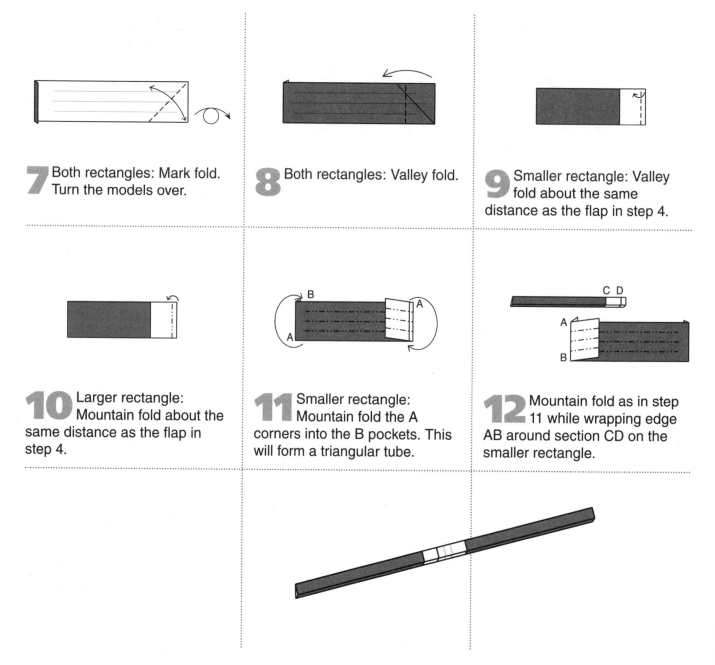

7 Both rectangles: Mark fold. Turn the models over.

8 Both rectangles: Valley fold.

9 Smaller rectangle: Valley fold about the same distance as the flap in step 4.

10 Larger rectangle: Mountain fold about the same distance as the flap in step 4.

11 Smaller rectangle: Mountain fold the A corners into the B pockets. This will form a triangular tube.

12 Mountain fold as in step 11 while wrapping edge AB around section CD on the smaller rectangle.

HOW TO FOLD: COUNT DOOKU'S LIGHTSABER

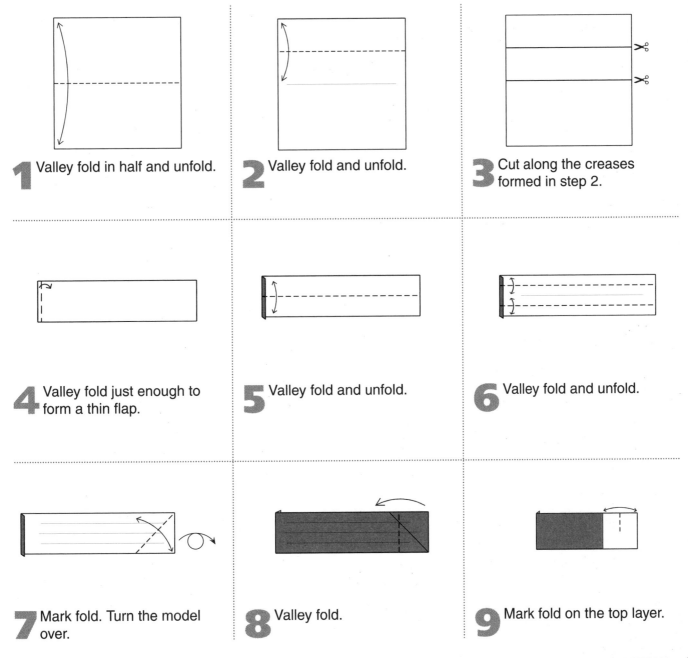

1 Valley fold in half and unfold.

2 Valley fold and unfold.

3 Cut along the creases formed in step 2.

4 Valley fold just enough to form a thin flap.

5 Valley fold and unfold.

6 Valley fold and unfold.

7 Mark fold. Turn the model over.

8 Valley fold.

9 Mark fold on the top layer.

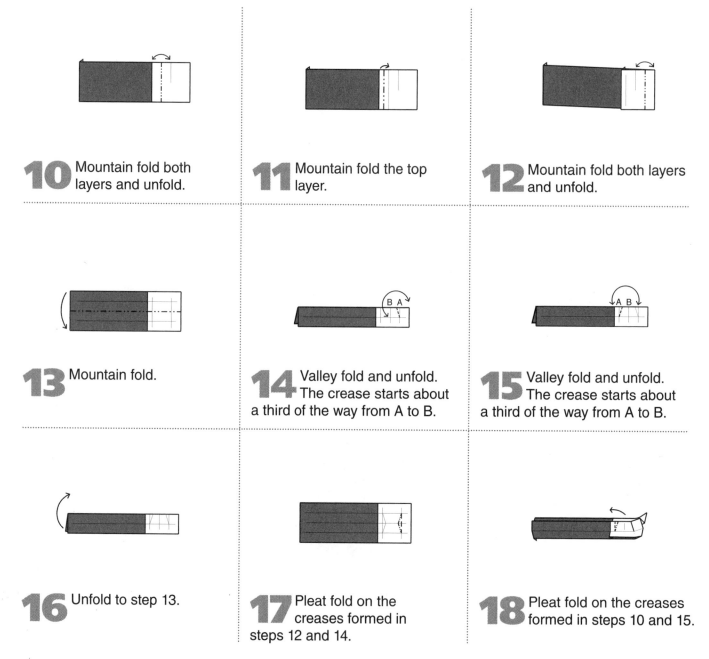

10 Mountain fold both layers and unfold.

11 Mountain fold the top layer.

12 Mountain fold both layers and unfold.

13 Mountain fold.

14 Valley fold and unfold. The crease starts about a third of the way from A to B.

15 Valley fold and unfold. The crease starts about a third of the way from A to B.

16 Unfold to step 13.

17 Pleat fold on the creases formed in steps 12 and 14.

18 Pleat fold on the creases formed in steps 10 and 15.

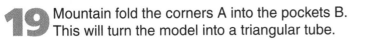

19 Mountain fold the corners A into the pockets B. This will turn the model into a triangular tube.

Qui-Gon Jinn's lightsaber, which Anakin Skywalker inherited.

Anakin Skywalker's own lightsaber.

Mace Windu's purple-bladed lightsaber.

Darth Maul's double-bladed lightsaber.

Count Dooku's lightsaber.

Obi-Wan Kenobi and Darth Maul battle at the Theed Power Generator on Naboo.

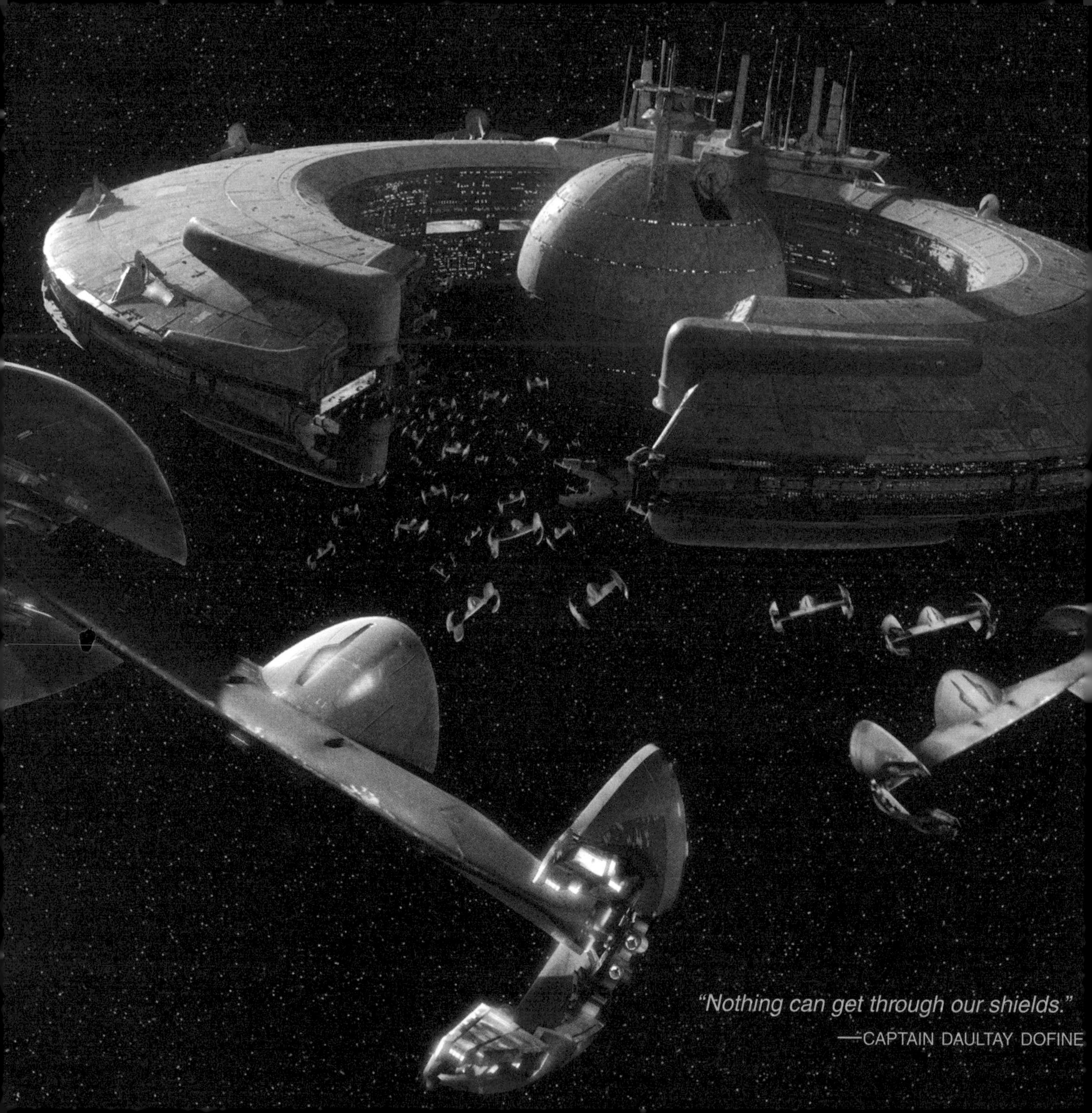

"Nothing can get through our shields."
—CAPTAIN DAULTAY DOFINE

TRADE FEDERATION BATTLESHIP

When the Trade Federation recognized a need for its own military, it converted some of its huge cargo carriers into battleships. These two-mile-wide carriers were ideal for the task. The enormous ships already had powerful engines, strong armor, and vast storage areas that could house up to 1,500 droid starfighters and 140,000 battle droids. After being refitted with stronger shields and powerful quad-laser batteries, any one of these ships could hold off an entire armada of Republic attack cruisers.

HOW TO FOLD: TRADE FEDERATION BATTLESHIP

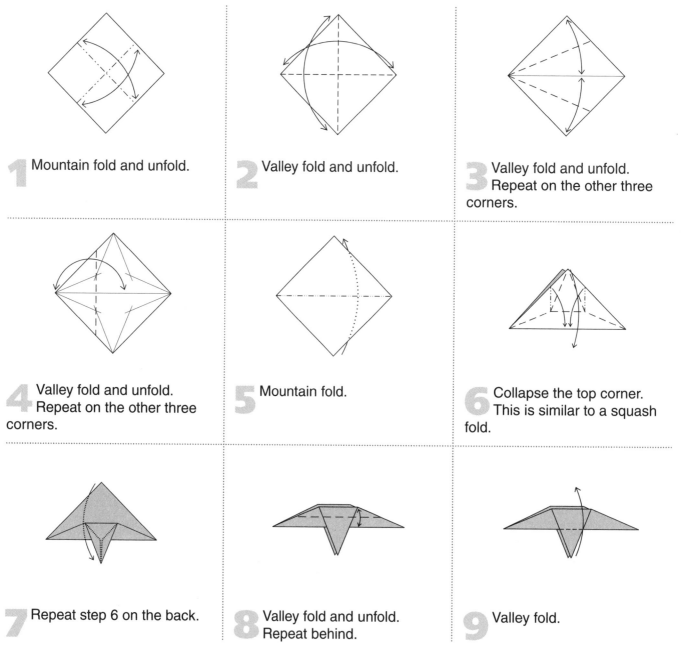

1 Mountain fold and unfold.

2 Valley fold and unfold.

3 Valley fold and unfold. Repeat on the other three corners.

4 Valley fold and unfold. Repeat on the other three corners.

5 Mountain fold.

6 Collapse the top corner. This is similar to a squash fold.

7 Repeat step 6 on the back.

8 Valley fold and unfold. Repeat behind.

9 Valley fold.

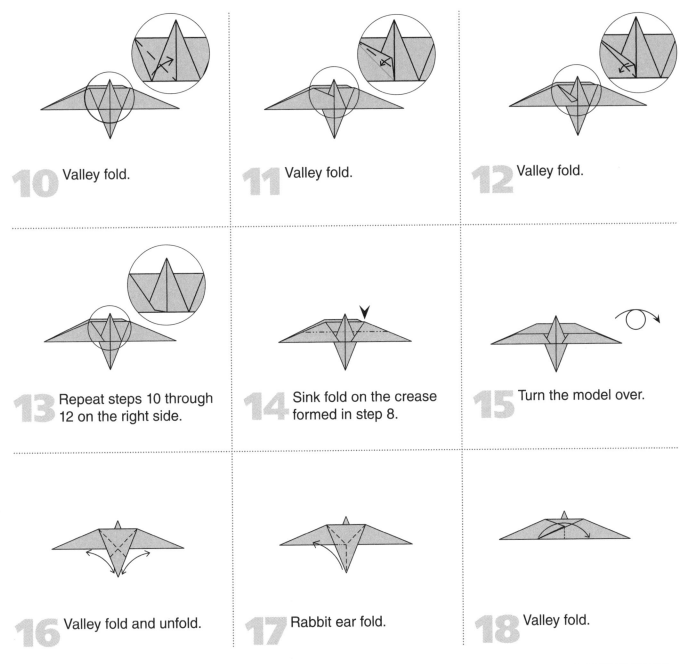

10 Valley fold.

11 Valley fold.

12 Valley fold.

13 Repeat steps 10 through 12 on the right side.

14 Sink fold on the crease formed in step 8.

15 Turn the model over.

16 Valley fold and unfold.

17 Rabbit ear fold.

18 Valley fold.

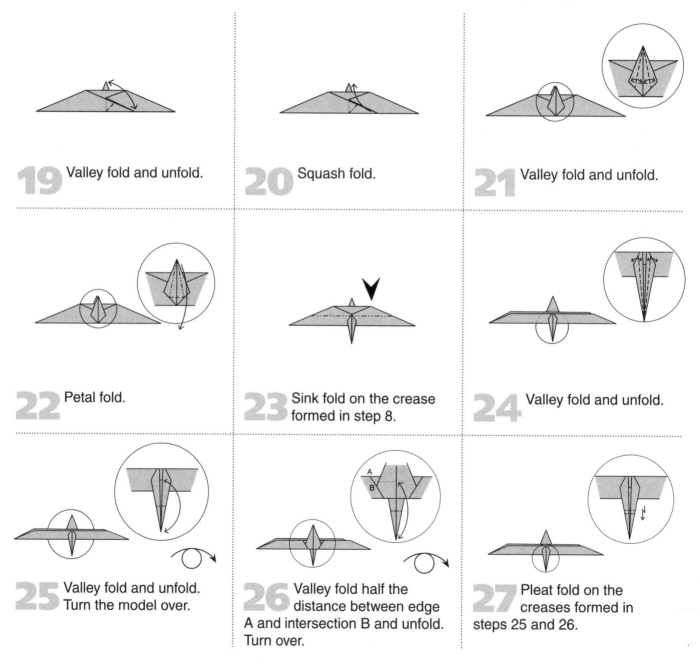

19 Valley fold and unfold.

20 Squash fold.

21 Valley fold and unfold.

22 Petal fold.

23 Sink fold on the crease formed in step 8.

24 Valley fold and unfold.

25 Valley fold and unfold. Turn the model over.

26 Valley fold half the distance between edge A and intersection B and unfold. Turn over.

27 Pleat fold on the creases formed in steps 25 and 26.

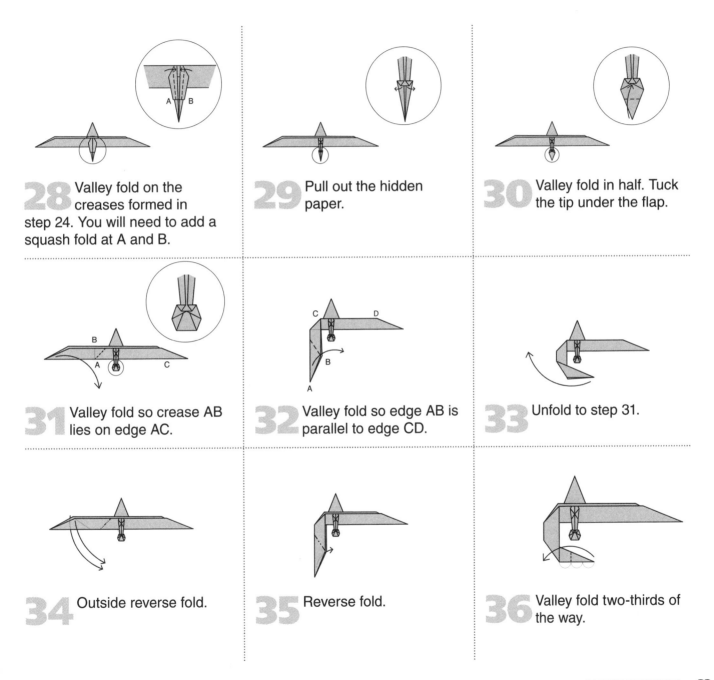

28 Valley fold on the creases formed in step 24. You will need to add a squash fold at A and B.

29 Pull out the hidden paper.

30 Valley fold in half. Tuck the tip under the flap.

31 Valley fold so crease AB lies on edge AC.

32 Valley fold so edge AB is parallel to edge CD.

33 Unfold to step 31.

34 Outside reverse fold.

35 Reverse fold.

36 Valley fold two-thirds of the way.

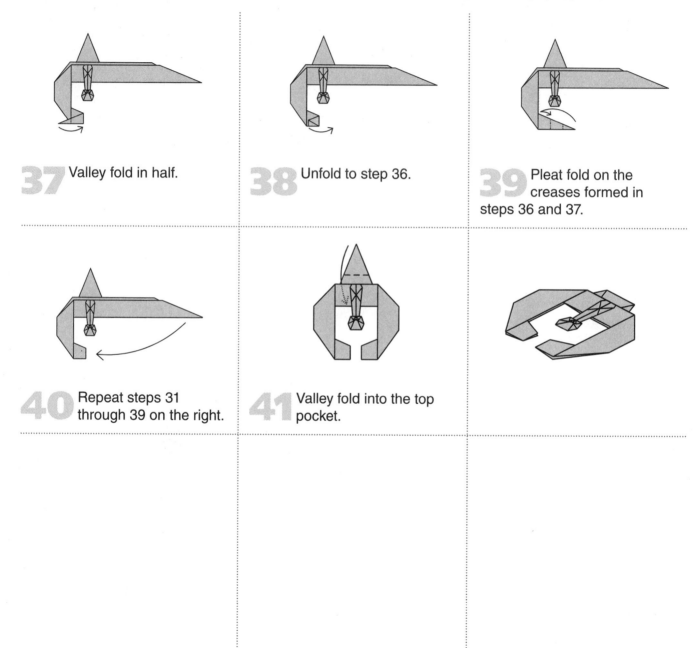

37 Valley fold in half.

38 Unfold to step 36.

39 Pleat fold on the creases formed in steps 36 and 37.

40 Repeat steps 31 through 39 on the right.

41 Valley fold into the top pocket.

WHO SAID IT?

Match the quote to the correct *Star Wars* character.

1. "The ability to destroy a planet is insignificant next to the power of the Force."

2. "I shall take you to Jabba now."

3. "The Chosen One the boy may be; nevertheless, grave danger I fear in his training."

4. "At last we will reveal ourselves to the Jedi. At last we will have revenge."

5. "Why, you slimy, double-crossing, no-good swindler."

6. "In his belly, you will find a new definition of pain and suffering as you are slowly digested over a thousand years."

A. Bib Fortuna

B. Lando Calrissian

C. C-3PO

D. Darth Maul

E. Darth Vader

F. Yoda

ANSWERS: 1.E; 2.A; 3.F; 4.D; 5.B; 6.C

"You catch on pretty quick."
—RIC OLIÉ TO ANAKIN SKYWALKER

NABOO ROYAL STARSHIP

Also called the J-type 327 Nubian royal starship, its primary mission was transportation to and from diplomatic functions. A luxurious ship, it was appointed with chambers for the queen, spacious quarters for the royal staff—even a throne room. While the ship had no offensive weapons, it was heavily shielded and armored. The defenses of this craft were so strong that Queen Amidala was able to run the Trade Federation blockade with several battleships firing on her. The shields collapsed and the hyperdrive was badly damaged, but, with R2-D2's help, the ship successfully made its escape.

HOW TO FOLD: NABOO ROYAL STARSHIP

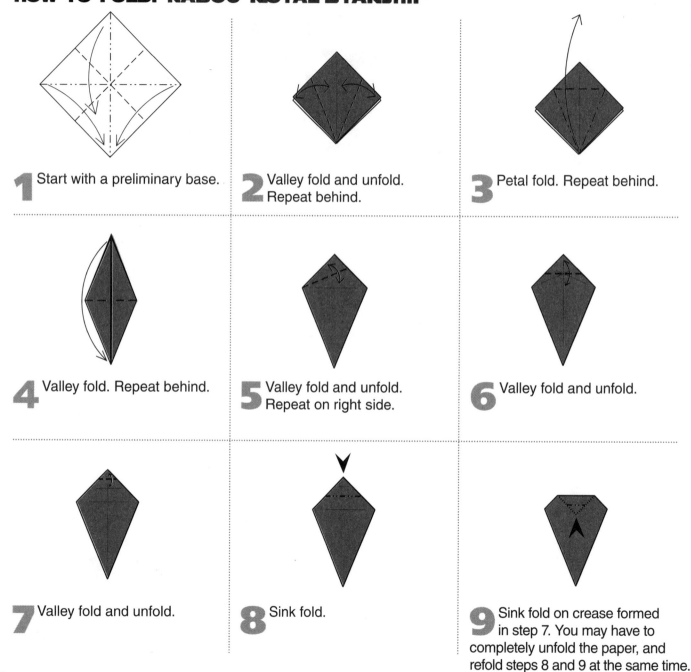

1 Start with a preliminary base.

2 Valley fold and unfold. Repeat behind.

3 Petal fold. Repeat behind.

4 Valley fold. Repeat behind.

5 Valley fold and unfold. Repeat on right side.

6 Valley fold and unfold.

7 Valley fold and unfold.

8 Sink fold.

9 Sink fold on crease formed in step 7. You may have to completely unfold the paper, and refold steps 8 and 9 at the same time.

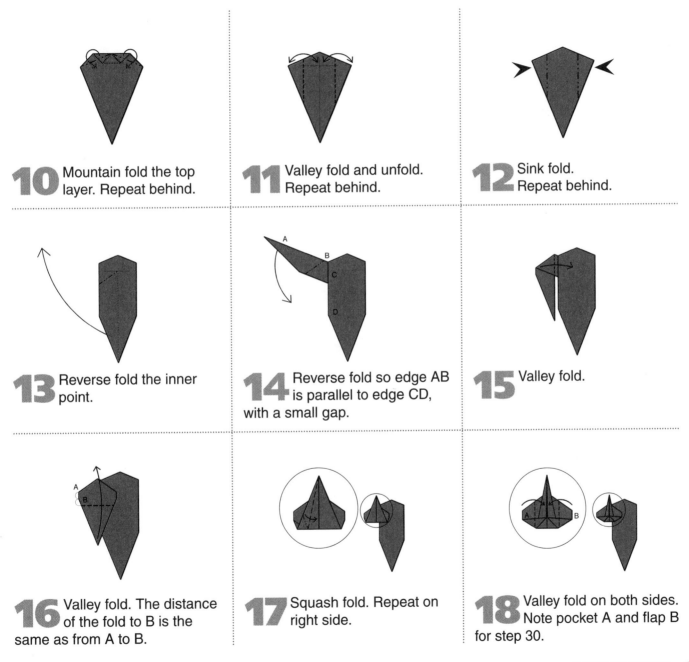

10 Mountain fold the top layer. Repeat behind.

11 Valley fold and unfold. Repeat behind.

12 Sink fold. Repeat behind.

13 Reverse fold the inner point.

14 Reverse fold so edge AB is parallel to edge CD, with a small gap.

15 Valley fold.

16 Valley fold. The distance of the fold to B is the same as from A to B.

17 Squash fold. Repeat on right side.

18 Valley fold on both sides. Note pocket A and flap B for step 30.

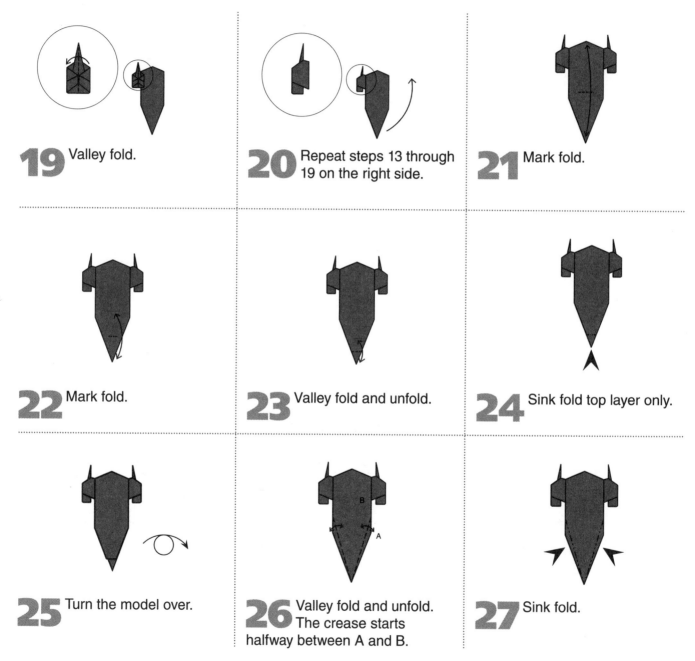

19 Valley fold.

20 Repeat steps 13 through 19 on the right side.

21 Mark fold.

22 Mark fold.

23 Valley fold and unfold.

24 Sink fold top layer only.

25 Turn the model over.

26 Valley fold and unfold. The crease starts halfway between A and B.

27 Sink fold.

28 Mountain fold the tip into the pocket formed in step 24.

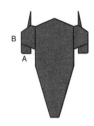

29 Valley fold the bottom edges into the pockets formed in step 27.

B
A

30 Insert flap B into pocket A. See step 18. The engines will be three-dimensional.

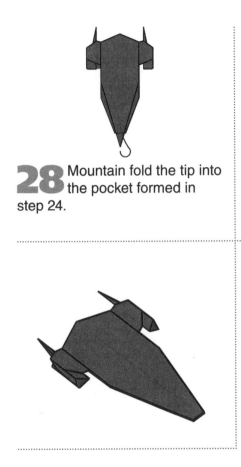

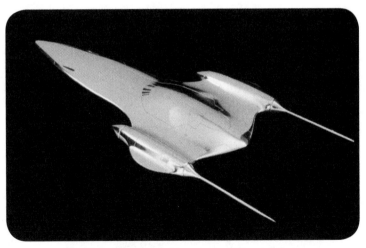

The Naboo Royal Starship measured 76 meters long.

"An extremely well-put-togethe
little droid, Your Highness."

—CAPTAIN PANA
TO QUEEN AMIDA

R2-D2

R2-D2, a bold, loyal, and spirited astromech droid, understood most forms of speech—but he spoke in a series of electronic chirps, whistles, and squeaks. And though astromechs were typically designed for starship management and repair, R2-D2's loyalty to Padmé and her family, and his long friendship with C-3PO, made him unique. That, and R2-D2 always seemed to be at the center of events in the galaxy. He repaired the shields on Queen Amidala's starship, allowing her to escape from Naboo. He carried the Death Star plans to the rebels and was on Luke's X-wing when Luke destroyed the Death Star. This little droid saved the lives of Padmé, Anakin, Luke, Han, and Leia.

HOW TO FOLD: R2-D2

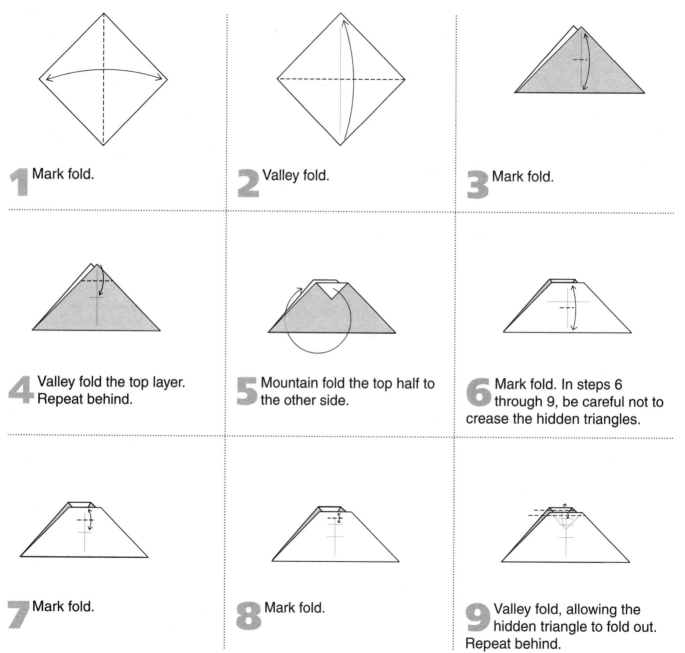

1 Mark fold.

2 Valley fold.

3 Mark fold.

4 Valley fold the top layer. Repeat behind.

5 Mountain fold the top half to the other side.

6 Mark fold. In steps 6 through 9, be careful not to crease the hidden triangles.

7 Mark fold.

8 Mark fold.

9 Valley fold, allowing the hidden triangle to fold out. Repeat behind.

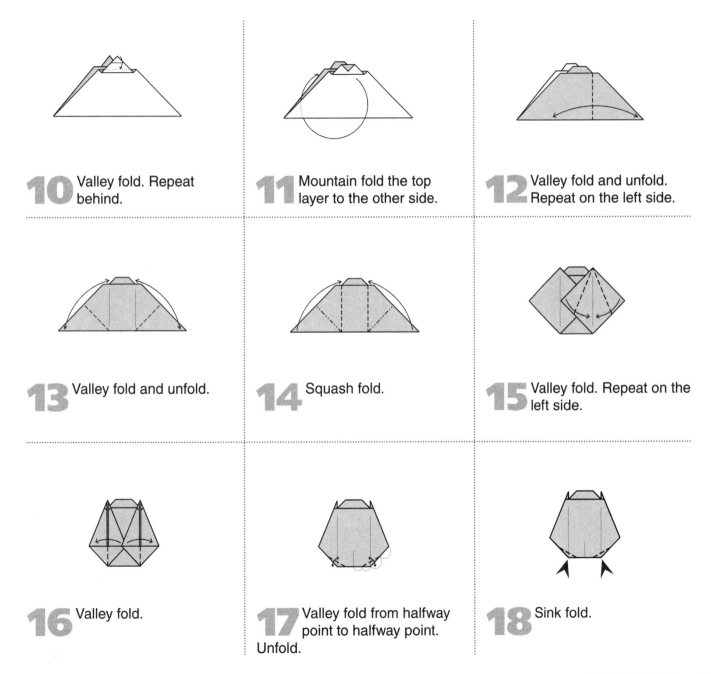

10 Valley fold. Repeat behind.

11 Mountain fold the top layer to the other side.

12 Valley fold and unfold. Repeat on the left side.

13 Valley fold and unfold.

14 Squash fold.

15 Valley fold. Repeat on the left side.

16 Valley fold.

17 Valley fold from halfway point to halfway point. Unfold.

18 Sink fold.

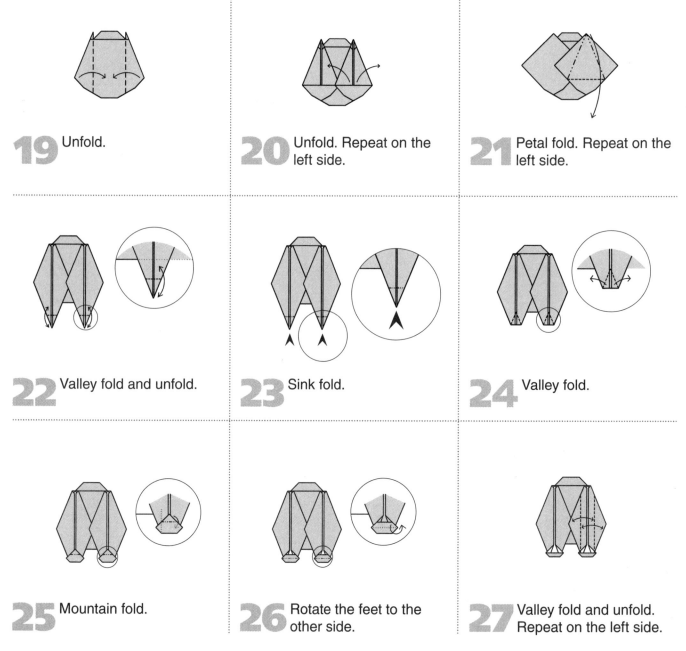

19 Unfold.

20 Unfold. Repeat on the left side.

21 Petal fold. Repeat on the left side.

22 Valley fold and unfold.

23 Sink fold.

24 Valley fold.

25 Mountain fold.

26 Rotate the feet to the other side.

27 Valley fold and unfold. Repeat on the left side.

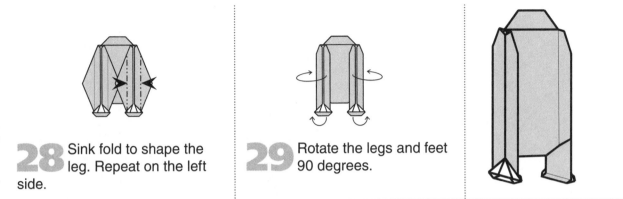

28 Sink fold to shape the leg. Repeat on the left side.

29 Rotate the legs and feet 90 degrees.

R2-D2 repairing the shields on Queen Amidala's starship.

"The dark side of the Force is a pathway to many abilities some consider to be unnatural."

—PALPATINE

DARTH SIDIOUS (EMPEROR PALPATINE)

Palpatine began his rise to power as the Senator of Naboo, eventually becoming Supreme Chancellor of the Galactic Republic. Then with his Sith apprentice, Darth Tyranus, he orchestrated a civil war. Half of the planetary systems remained loyal to him and the Republic, the other half followed Tyranus and the Separatists. With the galaxy in turmoil, the Jedi were spread thin leading the clone army against the Separatists. Sidious then seduced a confused Anakin Skywalker over to the dark side of the Force. With Anakin's help, the Jedi were destroyed, and Sidious announced the war was over. He brought an end to the Galactic Republic, declared himself Emperor Palpatine, and plunged the galaxy into darkness.

HOW TO FOLD: DARTH SIDIOUS (EMPEROR PALPATINE)

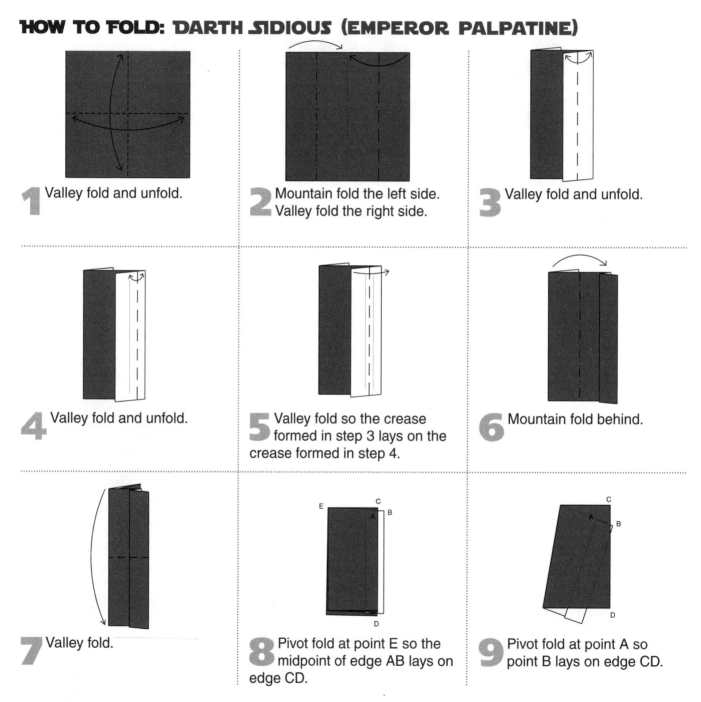

1 Valley fold and unfold.

2 Mountain fold the left side. Valley fold the right side.

3 Valley fold and unfold.

4 Valley fold and unfold.

5 Valley fold so the crease formed in step 3 lays on the crease formed in step 4.

6 Mountain fold behind.

7 Valley fold.

8 Pivot fold at point E so the midpoint of edge AB lays on edge CD.

9 Pivot fold at point A so point B lays on edge CD.

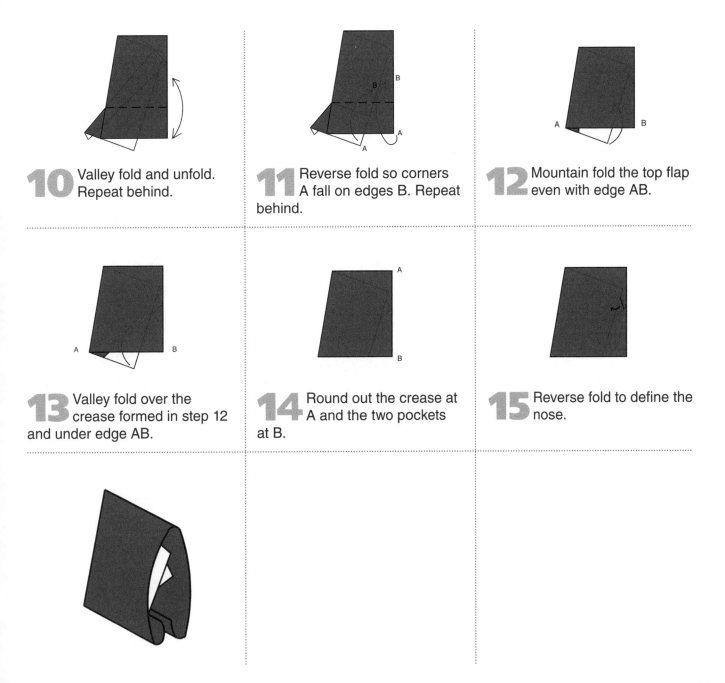

10 Valley fold and unfold. Repeat behind.

11 Reverse fold so corners A fall on edges B. Repeat behind.

12 Mountain fold the top flap even with edge AB.

13 Valley fold over the crease formed in step 12 and under edge AB.

14 Round out the crease at A and the two pockets at B.

15 Reverse fold to define the nose.

"They have Podracing on Malastare.
Very fast, very dangerous."

—QUI-GON JINN

ANAKIN SKYWALKER'S PODRACER

When Anakin Skywalker said of Podracing, "I'm the only human who can do it," he wasn't just bragging. He really was the first and only human to win a race. Podracers were made up of nothing more than a cockpit pulled by two racing engines. The engines were locked together by an energy binder, and the cockpit was dragged behind the engines by two Steelton control cables. The racers could reach speeds of more than 500 miles per hour, requiring either inhuman reflexes or Jedi skills.

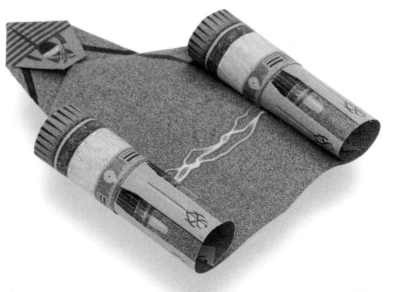

HOW TO FOLD: ANAKIN SKYWALKER'S PODRACER

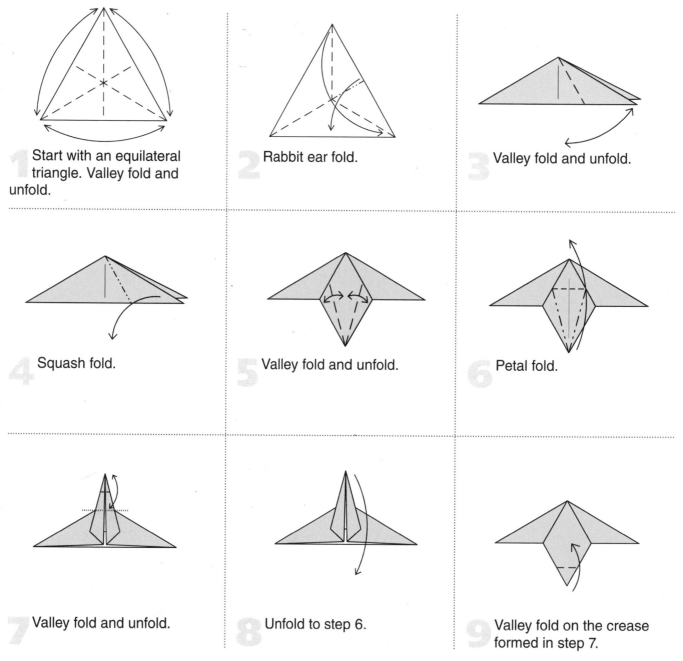

1 Start with an equilateral triangle. Valley fold and unfold.

2 Rabbit ear fold.

3 Valley fold and unfold.

4 Squash fold.

5 Valley fold and unfold.

6 Petal fold.

7 Valley fold and unfold.

8 Unfold to step 6.

9 Valley fold on the crease formed in step 7.

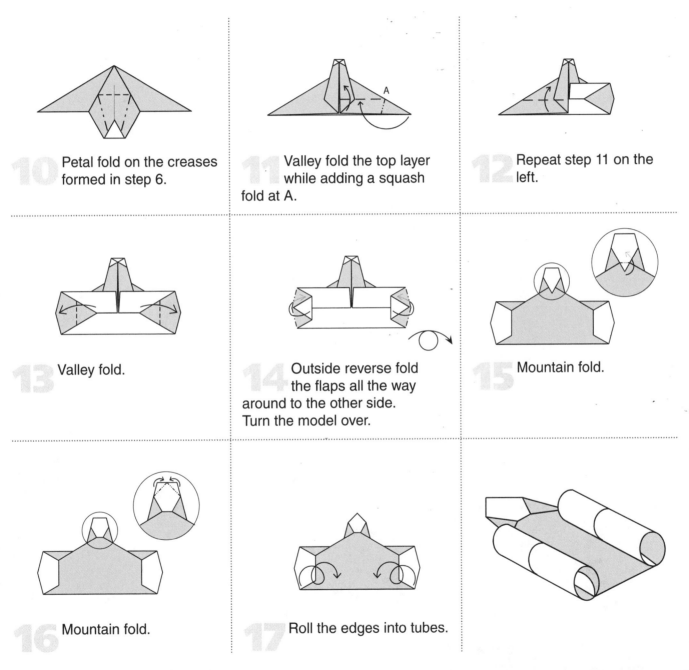

10 Petal fold on the creases formed in step 6.

11 Valley fold the top layer while adding a squash fold at A.

12 Repeat step 11 on the left.

13 Valley fold.

14 Outside reverse fold the flaps all the way around to the other side. Turn the model over.

15 Mountain fold.

16 Mountain fold.

17 Roll the edges into tubes.

"I shall enjoy watching you die."
—JABBA THE HUTT TO
LUKE SKYWALKER

JABBA THE HUTT

Tatooine's most infamous resident was Jabba the Hutt. The sluglike crime lord controlled a vast array of illegal activities, including slavery, extortion, gambling, and, of course, spice-running. Han Solo used to be one of Jabba's smugglers until, on a run, Han was about to be boarded by the authorities and was forced to jettison the spice he was carrying. Jabba demanded he pay for the lost shipment, and when Han couldn't, Jabba placed a bounty on his head. The bounty hunter Boba Fett presented Han encased in a carbonite block to Jabba, which he very happily displayed on his palace wall.

HOW TO FOLD: JABBA THE HUTT

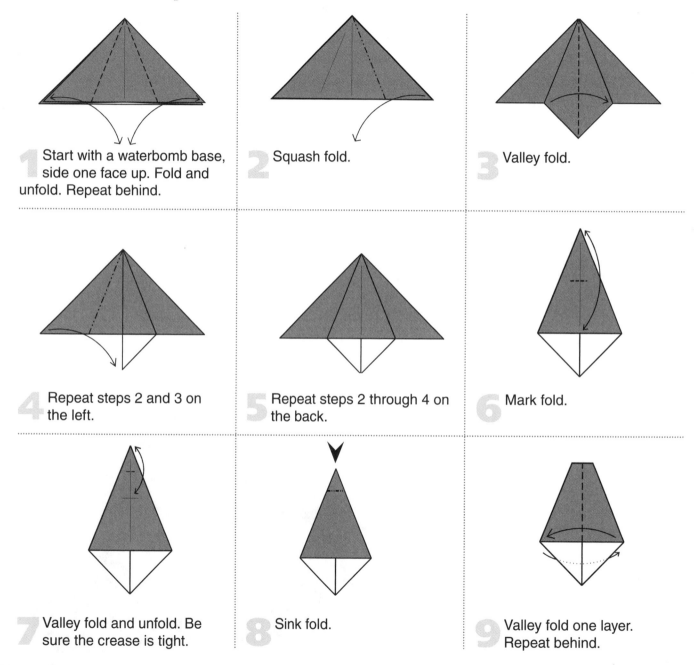

1. Start with a waterbomb base, side one face up. Fold and unfold. Repeat behind.

2. Squash fold.

3. Valley fold.

4. Repeat steps 2 and 3 on the left.

5. Repeat steps 2 through 4 on the back.

6. Mark fold.

7. Valley fold and unfold. Be sure the crease is tight.

8. Sink fold.

9. Valley fold one layer. Repeat behind.

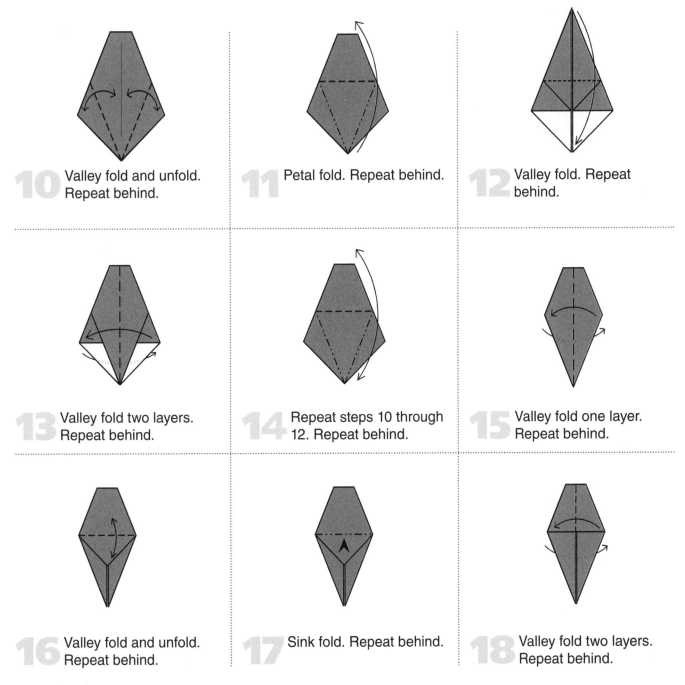

10 Valley fold and unfold. Repeat behind.

11 Petal fold. Repeat behind.

12 Valley fold. Repeat behind.

13 Valley fold two layers. Repeat behind.

14 Repeat steps 10 through 12. Repeat behind.

15 Valley fold one layer. Repeat behind.

16 Valley fold and unfold. Repeat behind.

17 Sink fold. Repeat behind.

18 Valley fold two layers. Repeat behind.

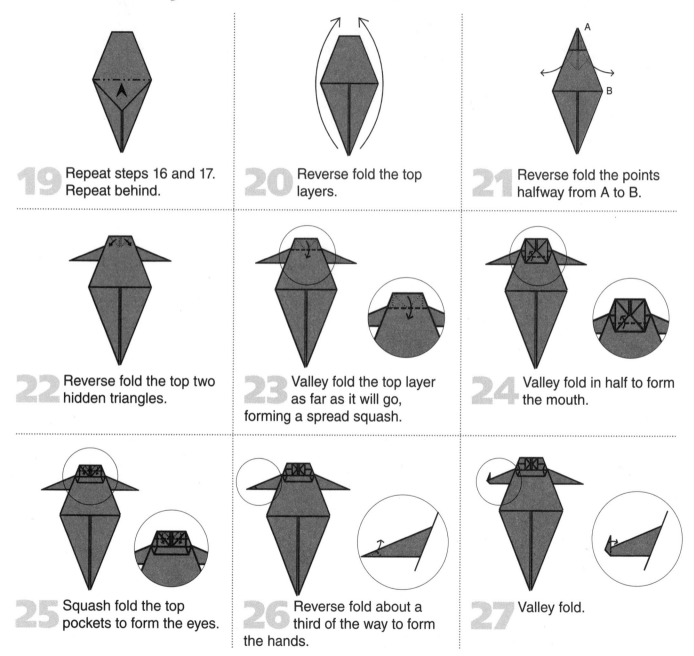

19 Repeat steps 16 and 17. Repeat behind.

20 Reverse fold the top layers.

21 Reverse fold the points halfway from A to B.

22 Reverse fold the top two hidden triangles.

23 Valley fold the top layer as far as it will go, forming a spread squash.

24 Valley fold in half to form the mouth.

25 Squash fold the top pockets to form the eyes.

26 Reverse fold about a third of the way to form the hands.

27 Valley fold.

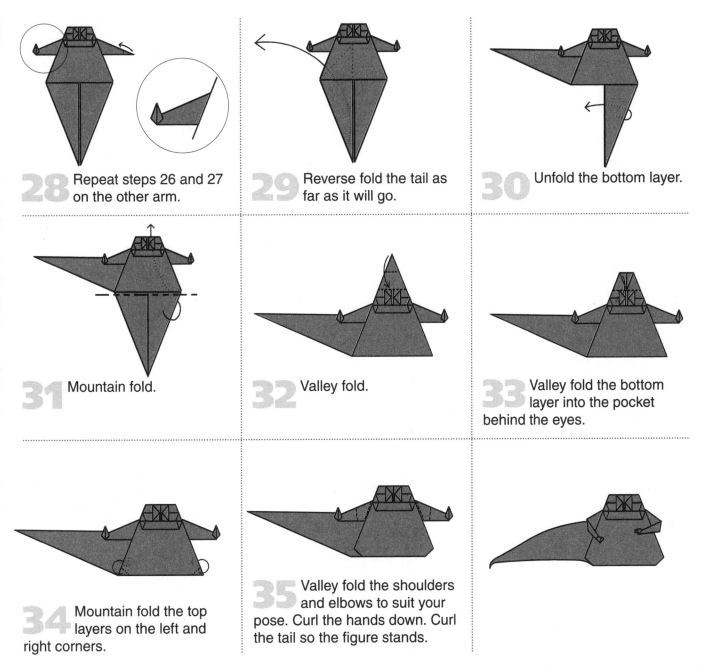

28 Repeat steps 26 and 27 on the other arm.

29 Reverse fold the tail as far as it will go.

30 Unfold the bottom layer.

31 Mountain fold.

32 Valley fold.

33 Valley fold the bottom layer into the pocket behind the eyes.

34 Mountain fold the top layers on the left and right corners.

35 Valley fold the shoulders and elbows to suit your pose. Curl the hands down. Curl the tail so the figure stands.

"[The Force's] energy surrounds us and binds us. Luminous beings are we, not this crude matter."

—YODA

YODA

A Master of the Jedi Council, Yoda was inarguably one of the most powerful Jedi of all time. For more than eight hundred years he trained Jedi Knights, until the Republic collapsed. When the new Emperor Palpatine instituted Order 66, calling for the execution of all the Jedi, only Yoda and Obi-Wan Kenobi managed to survive. After Yoda failed to defeat Palpatine, he exiled himself on the swamp planet, Dagobah, hiding until the time was right to restore the Jedi Order. This was where he met and trained Luke Skywalker in the ways of the Force. Yoda was the last of the original Jedi, and Luke was his last Padawan.

HOW TO FOLD: YODA

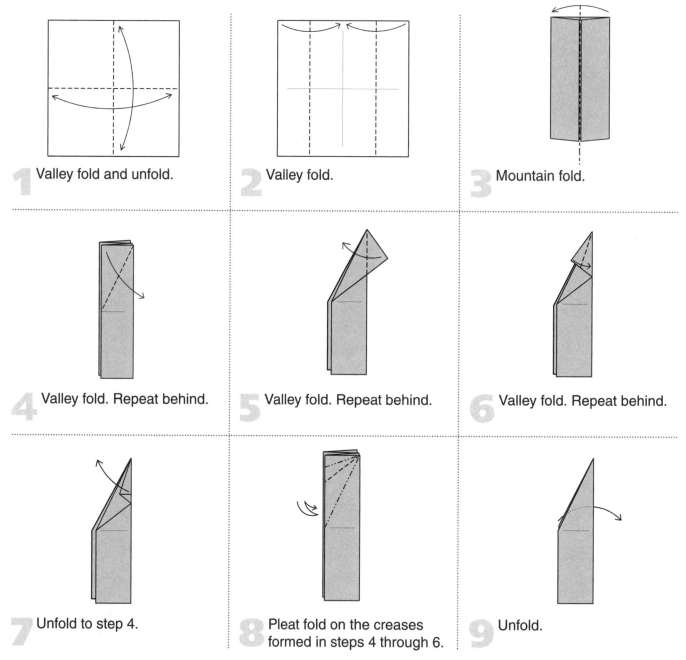

1 Valley fold and unfold.

2 Valley fold.

3 Mountain fold.

4 Valley fold. Repeat behind.

5 Valley fold. Repeat behind.

6 Valley fold. Repeat behind.

7 Unfold to step 4.

8 Pleat fold on the creases formed in steps 4 through 6.

9 Unfold.

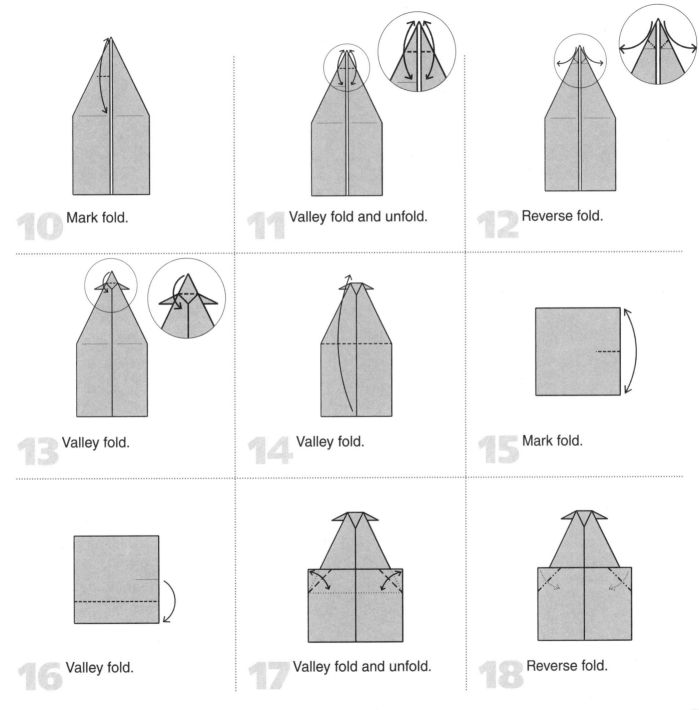

10 Mark fold.

11 Valley fold and unfold.

12 Reverse fold.

13 Valley fold.

14 Valley fold.

15 Mark fold.

16 Valley fold.

17 Valley fold and unfold.

18 Reverse fold.

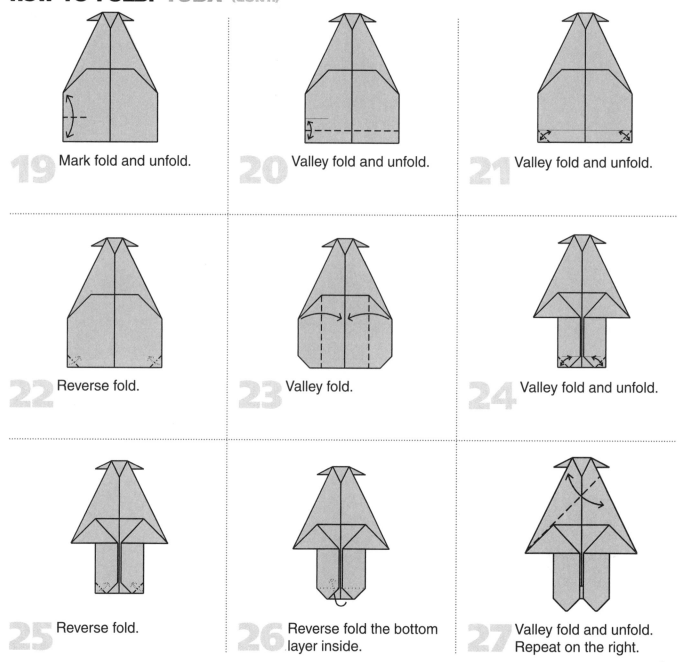

19 Mark fold and unfold.

20 Valley fold and unfold.

21 Valley fold and unfold.

22 Reverse fold.

23 Valley fold.

24 Valley fold and unfold.

25 Reverse fold.

26 Reverse fold the bottom layer inside.

27 Valley fold and unfold. Repeat on the right.

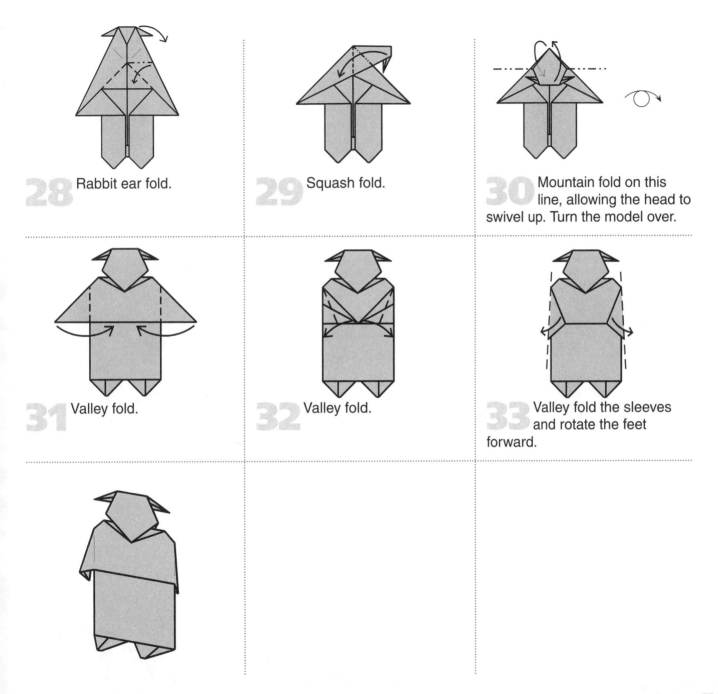

28 Rabbit ear fold.

29 Squash fold.

30 Mountain fold on this line, allowing the head to swivel up. Turn the model over.

31 Valley fold.

32 Valley fold.

33 Valley fold the sleeves and rotate the feet forward.

"Ouch time."
—CAPTAIN TARPALS

ARMORED ASSAULT TANK

The Armored Assault Tank (AAT) was the main battle tank used by the Trade Federation. It had a crew of four battle droids and was bursting with weaponry. Supporting the main long-range laser cannon were two side-mounted lasers and two forward short-range blasters. There were also six launch tubes that could fire either high-energy shells or solid projectiles. The heavy armor and weapons came at a price, though. This repulsor lift tank had a relatively low top speed, making it an easy target.

HOW TO FOLD: ARMORED ASSAULT TANK

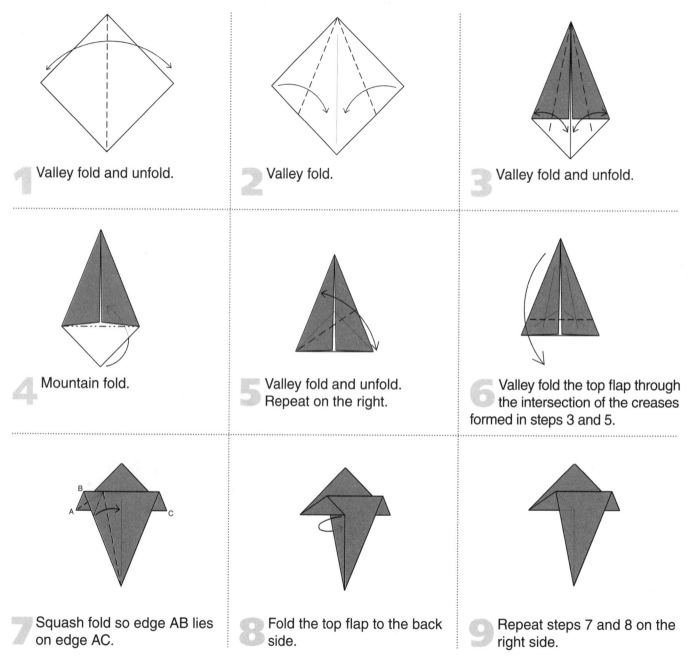

1 Valley fold and unfold.

2 Valley fold.

3 Valley fold and unfold.

4 Mountain fold.

5 Valley fold and unfold. Repeat on the right.

6 Valley fold the top flap through the intersection of the creases formed in steps 3 and 5.

7 Squash fold so edge AB lies on edge AC.

8 Fold the top flap to the back side.

9 Repeat steps 7 and 8 on the right side.

10 Rabbit ear fold.

11 Valley fold so edge AB is parallel to the center line.

12 Unfold.

13 Outside reverse fold.

14 Mountain fold.

15 Mark fold.

16 Valley fold so edge AB is parallel to line CD.

17 Valley fold so edge AB is parallel to line CB.

18 Unfold to step 16.

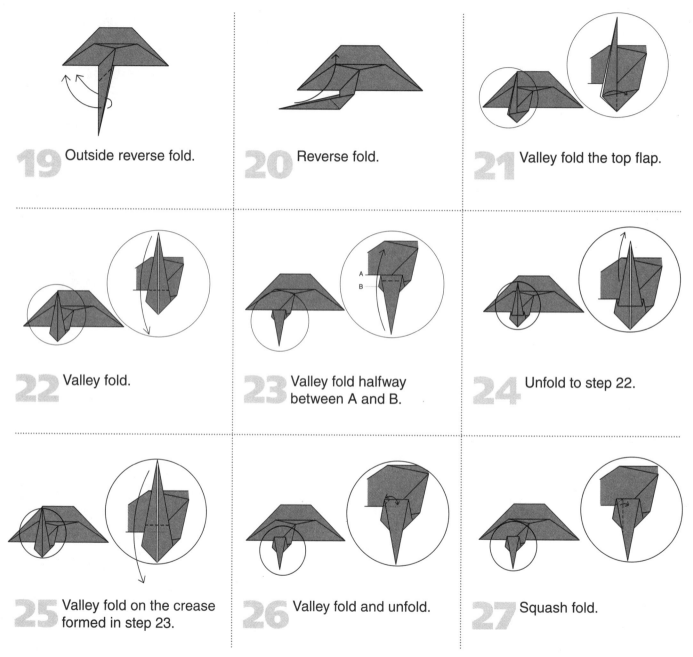

19 Outside reverse fold.

20 Reverse fold.

21 Valley fold the top flap.

22 Valley fold.

23 Valley fold halfway between A and B.

24 Unfold to step 22.

25 Valley fold on the crease formed in step 23.

26 Valley fold and unfold.

27 Squash fold.

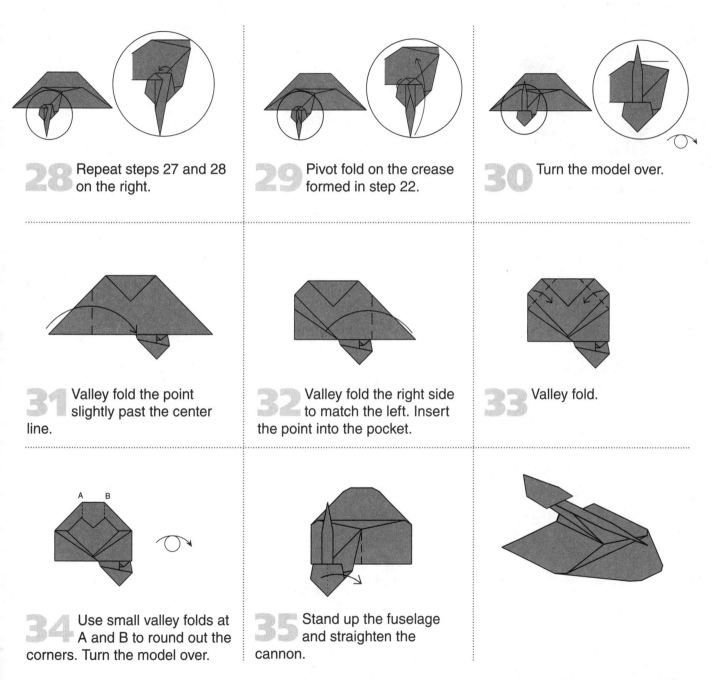

28 Repeat steps 27 and 28 on the right.

29 Pivot fold on the crease formed in step 22.

30 Turn the model over.

31 Valley fold the point slightly past the center line.

32 Valley fold the right side to match the left. Insert the point into the pocket.

33 Valley fold.

34 Use small valley folds at A and B to round out the corners. Turn the model over.

35 Stand up the fuselage and straighten the cannon.

"Go back?! Qui-Gon told me to stay in this cockpit and that's what I'm going to do."
—ANAKIN SKYWALKER

NABOO STARFIGHTER

A light-duty escort fighter, the Naboo starfighter was used primarily to escort the Queen's starship on her diplomatic travels. While highly maneuverable, it was under-armored and equipped with relatively light weapons; it had only a single torpedo launcher and two light laser cannons. Anakin Skywalker was flying one of these ships when he found himself in his first space battle, the Battle of Naboo. Deploying some well-placed torpedoes, he destroyed the Trade Federation's droid control ship and saved the day.

HOW TO FOLD: NABOO STARFIGHTER

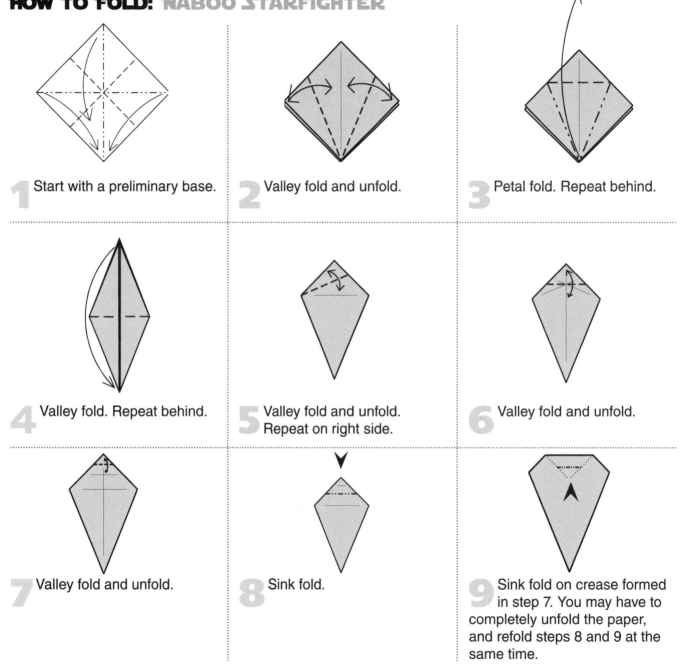

1 Start with a preliminary base.

2 Valley fold and unfold.

3 Petal fold. Repeat behind.

4 Valley fold. Repeat behind.

5 Valley fold and unfold. Repeat on right side.

6 Valley fold and unfold.

7 Valley fold and unfold.

8 Sink fold.

9 Sink fold on crease formed in step 7. You may have to completely unfold the paper, and refold steps 8 and 9 at the same time.

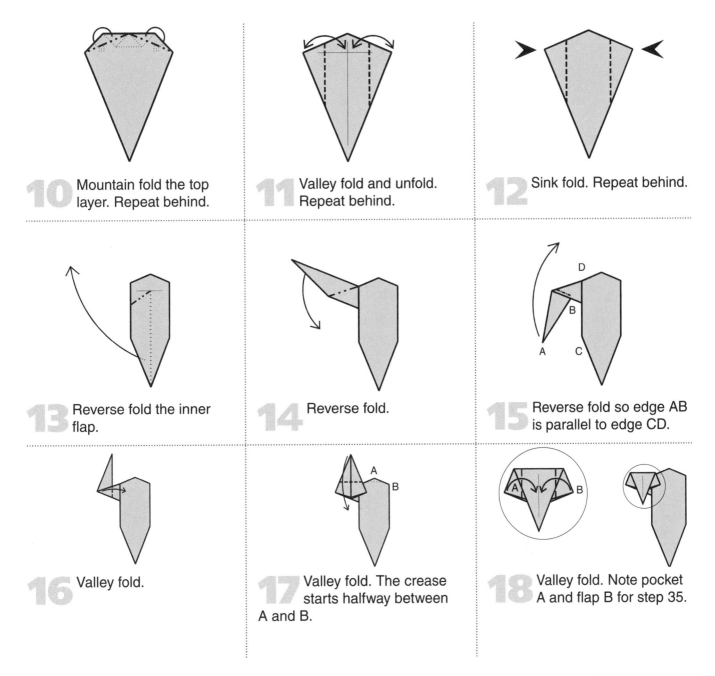

10 Mountain fold the top layer. Repeat behind.

11 Valley fold and unfold. Repeat behind.

12 Sink fold. Repeat behind.

13 Reverse fold the inner flap.

14 Reverse fold.

15 Reverse fold so edge AB is parallel to edge CD.

16 Valley fold.

17 Valley fold. The crease starts halfway between A and B.

18 Valley fold. Note pocket A and flap B for step 35.

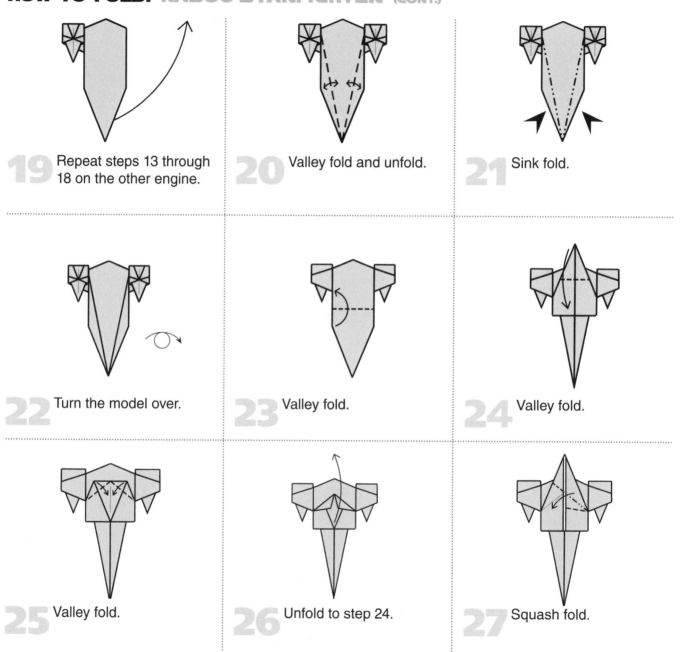

19 Repeat steps 13 through 18 on the other engine.

20 Valley fold and unfold.

21 Sink fold.

22 Turn the model over.

23 Valley fold.

24 Valley fold.

25 Valley fold.

26 Unfold to step 24.

27 Squash fold.

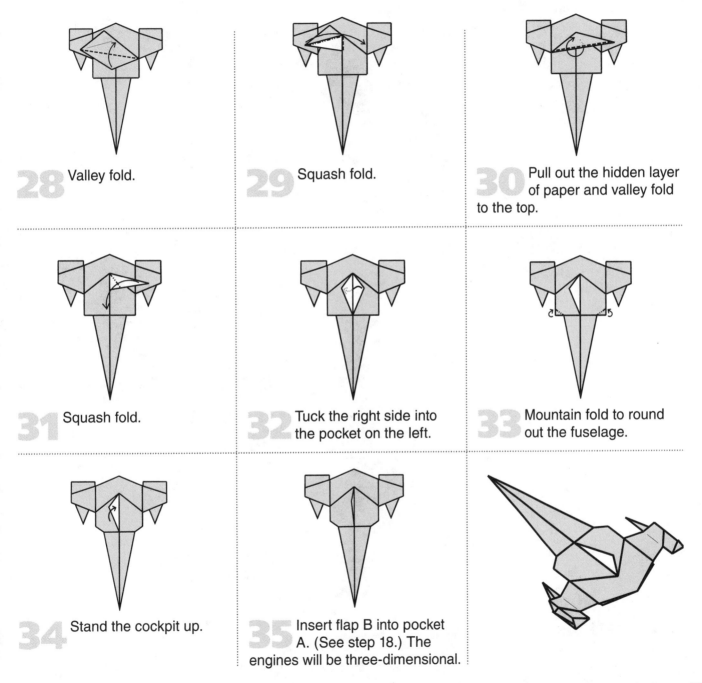

28 Valley fold.

29 Squash fold.

30 Pull out the hidden layer of paper and valley fold to the top.

31 Squash fold.

32 Tuck the right side into the pocket on the left.

33 Mountain fold to round out the fuselage.

34 Stand the cockpit up.

35 Insert flap B into pocket A. (See step 18.) The engines will be three-dimensional.

"General Grievous' ship is directly ahead, the one crawling with Vulture droids."

—ANAKIN SKYWALKER

VULTURE DROID STARFIGHTER

The Vulture droid was the Trade Federation's starfighter of choice. It was armed with four blaster cannons and two torpedo tubes, but lacked protective shields. A droid starfighter had several advantages over one with an organic pilot. Droid starfighters were cheaper to mass-produce, easier to train, required no life support systems, and wouldn't question orders. But a droid couldn't think creatively, and in an unusual situation, would fall back on its programming. This made it easy to anticipate in combat. Another weakness was its reliance on a central control computer. If the computer was knocked out, the droid would automatically shut down.

NOTE: You need three pieces of paper for this model. Steps 1 through 18 form one wing. You will need to make two wings. Steps 19 through 47 form the fuselage.

HOW TO FOLD: VULTURE DROID STARFIGHTER

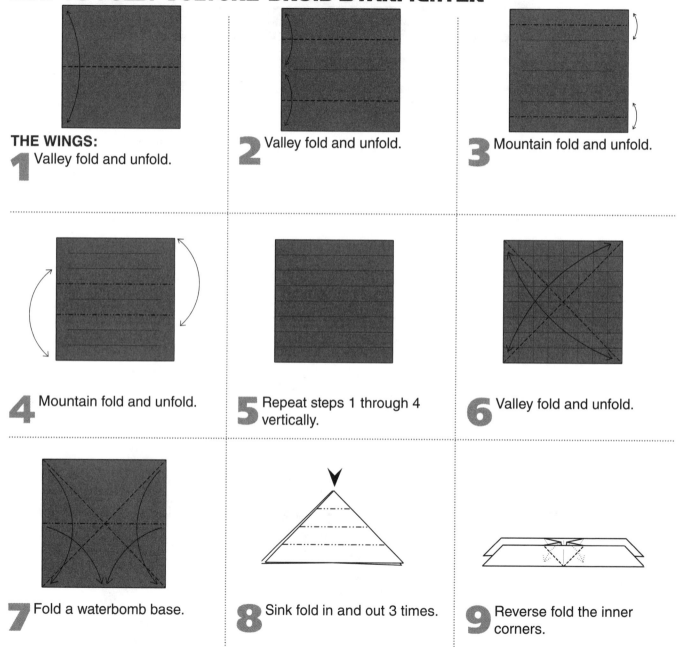

THE WINGS:

1 Valley fold and unfold.

2 Valley fold and unfold.

3 Mountain fold and unfold.

4 Mountain fold and unfold.

5 Repeat steps 1 through 4 vertically.

6 Valley fold and unfold.

7 Fold a waterbomb base.

8 Sink fold in and out 3 times.

9 Reverse fold the inner corners.

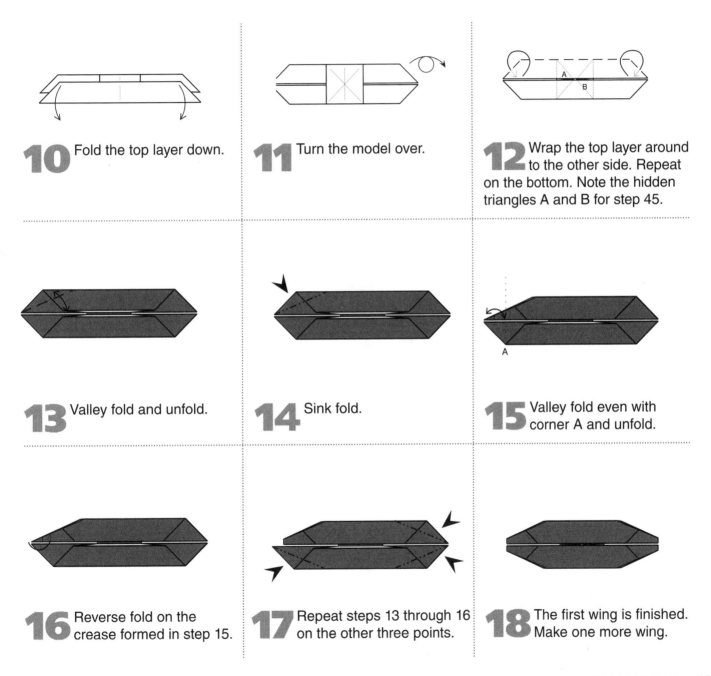

10 Fold the top layer down.

11 Turn the model over.

12 Wrap the top layer around to the other side. Repeat on the bottom. Note the hidden triangles A and B for step 45.

13 Valley fold and unfold.

14 Sink fold.

15 Valley fold even with corner A and unfold.

16 Reverse fold on the crease formed in step 15.

17 Repeat steps 13 through 16 on the other three points.

18 The first wing is finished. Make one more wing.

HOW TO FOLD: VULTURE DROID STARFIGHTER (CONT.)

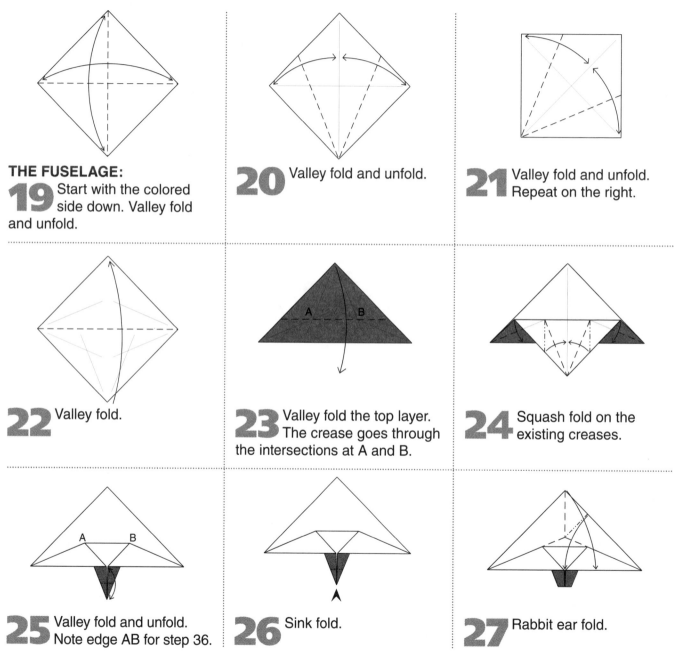

THE FUSELAGE:

19 Start with the colored side down. Valley fold and unfold.

20 Valley fold and unfold.

21 Valley fold and unfold. Repeat on the right.

22 Valley fold.

23 Valley fold the top layer. The crease goes through the intersections at A and B.

24 Squash fold on the existing creases.

25 Valley fold and unfold. Note edge AB for step 36.

26 Sink fold.

27 Rabbit ear fold.

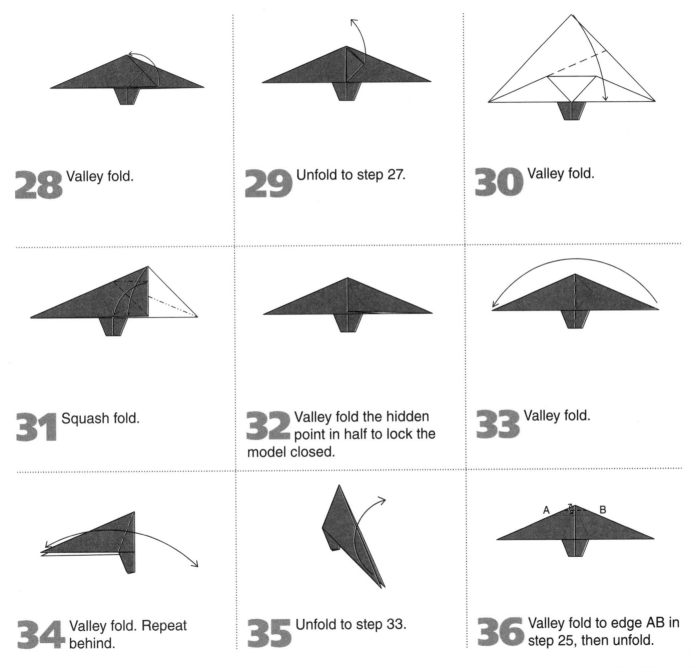

28 Valley fold.

29 Unfold to step 27.

30 Valley fold.

31 Squash fold.

32 Valley fold the hidden point in half to lock the model closed.

33 Valley fold.

34 Valley fold. Repeat behind.

35 Unfold to step 33.

36 Valley fold to edge AB in step 25, then unfold.

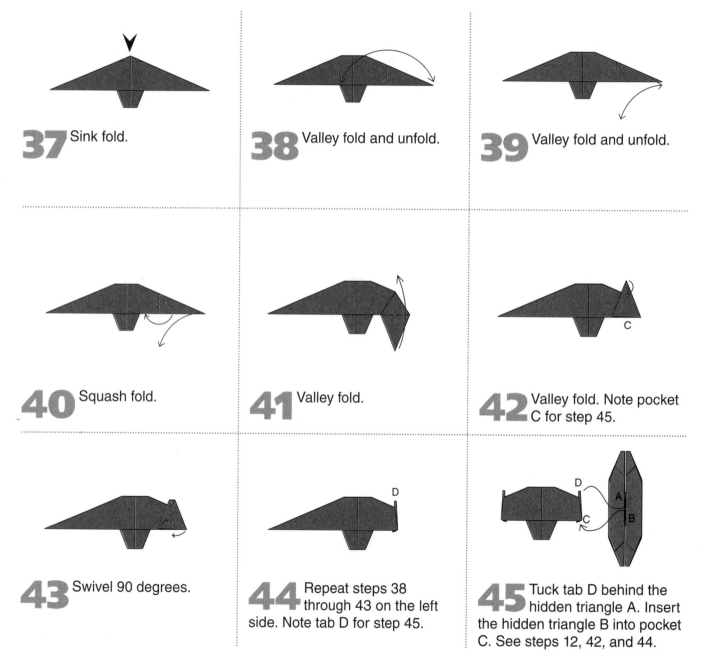

37 Sink fold.

38 Valley fold and unfold.

39 Valley fold and unfold.

40 Squash fold.

41 Valley fold.

42 Valley fold. Note pocket C for step 45.

43 Swivel 90 degrees.

44 Repeat steps 38 through 43 on the left side. Note tab D for step 45.

45 Tuck tab D behind the hidden triangle A. Insert the hidden triangle B into pocket C. See steps 12, 42, and 44.

46 Install the left wing the same way.

47 Rotate the wings 90 degrees and bend them in slightly. Give the cockpit a gentle squeeze to shape it.

Vulture droids take flight during the Battle of Utapau.

"No disintegrations."
—DARTH VADER TO BOBA FETT

JANGO FETT AND BOBA FETT

Jango Fett was a Mandalorian warrior who became a legendary bounty hunter. Ruthless yet honorable, he was selected by Darth Tyranus (Count Dooku) to become the genetic template for the clone army of the Republic. Aside from a cash payment, Jango also asked for an unaltered clone that he could raise as his son. Following in his father's footsteps, Boba Fett became the most notorious bounty hunter in the galaxy. While his armor looked battered and worn, it held many hidden weapons, including rocket darts, a flamethrower, and a rocket pack with a guided missile. But the most effective weapon the Fetts used was their cunning, preferring to outwit and trap their quarry rather than use pure force.

Boba Fett

Jango Fett

HOW TO FOLD: JANGO FETT AND BOBA FETT

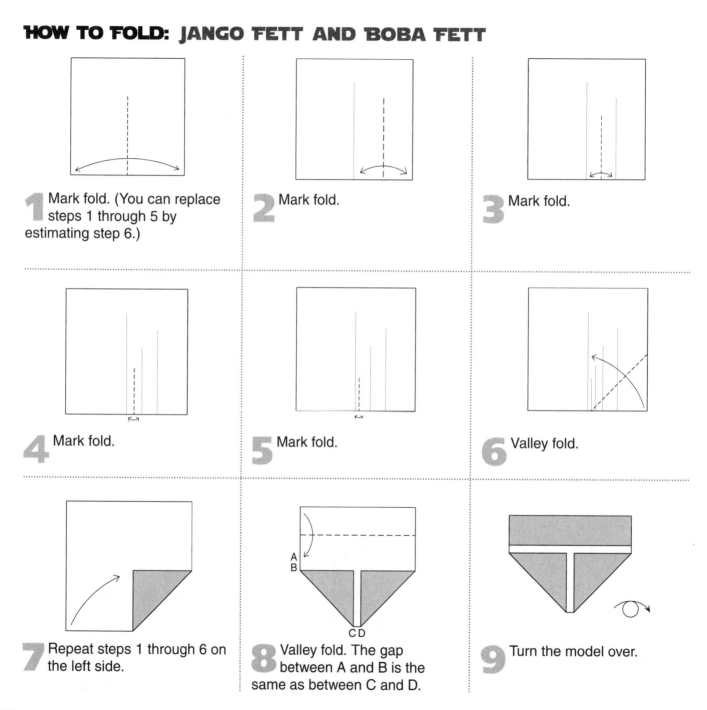

1 Mark fold. (You can replace steps 1 through 5 by estimating step 6.)

2 Mark fold.

3 Mark fold.

4 Mark fold.

5 Mark fold.

6 Valley fold.

7 Repeat steps 1 through 6 on the left side.

8 Valley fold. The gap between A and B is the same as between C and D.

9 Turn the model over.

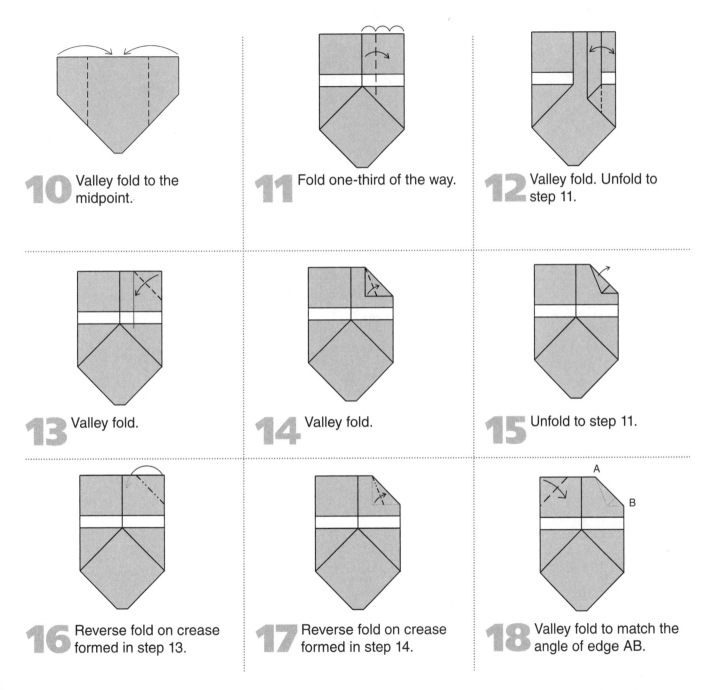

10 Valley fold to the midpoint.

11 Fold one-third of the way.

12 Valley fold. Unfold to step 11.

13 Valley fold.

14 Valley fold.

15 Unfold to step 11.

16 Reverse fold on crease formed in step 13.

17 Reverse fold on crease formed in step 14.

18 Valley fold to match the angle of edge AB.

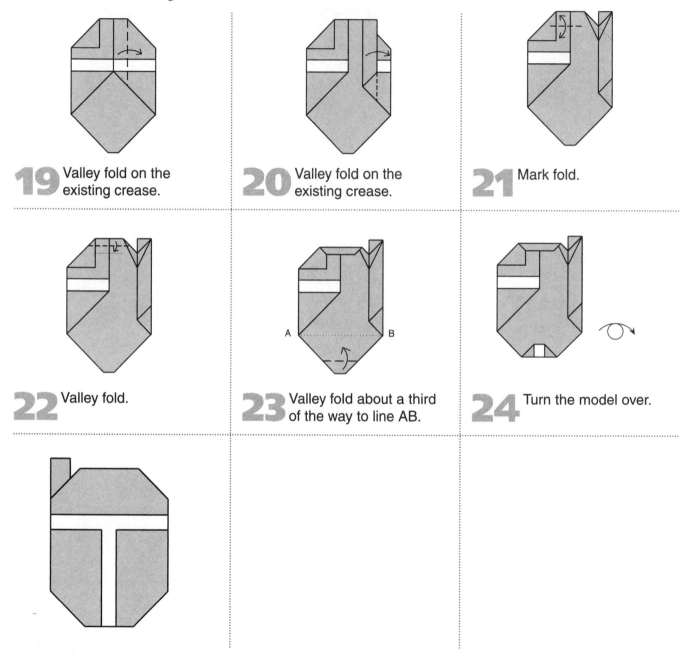

19 Valley fold on the existing crease.

20 Valley fold on the existing crease.

21 Mark fold.

22 Valley fold.

23 Valley fold about a third of the way to line AB.

24 Turn the model over.

TEST YOUR STAR WARS IQ:
MATCHUP

Match the *Star Wars* character to his or her home planet.

1. Padmé Amidala

A. Tatooine

2. Chewbacca

B. Stewjon

3. Luke Skywalker

C. Alderaan

4. Boba Fett

D. Kamino

5. Obi-Wan Kenobi

E. Naboo

6. Princess Leia Organa

F. Corellia

7. Han Solo

G. Kashyyyk

"Put Captain Solo in the cargo hold."
—BOBA FETT

SLAVE I

L ike the armor worn by its notorious owners, Jango Fett and Boba Fett, every inch of *Slave I* hid some weapon, sensor, or self-defense system. This fighter/bomber was modified and upgraded countless times and, in spite of its being considered an antique, was one of the top pursuit crafts in the galaxy. Jango Fett made this ship infamous before the Clone Wars, and his son, Boba, only increased its reputation long into the reign of the Empire.

HOW TO FOLD: *SLAVE I*

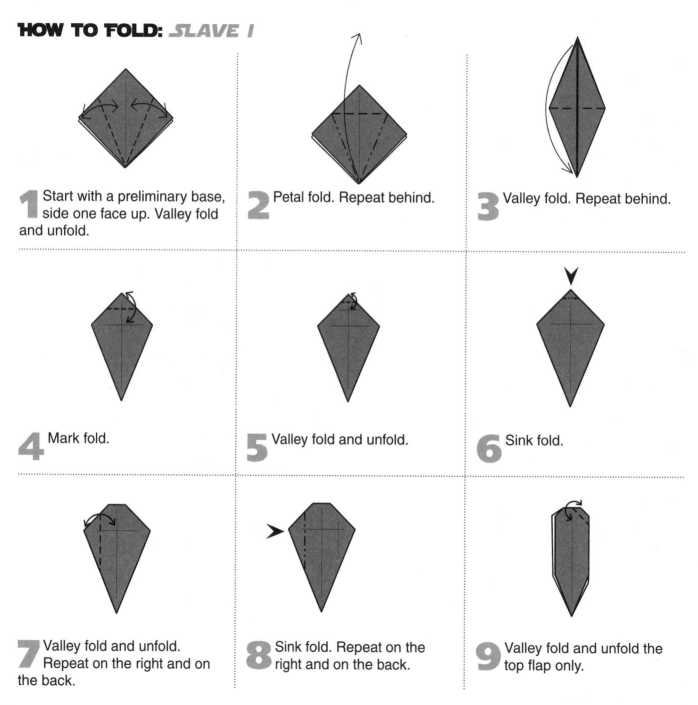

1 Start with a preliminary base, side one face up. Valley fold and unfold.

2 Petal fold. Repeat behind.

3 Valley fold. Repeat behind.

4 Mark fold.

5 Valley fold and unfold.

6 Sink fold.

7 Valley fold and unfold. Repeat on the right and on the back.

8 Sink fold. Repeat on the right and on the back.

9 Valley fold and unfold the top flap only.

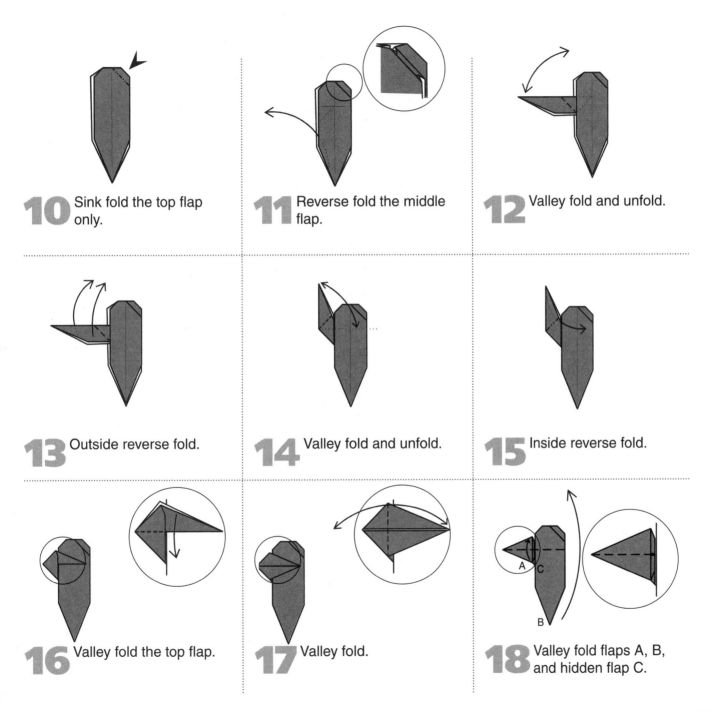

10 Sink fold the top flap only.

11 Reverse fold the middle flap.

12 Valley fold and unfold.

13 Outside reverse fold.

14 Valley fold and unfold.

15 Inside reverse fold.

16 Valley fold the top flap.

17 Valley fold.

18 Valley fold flaps A, B, and hidden flap C.

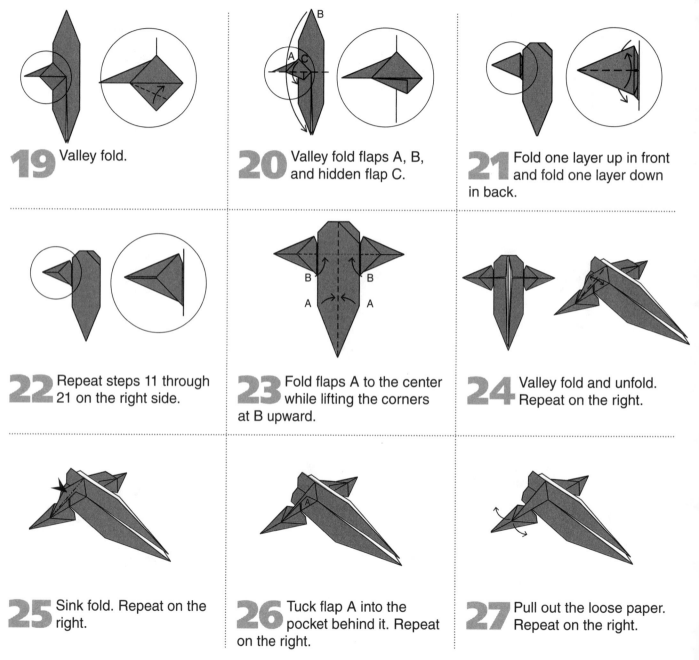

19 Valley fold.

20 Valley fold flaps A, B, and hidden flap C.

21 Fold one layer up in front and fold one layer down in back.

22 Repeat steps 11 through 21 on the right side.

23 Fold flaps A to the center while lifting the corners at B upward.

24 Valley fold and unfold. Repeat on the right.

25 Sink fold. Repeat on the right.

26 Tuck flap A into the pocket behind it. Repeat on the right.

27 Pull out the loose paper. Repeat on the right.

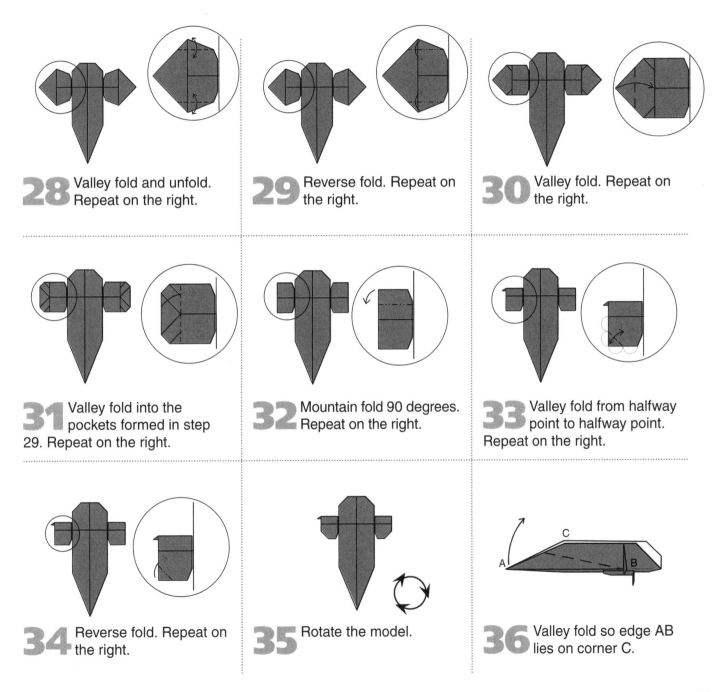

28 Valley fold and unfold. Repeat on the right.

29 Reverse fold. Repeat on the right.

30 Valley fold. Repeat on the right.

31 Valley fold into the pockets formed in step 29. Repeat on the right.

32 Mountain fold 90 degrees. Repeat on the right.

33 Valley fold from halfway point to halfway point. Repeat on the right.

34 Reverse fold. Repeat on the right.

35 Rotate the model.

36 Valley fold so edge AB lies on corner C.

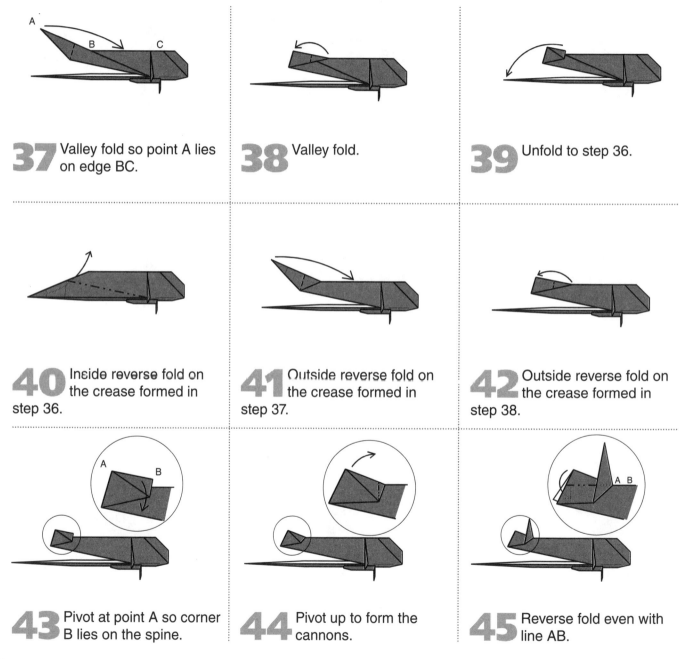

37 Valley fold so point A lies on edge BC.

38 Valley fold.

39 Unfold to step 36.

40 Inside reverse fold on the crease formed in step 36.

41 Outside reverse fold on the crease formed in step 37.

42 Outside reverse fold on the crease formed in step 38.

43 Pivot at point A so corner B lies on the spine.

44 Pivot up to form the cannons.

45 Reverse fold even with line AB.

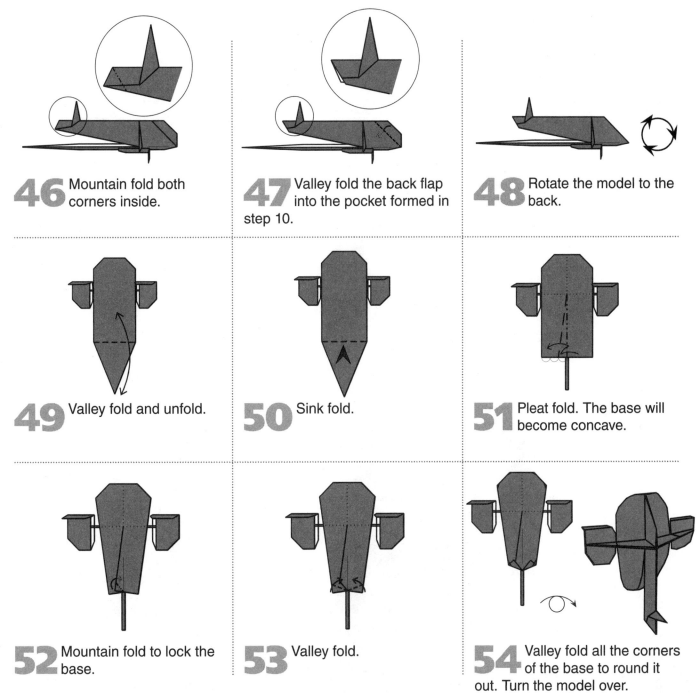

46 Mountain fold both corners inside.

47 Valley fold the back flap into the pocket formed in step 10.

48 Rotate the model to the back.

49 Valley fold and unfold.

50 Sink fold.

51 Pleat fold. The base will become concave.

52 Mountain fold to lock the base.

53 Valley fold.

54 Valley fold all the corners of the base to round it out. Turn the model over.

"These Kaminoans keep to themselves; they're cloners . . . good ones, too."

—DEXTER JETTSTER

TAUN WE

Kaminoans were tall, slender, and graceful humanoids. As a race they were gentle, artistic, and intelligent, but often a bit naive. They excelled in scientific fields and were considered the best cloners in the galaxy. Because of this skill, Taun We was chosen as the project coordinator for the clone army commissioned by the Jedi Master Sifo-Dyas. Using legendary bounty hunter Jango Fett as the genetic template, she developed the clones into a fighting force of exceptional ability.

HOW TO FOLD: TAUN WE

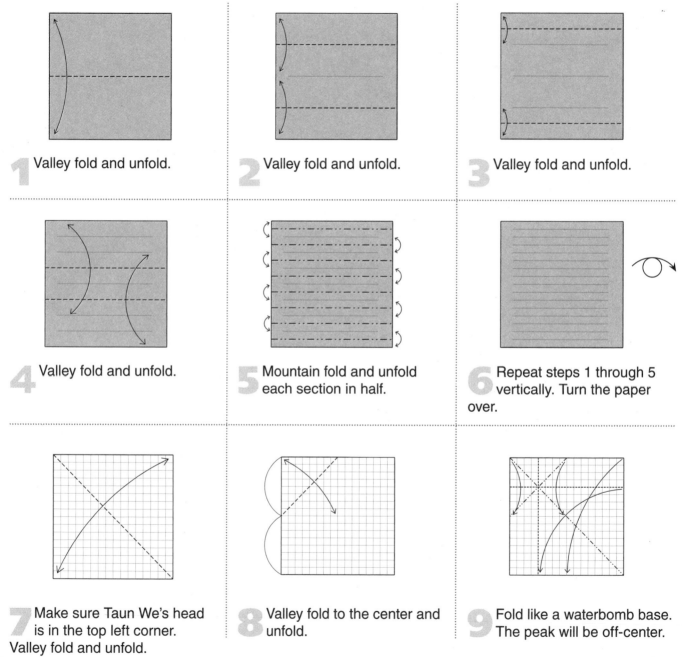

1 Valley fold and unfold.

2 Valley fold and unfold.

3 Valley fold and unfold.

4 Valley fold and unfold.

5 Mountain fold and unfold each section in half.

6 Repeat steps 1 through 5 vertically. Turn the paper over.

7 Make sure Taun We's head is in the top left corner. Valley fold and unfold.

8 Valley fold to the center and unfold.

9 Fold like a waterbomb base. The peak will be off-center.

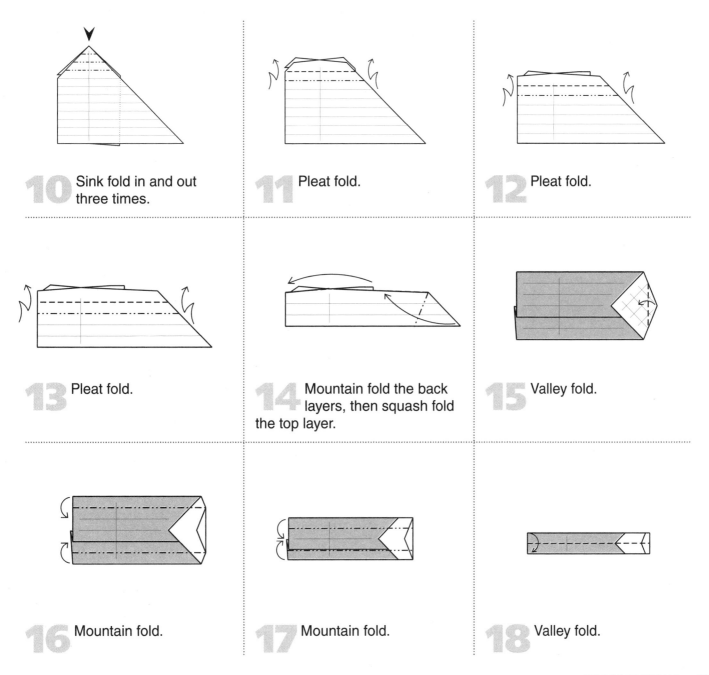

10 Sink fold in and out three times.

11 Pleat fold.

12 Pleat fold.

13 Pleat fold.

14 Mountain fold the back layers, then squash fold the top layer.

15 Valley fold.

16 Mountain fold.

17 Mountain fold.

18 Valley fold.

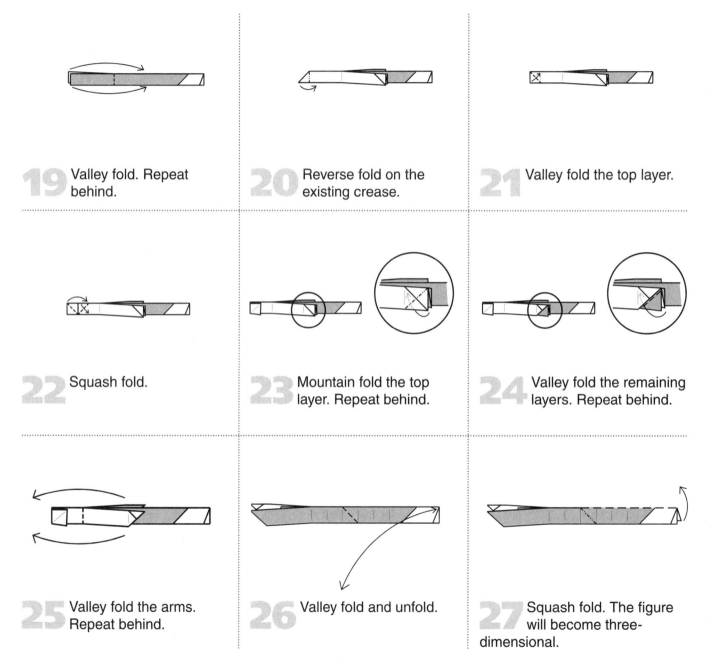

19 Valley fold. Repeat behind.

20 Reverse fold on the existing crease.

21 Valley fold the top layer.

22 Squash fold.

23 Mountain fold the top layer. Repeat behind.

24 Valley fold the remaining layers. Repeat behind.

25 Valley fold the arms. Repeat behind.

26 Valley fold and unfold.

27 Squash fold. The figure will become three-dimensional.

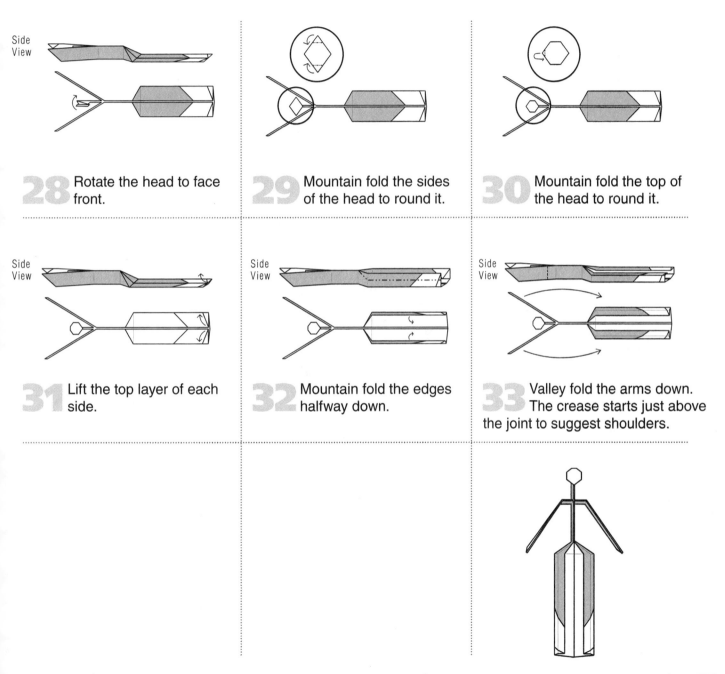

28 Rotate the head to face front.

29 Mountain fold the sides of the head to round it.

30 Mountain fold the top of the head to round it.

31 Lift the top layer of each side.

32 Mountain fold the edges halfway down.

33 Valley fold the arms down. The crease starts just above the joint to suggest shoulders.

"I do believe they think I am some sort of god."

—C-3PO

C-3PO

Like all protocol droids, C-3PO specialized in interpretation and communication with intelligent species and droids throughout the galaxy. Fluent in more than six million galactic languages, he was most drawn to the nuances of human interaction. And while C-3PO might have been a bit fussy, he was incredibly loyal to his masters and his counterpart, R2-D2. Originally built from parts that a young Anakin Skywalker scavenged in Watto's junkyard, C-3PO stayed in the extended Skywalker family, working for Padmé Amidala, Bail Organa, Princess Leia Organa, and Luke Skywalker.

NOTE: You will need two pieces of paper for this model. Steps 1 through 19 form the lower half. Steps 20 through 51 form the upper half.

HOW TO FOLD: C-3PO

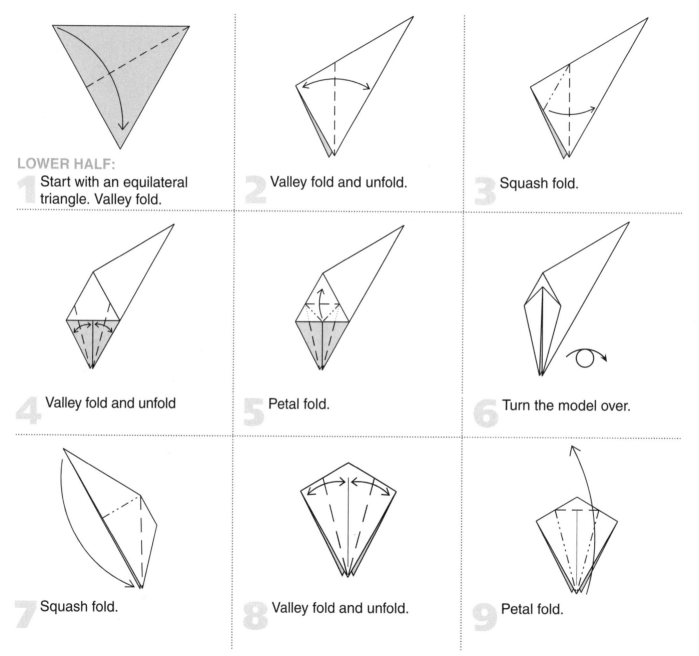

LOWER HALF:

1 Start with an equilateral triangle. Valley fold.

2 Valley fold and unfold.

3 Squash fold.

4 Valley fold and unfold

5 Petal fold.

6 Turn the model over.

7 Squash fold.

8 Valley fold and unfold.

9 Petal fold.

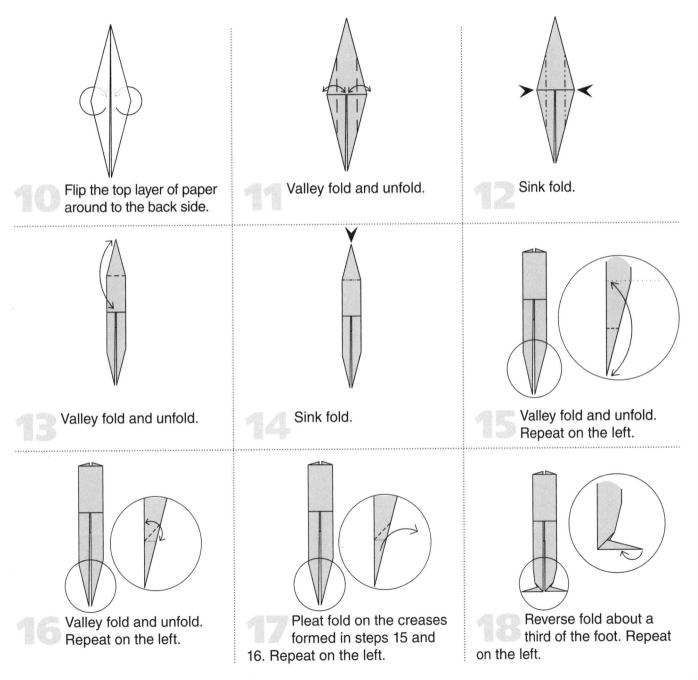

10 Flip the top layer of paper around to the back side.

11 Valley fold and unfold.

12 Sink fold.

13 Valley fold and unfold.

14 Sink fold.

15 Valley fold and unfold. Repeat on the left.

16 Valley fold and unfold. Repeat on the left.

17 Pleat fold on the creases formed in steps 15 and 16. Repeat on the left.

18 Reverse fold about a third of the foot. Repeat on the left.

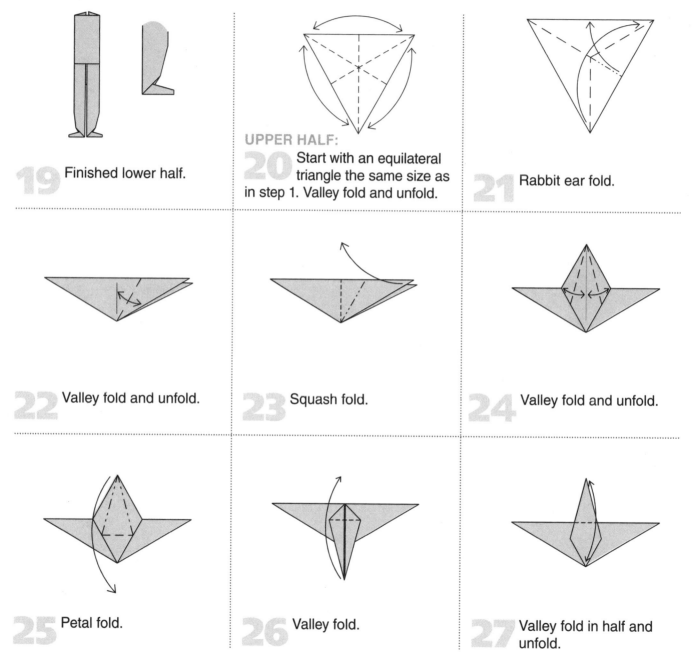

19 Finished lower half.

UPPER HALF:
20 Start with an equilateral triangle the same size as in step 1. Valley fold and unfold.

21 Rabbit ear fold.

22 Valley fold and unfold.

23 Squash fold.

24 Valley fold and unfold.

25 Petal fold.

26 Valley fold.

27 Valley fold in half and unfold.

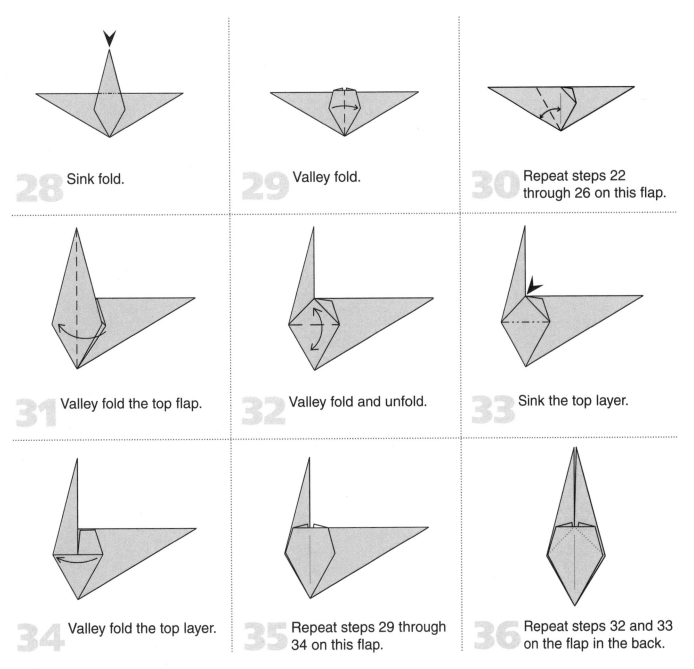

28 Sink fold.

29 Valley fold.

30 Repeat steps 22 through 26 on this flap.

31 Valley fold the top flap.

32 Valley fold and unfold.

33 Sink the top layer.

34 Valley fold the top layer.

35 Repeat steps 29 through 34 on this flap.

36 Repeat steps 32 and 33 on the flap in the back.

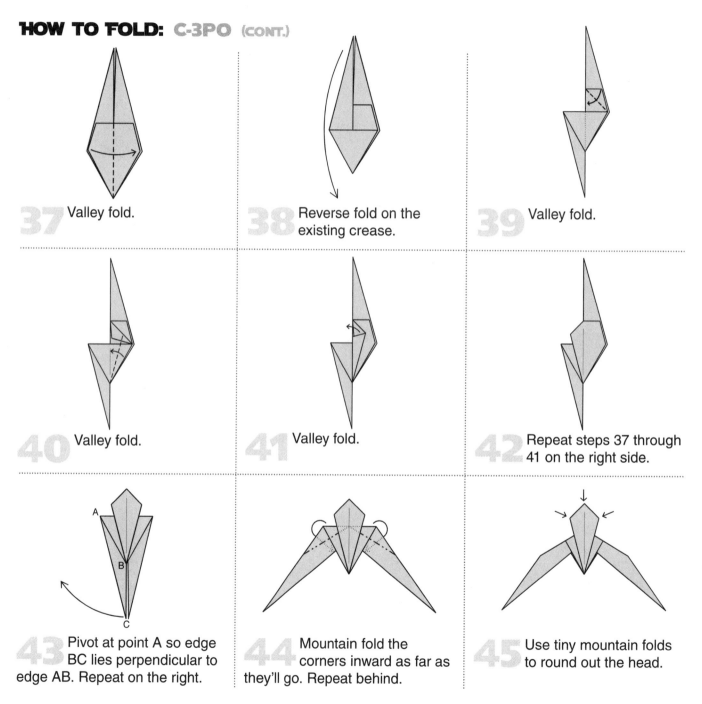

37 Valley fold.

38 Reverse fold on the existing crease.

39 Valley fold.

40 Valley fold.

41 Valley fold.

42 Repeat steps 37 through 41 on the right side.

43 Pivot at point A so edge BC lies perpendicular to edge AB. Repeat on the right.

44 Mountain fold the corners inward as far as they'll go. Repeat behind.

45 Use tiny mountain folds to round out the head.

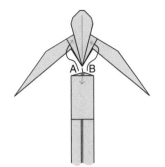

46 Insert the upper half into the pocket of the lower half, while inserting tabs A and B into the top pockets of the lower half. Keep the tabs above the arms.

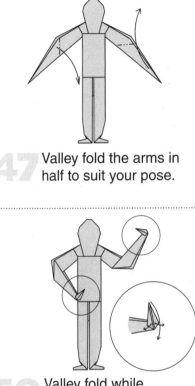

47 Valley fold the arms in half to suit your pose.

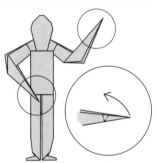

48 Squash fold about one-fourth of the arm to form hands.

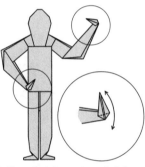

49 Valley fold and unfold.

50 Valley fold while spreading the loose paper to the sides.

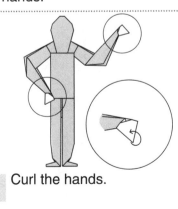

51 Curl the hands.

"They are totally obedient, taking any order without question."

—LAMA SU TO OBI-WAN KENOBI

REPUBLIC CLONE TROOPER

Clone troopers were created by the Republic for one purpose: combat. Bred in the Kamino clone hatcheries using the bounty hunter Jango Fett as the template, clone troopers were considered the future of warfare. They were first used in combat after the Separatists put an army of battle droids into the field, forcing the Republic to use the clone army in response. Units of clone troopers were led by the Jedi and eventually put down the Separatist threat. At the end of the Clone Wars, Darth Sidious issued Order 66, which identified the Jedi as traitors. The clones turned on the unsuspecting Jedi and extinguished their light from the galaxy.

HOW TO FOLD: REPUBLIC CLONE TROOPER

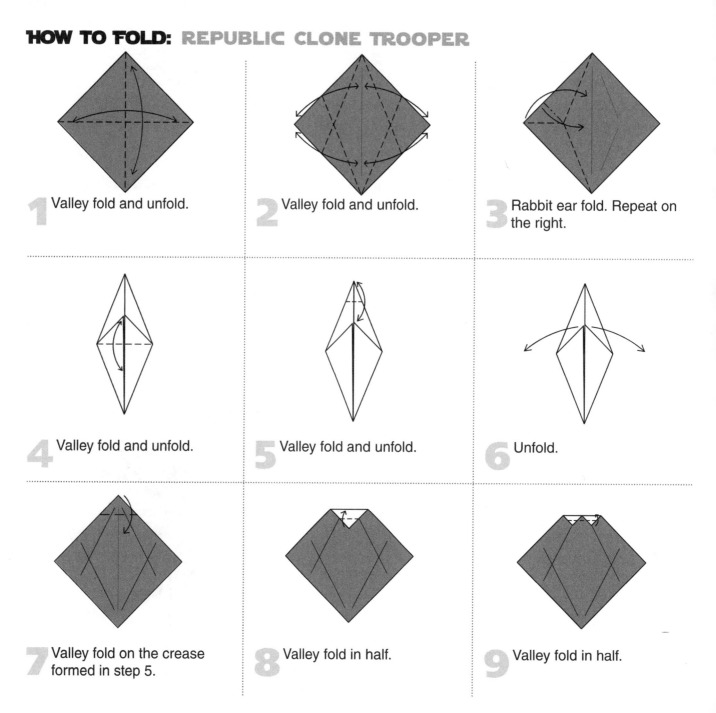

1 Valley fold and unfold.

2 Valley fold and unfold.

3 Rabbit ear fold. Repeat on the right.

4 Valley fold and unfold.

5 Valley fold and unfold.

6 Unfold.

7 Valley fold on the crease formed in step 5.

8 Valley fold in half.

9 Valley fold in half.

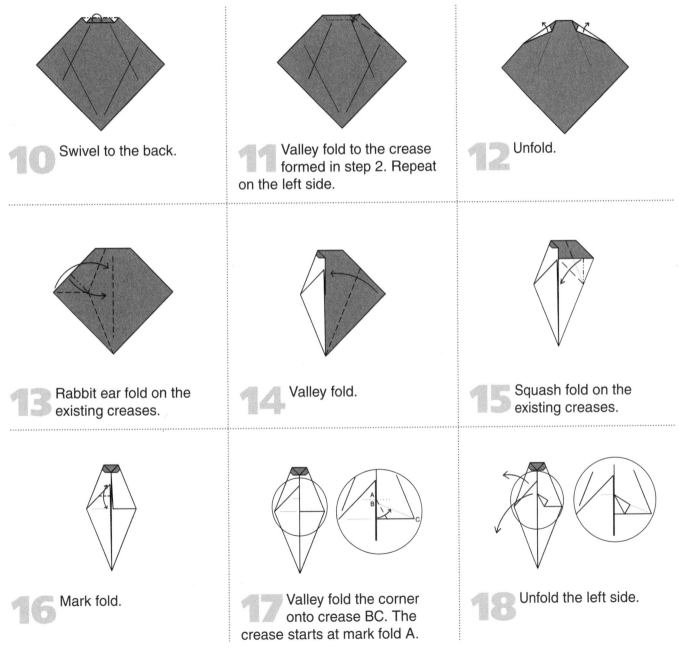

10 Swivel to the back.

11 Valley fold to the crease formed in step 2. Repeat on the left side.

12 Unfold.

13 Rabbit ear fold on the existing creases.

14 Valley fold.

15 Squash fold on the existing creases.

16 Mark fold.

17 Valley fold the corner onto crease BC. The crease starts at mark fold A.

18 Unfold the left side.

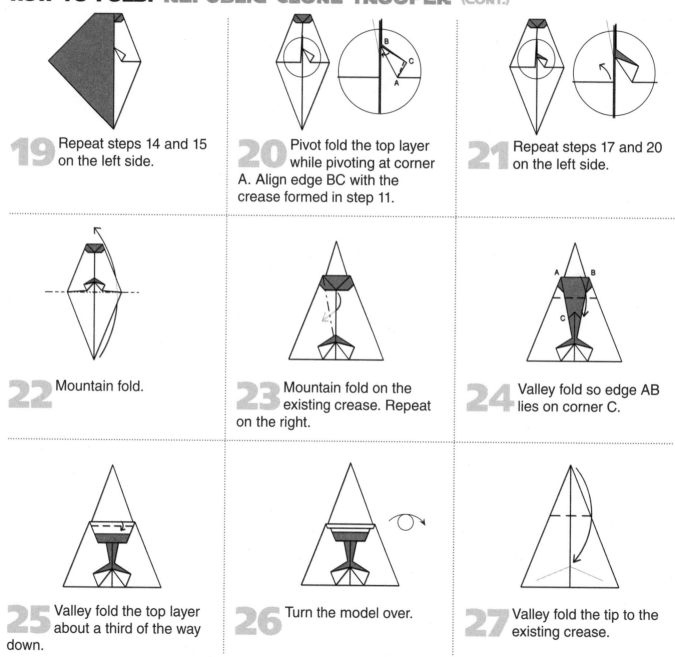

19 Repeat steps 14 and 15 on the left side.

20 Pivot fold the top layer while pivoting at corner A. Align edge BC with the crease formed in step 11.

21 Repeat steps 17 and 20 on the left side.

22 Mountain fold.

23 Mountain fold on the existing crease. Repeat on the right.

24 Valley fold so edge AB lies on corner C.

25 Valley fold the top layer about a third of the way down.

26 Turn the model over.

27 Valley fold the tip to the existing crease.

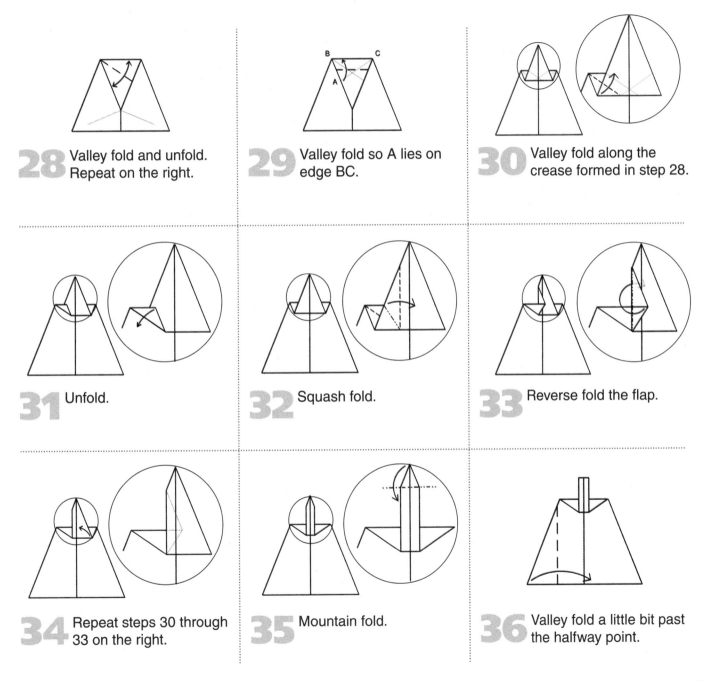

28 Valley fold and unfold. Repeat on the right.

29 Valley fold so A lies on edge BC.

30 Valley fold along the crease formed in step 28.

31 Unfold.

32 Squash fold.

33 Reverse fold the flap.

34 Repeat steps 30 through 33 on the right.

35 Mountain fold.

36 Valley fold a little bit past the halfway point.

HOW TO FOLD: REPUBLIC CLONE TROOPER (CONT.)

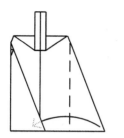

37 Valley fold as in step 36. Insert the corner into the pocket.

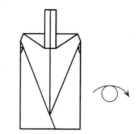

38 Turn the model over.

39 Mountain fold halfway between A and B. Repeat on the right.

40 Valley fold.

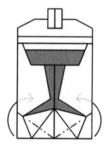

41 Mountain fold.

TEST YOUR STAR WARS IQ:
TRIVIA

1. Who is believed to be the Chosen One of an ancient Jedi prophecy?

2. Which Jedi has green blood?

3. Who disfigured Emperor Palpatine's face in battle?

4. What were the names of Luke Skywalker's aunt and uncle?

5. Which character was sent to deliver the stolen Death Star plans to Obi-Wan Kenobi?

6. In the movies, how many times did Luke Skywalker say, "May the Force be with you"?

ANSWERS: 1. Anakin Skywalker. 2. Yoda. 3. Mace Windu. 4. Owen and Beru Lars. 5. R2-D2. 6. Zero

"This is where the fun begins!"

—ANAKIN SKYWALKER

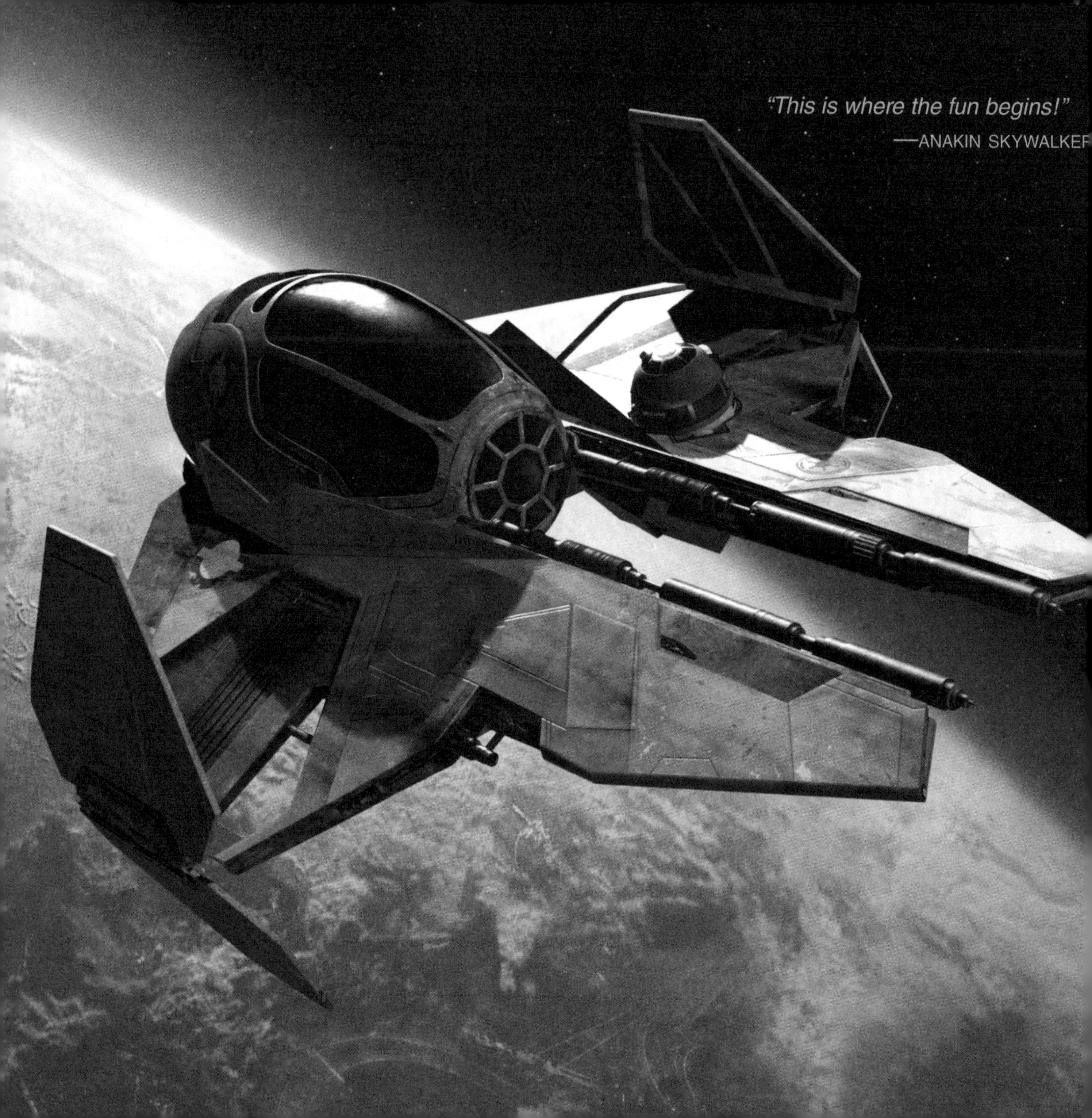

ETA-2 JEDI STARFIGHTER

N ear the end of the Clone Wars, a new starfighter gained preference among the Jedi pilots, the Eta-2 Actis-class light interceptor. This tiny ship was barely ten feet long, but was extremely well armed and very maneuverable. It carried an R2 unit on the left mandible for in-flight repairs and to manage onboard systems, such as navigation and fire control. S-foils on the wings also extended for added agility and retracted for landings. Improved maneuverability and increased firepower were two very good reasons why this fighter became the preferred choice for Jedi pilots.

HOW TO FOLD: ETA-2 JEDI STARFIGHTER

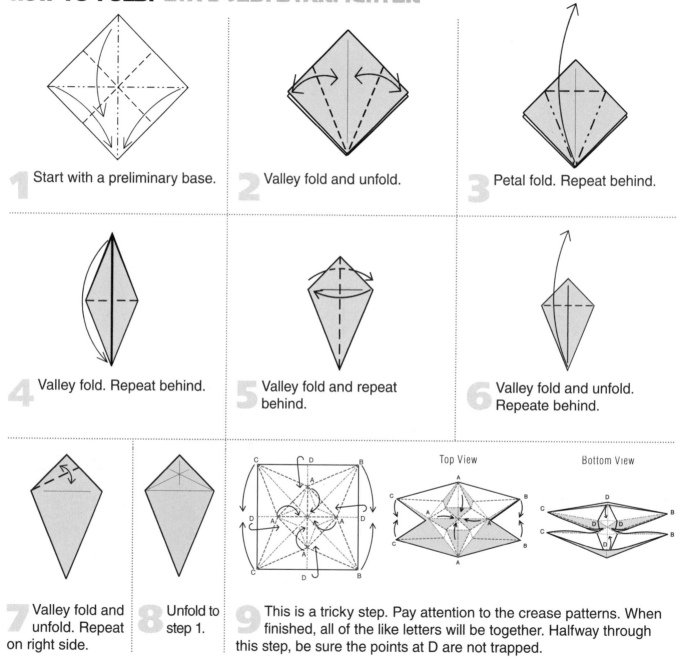

1 Start with a preliminary base.

2 Valley fold and unfold.

3 Petal fold. Repeat behind.

4 Valley fold. Repeat behind.

5 Valley fold and repeat behind.

6 Valley fold and unfold. Repeate behind.

7 Valley fold and unfold. Repeat on right side.

8 Unfold to step 1.

9 This is a tricky step. Pay attention to the crease patterns. When finished, all of the like letters will be together. Halfway through this step, be sure the points at D are not trapped.

Top View

Bottom View

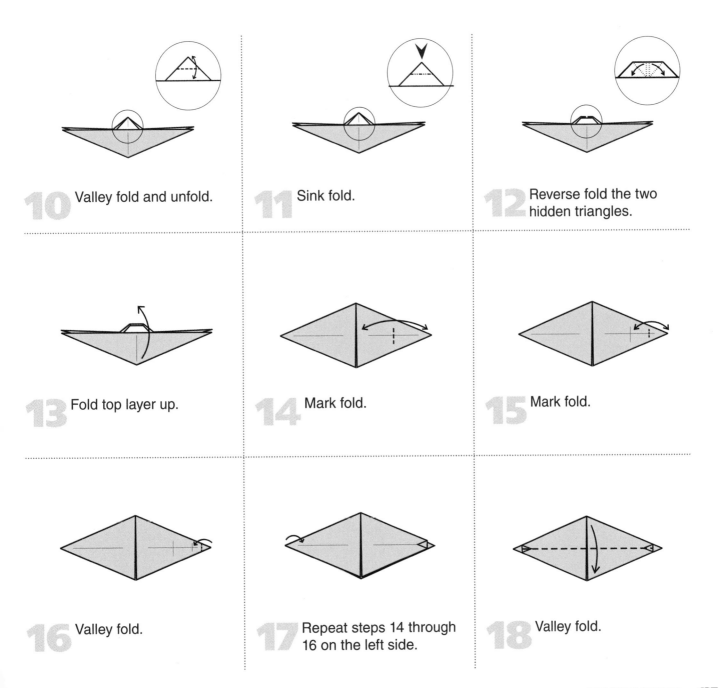

10 Valley fold and unfold.

11 Sink fold.

12 Reverse fold the two hidden triangles.

13 Fold top layer up.

14 Mark fold.

15 Mark fold.

16 Valley fold.

17 Repeat steps 14 through 16 on the left side.

18 Valley fold.

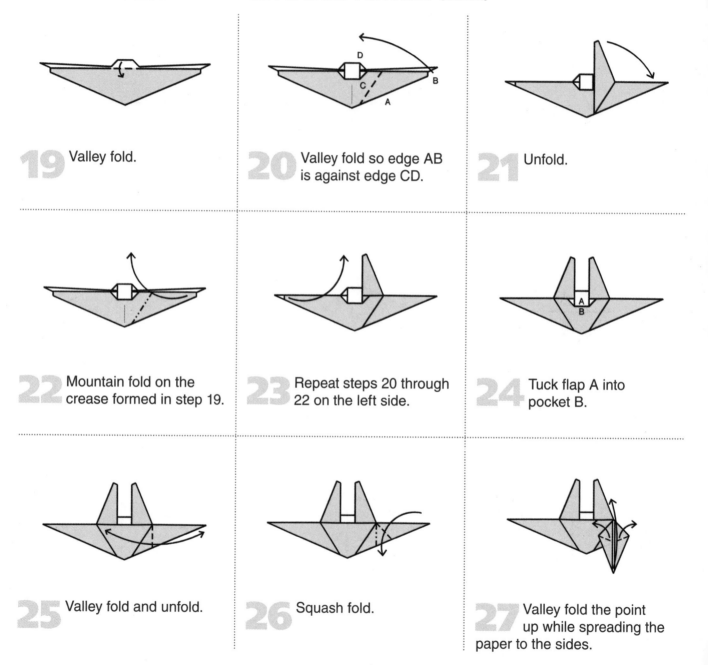

19 Valley fold.

20 Valley fold so edge AB is against edge CD.

21 Unfold.

22 Mountain fold on the crease formed in step 19.

23 Repeat steps 20 through 22 on the left side.

24 Tuck flap A into pocket B.

25 Valley fold and unfold.

26 Squash fold.

27 Valley fold the point up while spreading the paper to the sides.

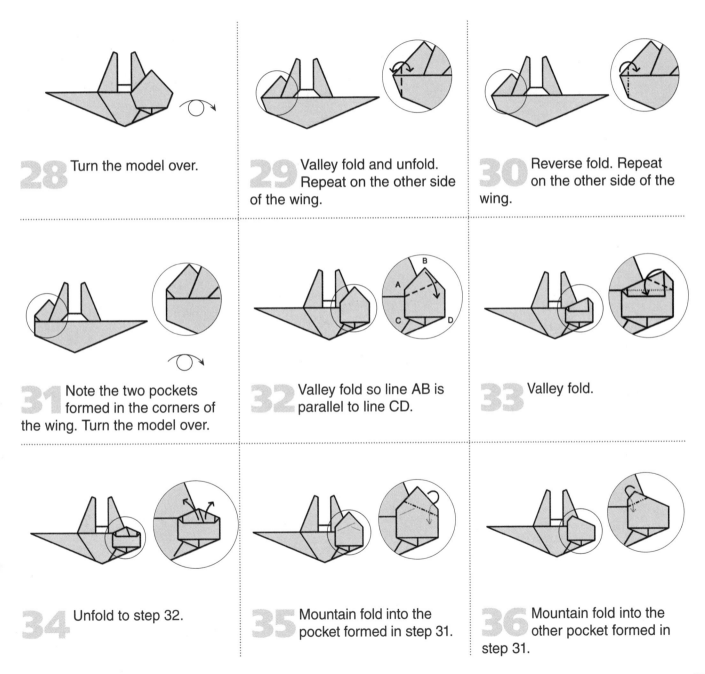

28 Turn the model over.

29 Valley fold and unfold. Repeat on the other side of the wing.

30 Reverse fold. Repeat on the other side of the wing.

31 Note the two pockets formed in the corners of the wing. Turn the model over.

32 Valley fold so line AB is parallel to line CD.

33 Valley fold.

34 Unfold to step 32.

35 Mountain fold into the pocket formed in step 31.

36 Mountain fold into the other pocket formed in step 31.

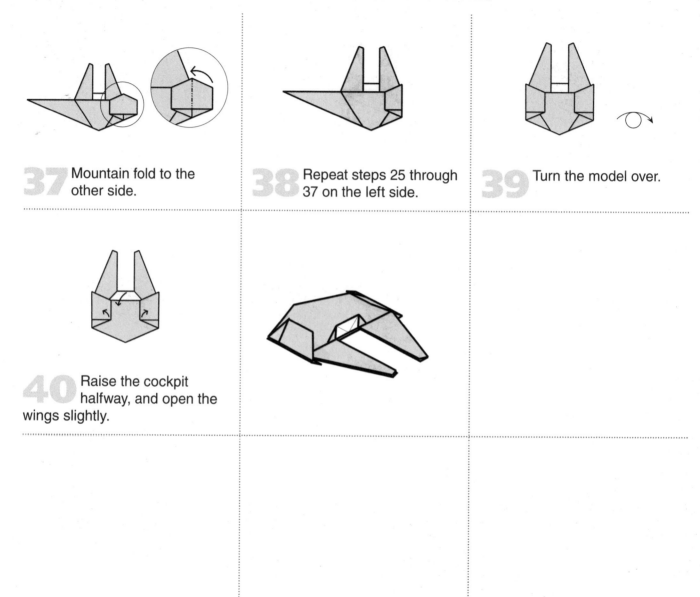

37 Mountain fold to the other side.

38 Repeat steps 25 through 37 on the left side.

39 Turn the model over.

40 Raise the cockpit halfway, and open the wings slightly.

TEST YOUR STAR WARS IQ:

WHO SAID IT?

Match the quote to the correct *Star Wars* character.

1. "I have become more powerful than any Jedi."

 A. Admiral Ackbar

2. "I want to learn the ways of the Force and become a Jedi like my father."

B. Count Dooku (Darth Tyranus)

3. "The Emperor has made a critical error and the time for our attack has come."

C. Admiral Piett

4. "Commence attack on the Death Star's main reactor."

D. Mon Mothma

5. "You Rebel scum!"

 E. Imperial Lieutenant Renz

6. "I have my orders from the Emperor himself."

F. Luke Skywalker

"They're all over me!
Get them off my . . ."
—LAST WORDS OF A CLONE PILOT

DROID TRI-FIGHTER

The droid tri-fighter was a short-range fighter used mostly for fleet support by the Separatists during the Clone Wars. The central fuselage housed a medium laser, a droid brain, and a compartment for ordinance, such as buzz droids or dumb bombs. Its power plant was more advanced than that of the older Vulture droid starfighter. Surrounding the fuselage were three wings, each armed with a laser cannon and two to six missiles. The tri-fighter was the last generation of droid starfighters.

HOW TO FOLD: DROID TRI-FIGHTER

1 Start with an equilateral triangle. Valley fold and unfold.

2 Rabbit ear fold.

3 Valley fold and unfold.

4 Squash fold.

5 Valley fold.

6 Repeat steps 3 and 4 on the left side.

7 Valley fold 2 flaps to the left.

8 Repeat steps 5 through 7 on the right side.

9 Valley fold and unfold.

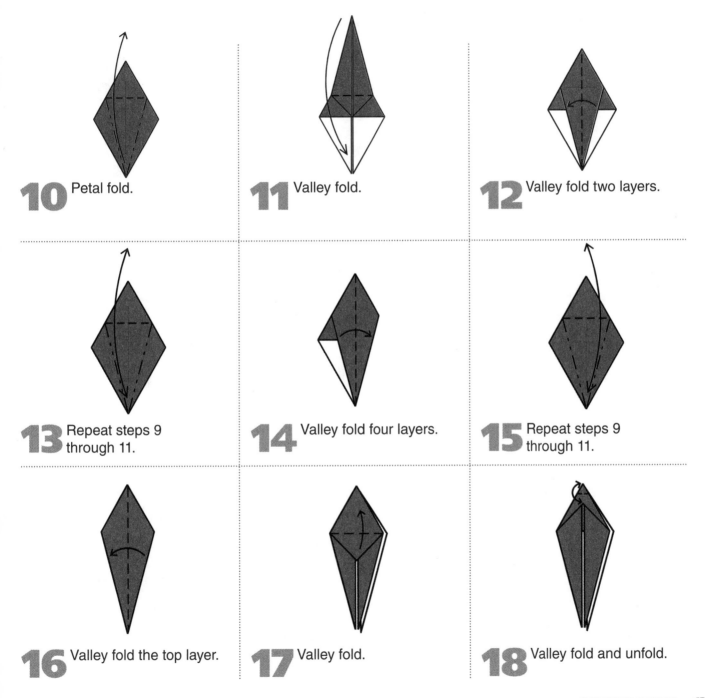

10 Petal fold.

11 Valley fold.

12 Valley fold two layers.

13 Repeat steps 9 through 11.

14 Valley fold four layers.

15 Repeat steps 9 through 11.

16 Valley fold the top layer.

17 Valley fold.

18 Valley fold and unfold.

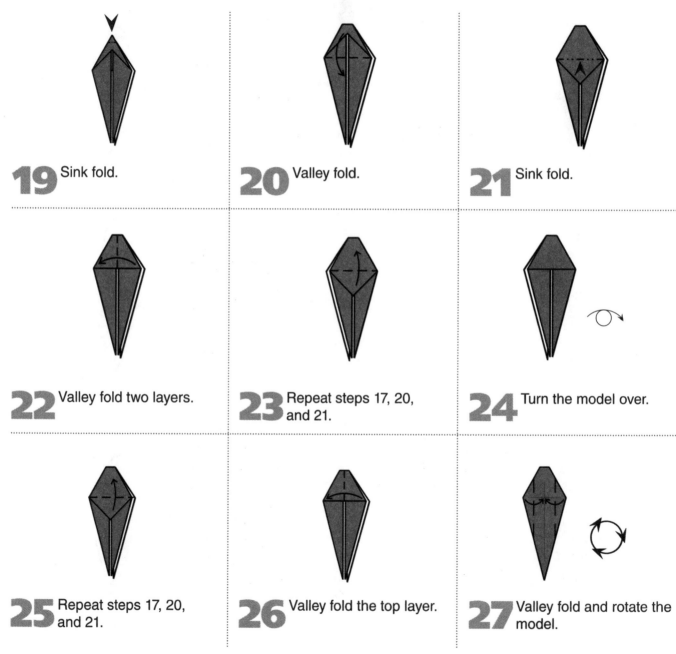

19 Sink fold.

20 Valley fold.

21 Sink fold.

22 Valley fold two layers.

23 Repeat steps 17, 20, and 21.

24 Turn the model over.

25 Repeat steps 17, 20, and 21.

26 Valley fold the top layer.

27 Valley fold and rotate the model.

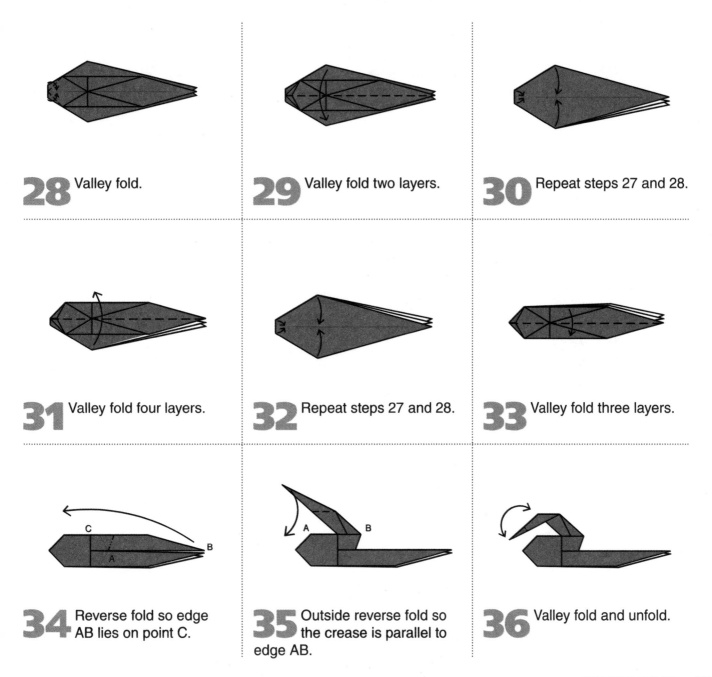

28 Valley fold.

29 Valley fold two layers.

30 Repeat steps 27 and 28.

31 Valley fold four layers.

32 Repeat steps 27 and 28.

33 Valley fold three layers.

34 Reverse fold so edge AB lies on point C.

35 Outside reverse fold so the crease is parallel to edge AB.

36 Valley fold and unfold.

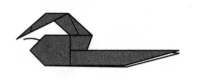

37 Reverse fold along the crease formed in step 36. Insert the point into the pocket.

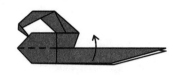

38 Fold one flap up.

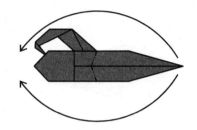

39 Repeat steps 35 through 37 on both wings.

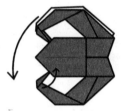

40 Spread the 3 wings apart equally.

TEST YOUR STAR WARS IQ:
MATCHUP

Match the *Star Wars* character to his or her preferred vehicle.
You may use each vehicle more than once.

1. Lando Calrissian

A. *Slave I*

2. Jango Fett

B. ARC-170 starfighter

3. Han Solo

C. *Millennium Falcon*

4. Jabba the Hutt

D. Sail barge

5. Princess Leia Organa

E. X-wing starfighter

6. Luke Skywalker

F. Rebel Blockade Runner

7. Boba Fett

G. Y-wing starfighter

"Your lightsabers will make a fine addition to my collection."

—GENERAL GRIEVOUS TO OBI-WAN KENOBI AND ANAKIN SKYWALKER

GENERAL GRIEVOUS

General Grievous was the leader of the Separatist droid army in the revolt against the Republic. Once a fearsome Kaleesh warlord, General Grievous was more machine than man. Rescued from a terrible accident, only his brain, eyes, and a few select organs remained of his human form; the rest was droid. With an organic brain and the reflexes and strength of a combat droid, Grievous was a formidable foe who took particular delight in keeping defeated Jedis' lightsabers. Grievous was finally defeated by Obi-Wan Kenobi after an epic battle on Utapau. A shot from Obi-Wan's blaster pierced the general's gut-sack, killing him.

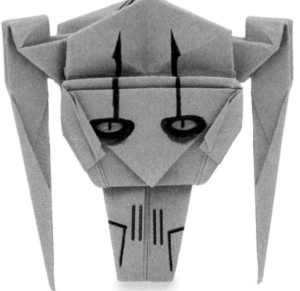

HOW TO FOLD: GENERAL GRIEVOUS

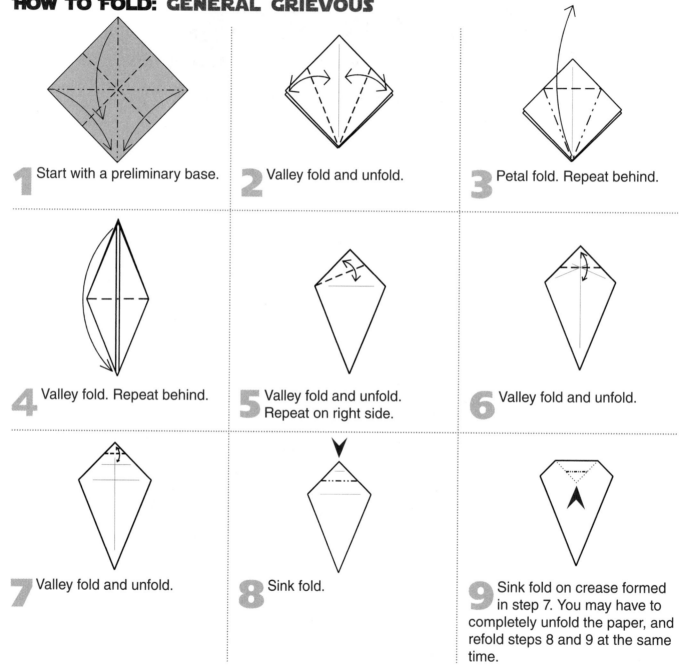

1 Start with a preliminary base.

2 Valley fold and unfold.

3 Petal fold. Repeat behind.

4 Valley fold. Repeat behind.

5 Valley fold and unfold. Repeat on right side.

6 Valley fold and unfold.

7 Valley fold and unfold.

8 Sink fold.

9 Sink fold on crease formed in step 7. You may have to completely unfold the paper, and refold steps 8 and 9 at the same time.

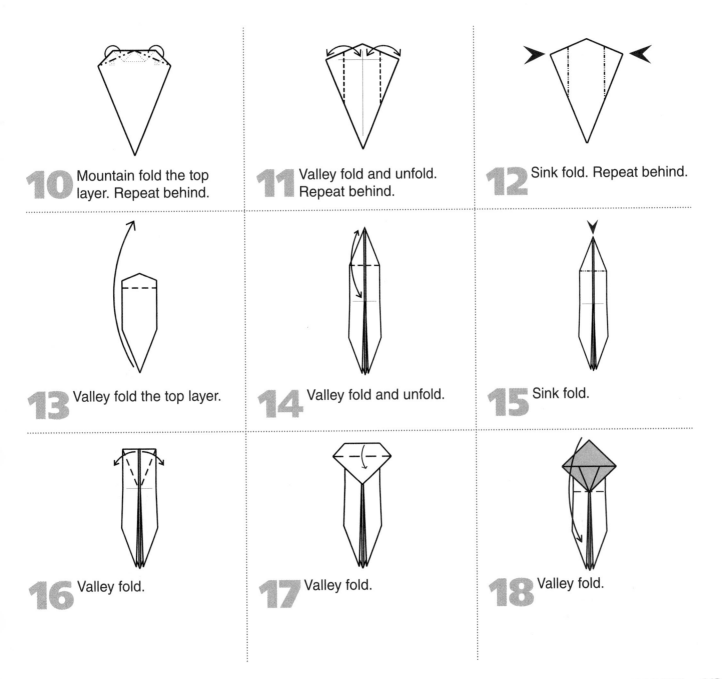

10 Mountain fold the top layer. Repeat behind.

11 Valley fold and unfold. Repeat behind.

12 Sink fold. Repeat behind.

13 Valley fold the top layer.

14 Valley fold and unfold.

15 Sink fold.

16 Valley fold.

17 Valley fold.

18 Valley fold.

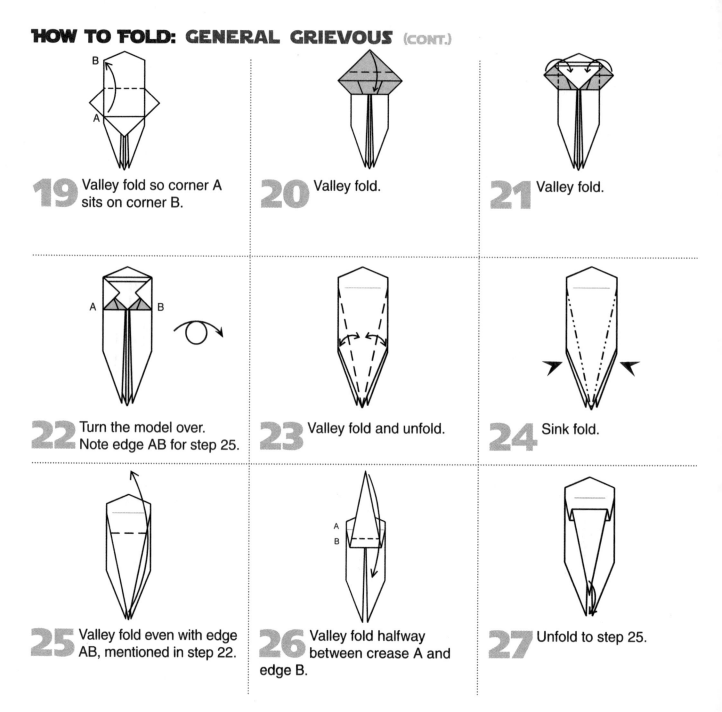

HOW TO FOLD: GENERAL GRIEVOUS (CONT.)

19 Valley fold so corner A sits on corner B.

20 Valley fold.

21 Valley fold.

22 Turn the model over. Note edge AB for step 25.

23 Valley fold and unfold.

24 Sink fold.

25 Valley fold even with edge AB, mentioned in step 22.

26 Valley fold halfway between crease A and edge B.

27 Unfold to step 25.

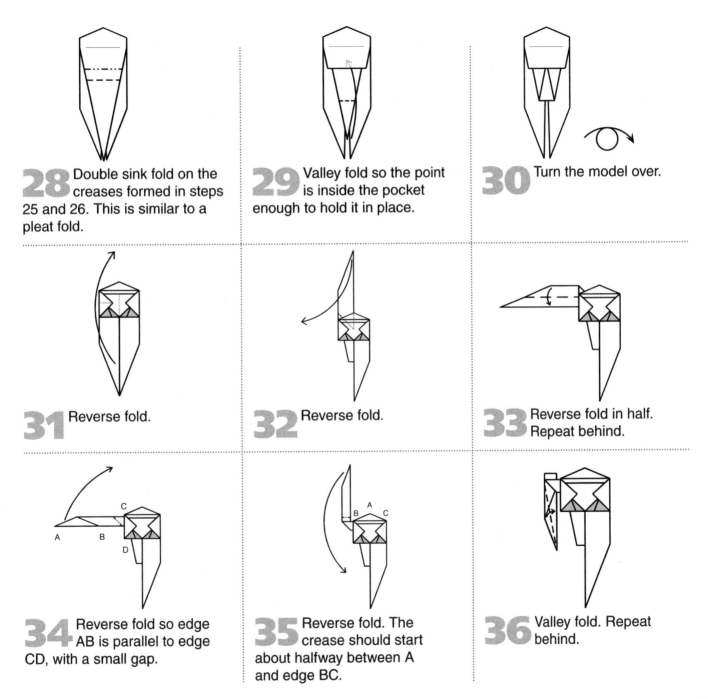

28 Double sink fold on the creases formed in steps 25 and 26. This is similar to a pleat fold.

29 Valley fold so the point is inside the pocket enough to hold it in place.

30 Turn the model over.

31 Reverse fold.

32 Reverse fold.

33 Reverse fold in half. Repeat behind.

34 Reverse fold so edge AB is parallel to edge CD, with a small gap.

35 Reverse fold. The crease should start about halfway between A and edge BC.

36 Valley fold. Repeat behind.

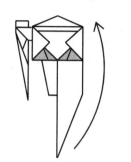

37 Repeat steps 31 through 36 on the right side.

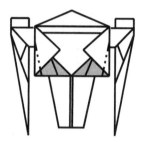

38 Mountain fold to match the edges in the back.

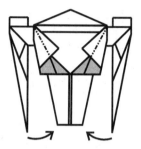

39 Mountain fold. Pivot the ear flaps in toward the face.

TRIVIA

1. What was Padmé Amidala's middle name?
  A. Jobal
  B. Ruwee
  C. Naberrie

2. There were always how many Sith at a time?
  A. one
  B. two
  C. three

3. Which was NOT a Jedi ability?
  A. sensing other Jedi or disturbances in the Force
  B. invisibility
  C. healing

4. Who gave Luke Skywalker his first lightsaber?
  A. Obi-Wan Kenobi
  B. Yoda
  C. Anakin Skywalker

5. In what substance was Han Solo encased on Bespin?
  A. platinum
  B. cryogerium
  C. carbonite

6. Who called Han Solo a "scruffy-looking nerf herder"?
  A. Princess Leia Organa
  B. C-3PO
  C. Jabba the Hutt

"I think I'm beginning to get the hang of this flying business."

—C-3PO

NABOO STAR SKIFF

Also known as the J-type star skiff, this ship was used by the Royal House of Naboo near the end of the Clone Wars. Like other royal yachts, the entire ship was finished in chromium. Unlike the previous ships, two laser cannons were added to the top wing for protection. This marked the first time a royal Naboo yacht was armed. Senator Amidala used this ship on her ill-fated journey to Mustafar in an attempt to find her husband, Anakin Skywalker.

HOW TO FOLD: NABOO STAR SKIFF

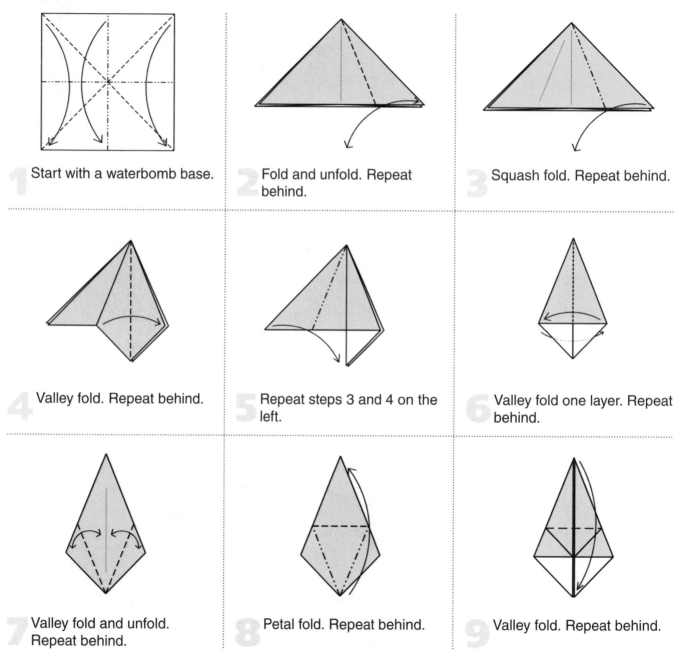

1. Start with a waterbomb base.

2. Fold and unfold. Repeat behind.

3. Squash fold. Repeat behind.

4. Valley fold. Repeat behind.

5. Repeat steps 3 and 4 on the left.

6. Valley fold one layer. Repeat behind.

7. Valley fold and unfold. Repeat behind.

8. Petal fold. Repeat behind.

9. Valley fold. Repeat behind.

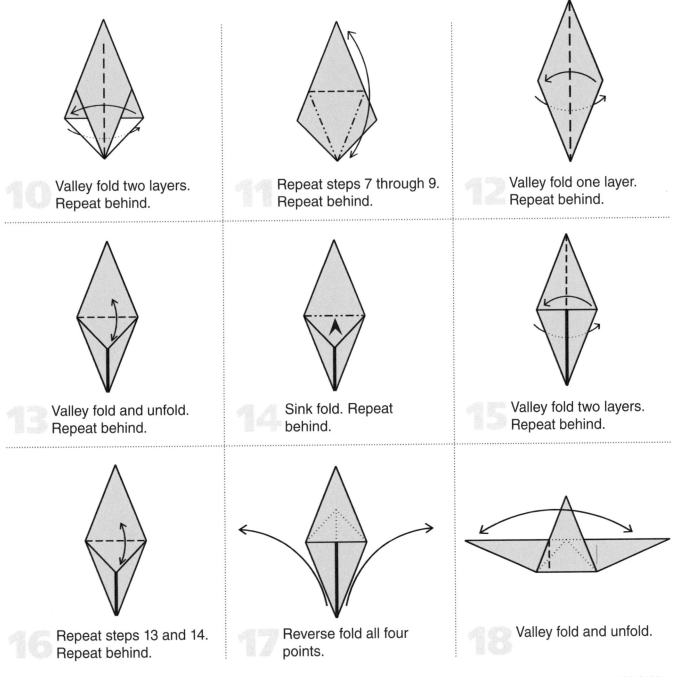

10 Valley fold two layers. Repeat behind.

11 Repeat steps 7 through 9. Repeat behind.

12 Valley fold one layer. Repeat behind.

13 Valley fold and unfold. Repeat behind.

14 Sink fold. Repeat behind.

15 Valley fold two layers. Repeat behind.

16 Repeat steps 13 and 14. Repeat behind.

17 Reverse fold all four points.

18 Valley fold and unfold.

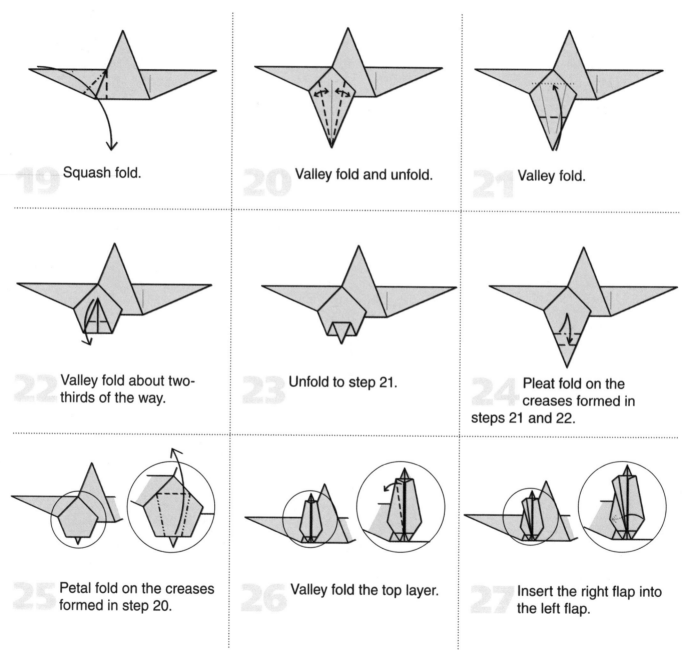

19 Squash fold.

20 Valley fold and unfold.

21 Valley fold.

22 Valley fold about two-thirds of the way.

23 Unfold to step 21.

24 Pleat fold on the creases formed in steps 21 and 22.

25 Petal fold on the creases formed in step 20.

26 Valley fold the top layer.

27 Insert the right flap into the left flap.

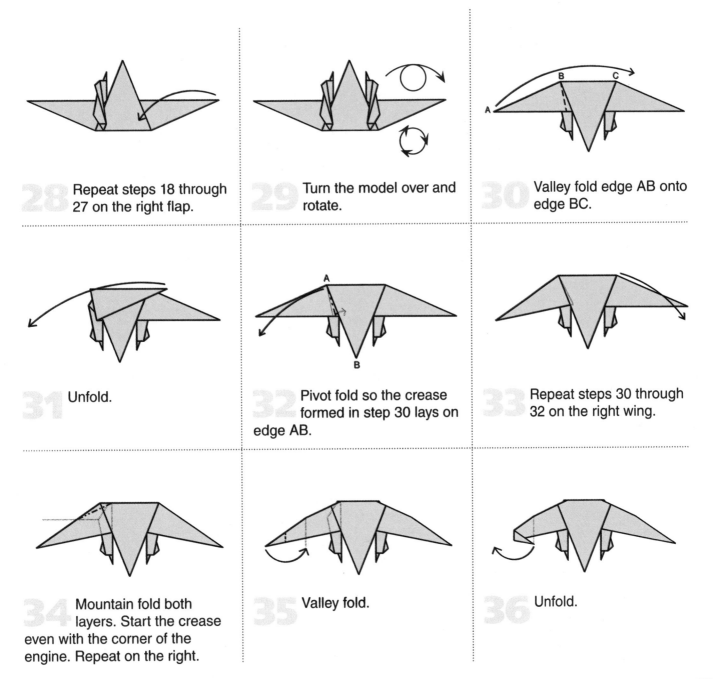

28 Repeat steps 18 through 27 on the right flap.

29 Turn the model over and rotate.

30 Valley fold edge AB onto edge BC.

31 Unfold.

32 Pivot fold so the crease formed in step 30 lays on edge AB.

33 Repeat steps 30 through 32 on the right wing.

34 Mountain fold both layers. Start the crease even with the corner of the engine. Repeat on the right.

35 Valley fold.

36 Unfold.

HOW TO FOLD: NABOO STAR SKIFF (CONT.)

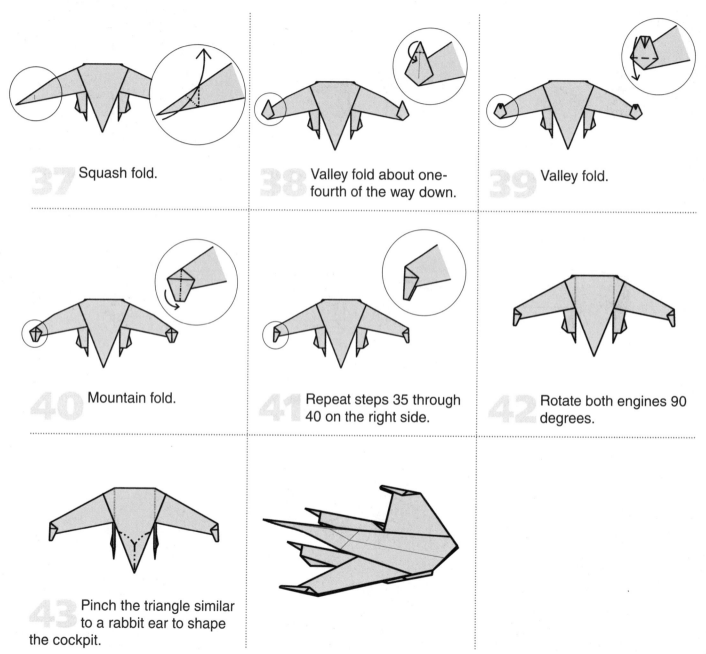

37 Squash fold.

38 Valley fold about one-fourth of the way down.

39 Valley fold.

40 Mountain fold.

41 Repeat steps 35 through 40 on the right side.

42 Rotate both engines 90 degrees.

43 Pinch the triangle similar to a rabbit ear to shape the cockpit.

TEST YOUR STAR WARS IQ:

WHO SAID IT?

Match the quote to the correct *Star Wars* character.

1. "Help me, Obi-Wan Kenobi, you're my only hope."

2. "Anakin, you're breaking my heart! And you're going down a path I cannot follow!"

3. "My wife and I will take the girl . . . She will be loved with us."

4. "Everything is proceeding as I have foreseen."

5. "I shall do what I must, Obi-Wan."

6. "The Force will be with you. Always."

A. Qui-Gon Jinn

B. Bail Organa

C. Padmé Amidala

D. Princess Leia Organa

E. Emperor Palpatine

F. Obi-Wan Kenobi

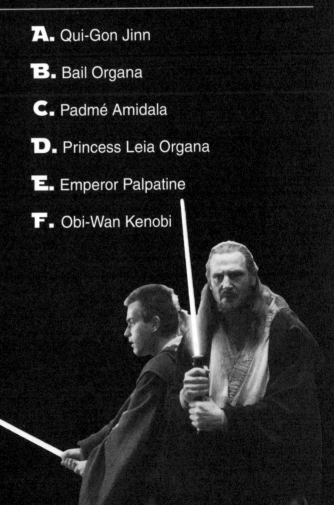

ANSWERS: 1.D Princess Leia Organa, 2.C Padmé Amidala, 3.B Bail Organa, on Leia, 4.E Emperor Palpatine, 5.A Qui-Gon Jinn, 6.F Obi-Wan Kenobi to Luke Skywalker

"Sir, the odds of surviving a direct assault on an Imperial Star Destroyer—"

—C-3PO

IMPERIAL STAR DESTROYER

The Star Destroyer was the backbone of the Imperial Navy. Over a mile long and armed with sixty turbolasers and sixty ion cannons, it overwhelmed just about any other starship. And its fleet of seventy-two TIE fighters fended off attacks from smaller snub ships. Usually just the presence of a destroyer in orbit was enough to restore order to an unruly planet.

HOW TO FOLD: IMPERIAL STAR DESTROYER

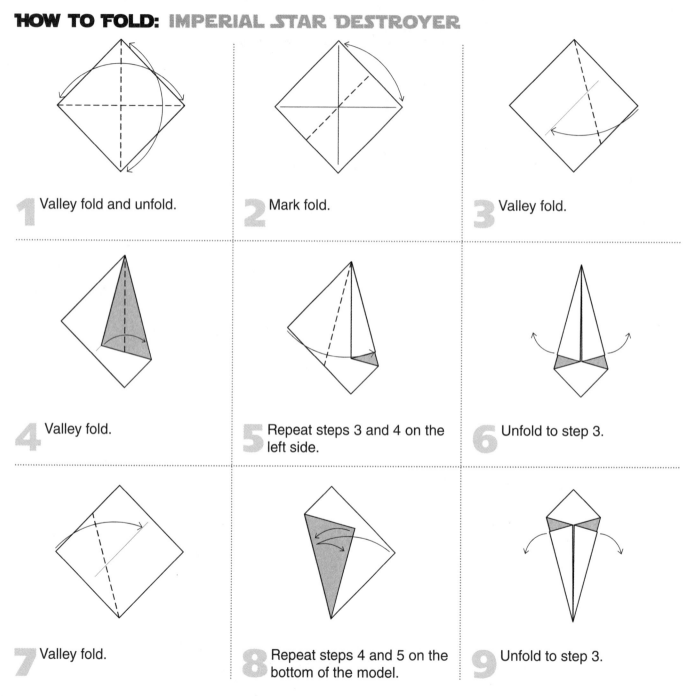

1 Valley fold and unfold.

2 Mark fold.

3 Valley fold.

4 Valley fold.

5 Repeat steps 3 and 4 on the left side.

6 Unfold to step 3.

7 Valley fold.

8 Repeat steps 4 and 5 on the bottom of the model.

9 Unfold to step 3.

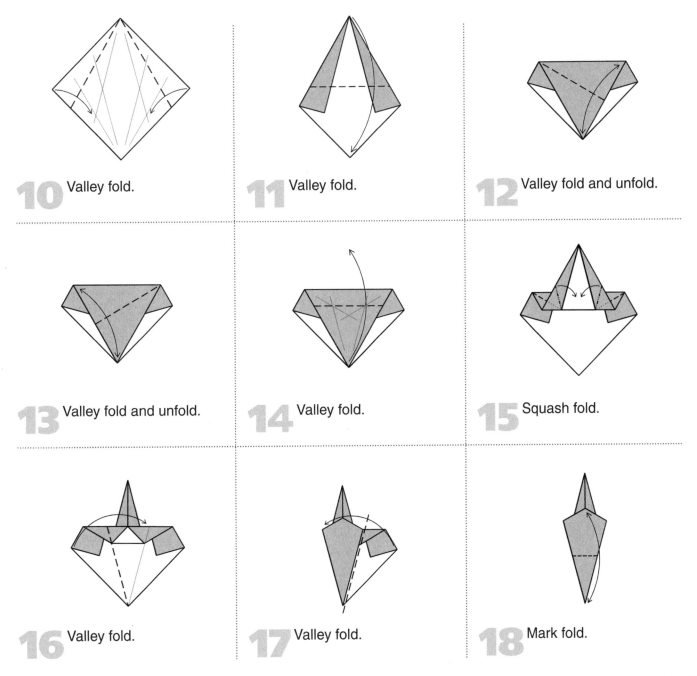

10 Valley fold.

11 Valley fold.

12 Valley fold and unfold.

13 Valley fold and unfold.

14 Valley fold.

15 Squash fold.

16 Valley fold.

17 Valley fold.

18 Mark fold.

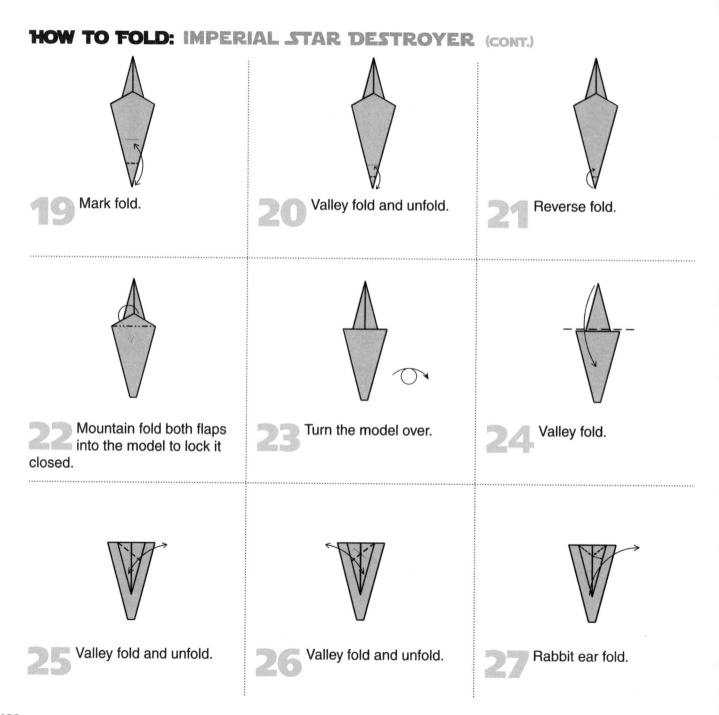

19 Mark fold.

20 Valley fold and unfold.

21 Reverse fold.

22 Mountain fold both flaps into the model to lock it closed.

23 Turn the model over.

24 Valley fold.

25 Valley fold and unfold.

26 Valley fold and unfold.

27 Rabbit ear fold.

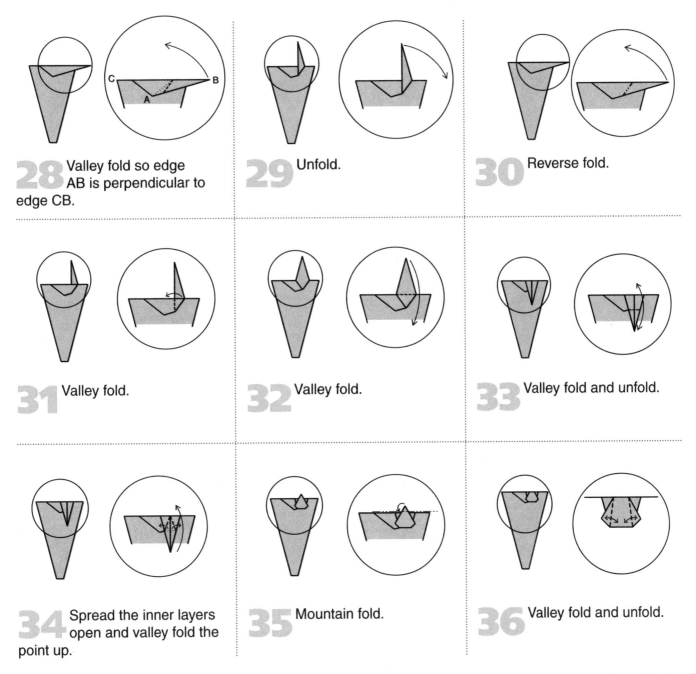

28 Valley fold so edge AB is perpendicular to edge CB.

29 Unfold.

30 Reverse fold.

31 Valley fold.

32 Valley fold.

33 Valley fold and unfold.

34 Spread the inner layers open and valley fold the point up.

35 Mountain fold.

36 Valley fold and unfold.

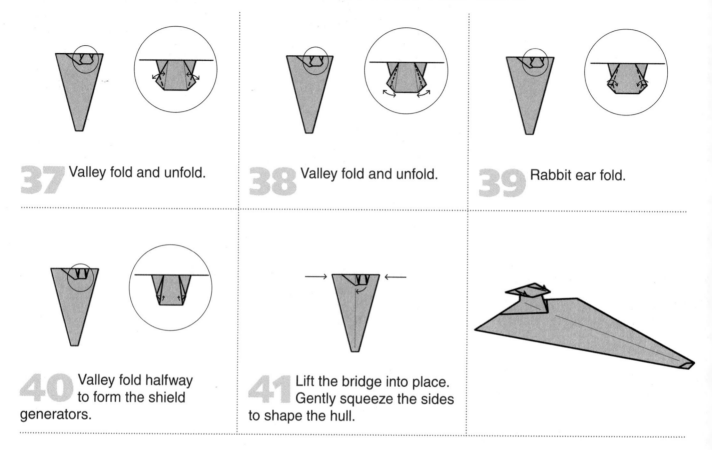

37 Valley fold and unfold.

38 Valley fold and unfold.

39 Rabbit ear fold.

40 Valley fold halfway to form the shield generators.

41 Lift the bridge into place. Gently squeeze the sides to shape the hull.

TEST YOUR STAR WARS IQ:

TRIVIA

1. How many starships survived the Battle of Yavin?

2. Which two characters were the only witnesses to Anakin Skywalker and Padmé Amidala's wedding?

3. Who called Chewbacca a "big walking carpet"?

4. On what kind of farm did Luke Skywalker grow up?

5. Who was the youngest person to hold a seat in the Senate?

6. How did Lando Calrissian lose the *Millennium Falcon* to Han Solo?

ANSWERS: 1. 5 (2 X-wings, 1 Y-wing, the *Millennium Falcon*, Darth Vader's TIE fighter). 2. C-3PO and R2-D2. 3. Princess Leia Organa. 4. A moisture farm. 5. Princess Leia Organa. 6. In a card game called sabacc.

"If you only knew the power of the dark side."

—DARTH VADER

DARTH VADER

Darth Vader, Dark Lord of the Sith, wasn't always evil. Born Anakin Skywalker, he was once a pupil of Obi-Wan Kenobi— the Chosen One spoken of in an ancient Jedi prophecy. But when Supreme Chancellor Palpatine (Darth Sidious) convinced Anakin that the only way to save his wife Padmé's life was to help him destroy The Republic, Anakin was seduced to the dark side of the Force. As a Sith apprentice, Darth Vader nearly died at the hands of Obi-Wan. Darth Sidious saved Vader's life by encasing him in a mostly cybernetic body. In the end, Vader was forced to choose between saving the life of his son, Luke Skywalker, or serving Sidious. Vader chose to kill Sidious, thereby bringing balance to the Force and fulfilling the ancient Jedi prophecy.

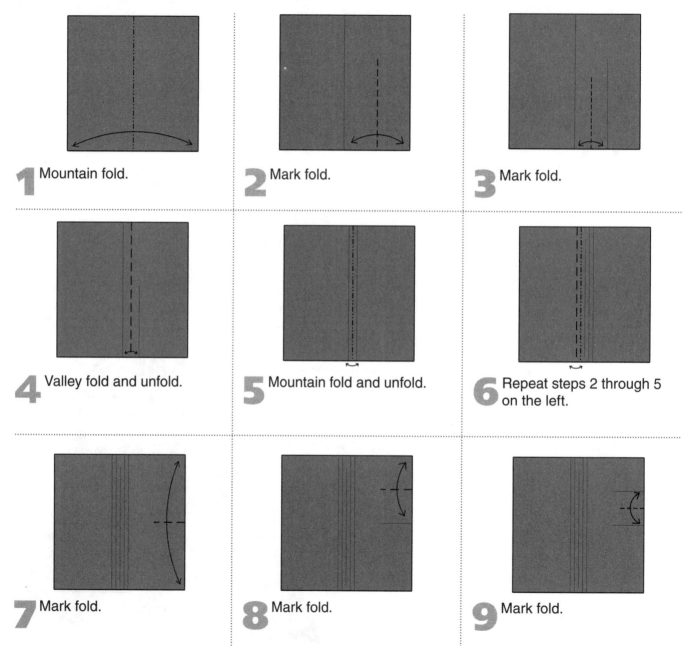

1 Mountain fold.

2 Mark fold.

3 Mark fold.

4 Valley fold and unfold.

5 Mountain fold and unfold.

6 Repeat steps 2 through 5 on the left.

7 Mark fold.

8 Mark fold.

9 Mark fold.

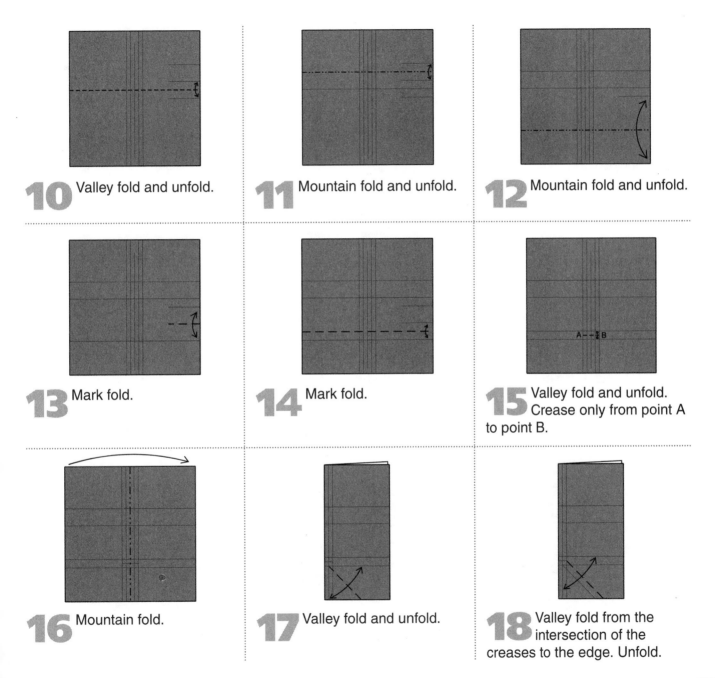

10 Valley fold and unfold.

11 Mountain fold and unfold.

12 Mountain fold and unfold.

13 Mark fold.

14 Mark fold.

15 Valley fold and unfold. Crease only from point A to point B.

16 Mountain fold.

17 Valley fold and unfold.

18 Valley fold from the intersection of the creases to the edge. Unfold.

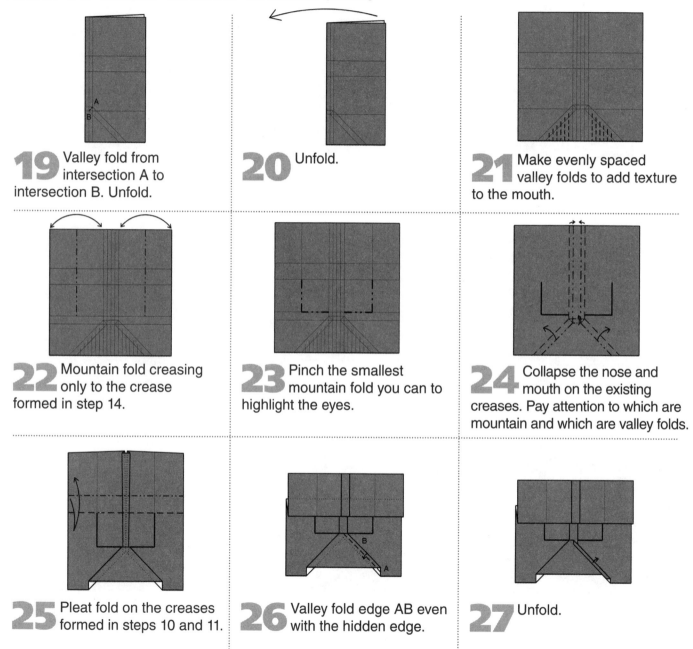

19 Valley fold from intersection A to intersection B. Unfold.

20 Unfold.

21 Make evenly spaced valley folds to add texture to the mouth.

22 Mountain fold creasing only to the crease formed in step 14.

23 Pinch the smallest mountain fold you can to highlight the eyes.

24 Collapse the nose and mouth on the existing creases. Pay attention to which are mountain and which are valley folds.

25 Pleat fold on the creases formed in steps 10 and 11.

26 Valley fold edge AB even with the hidden edge.

27 Unfold.

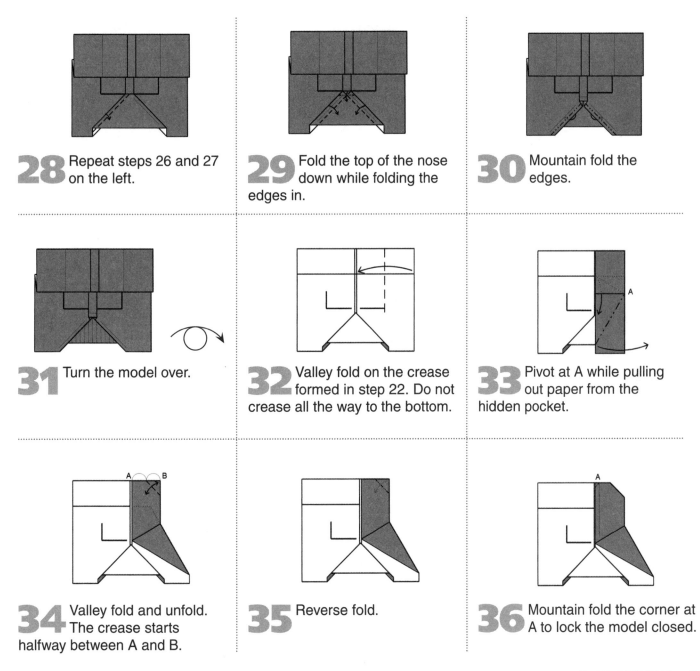

28 Repeat steps 26 and 27 on the left.

29 Fold the top of the nose down while folding the edges in.

30 Mountain fold the edges.

31 Turn the model over.

32 Valley fold on the crease formed in step 22. Do not crease all the way to the bottom.

33 Pivot at A while pulling out paper from the hidden pocket.

34 Valley fold and unfold. The crease starts halfway between A and B.

35 Reverse fold.

36 Mountain fold the corner at A to lock the model closed.

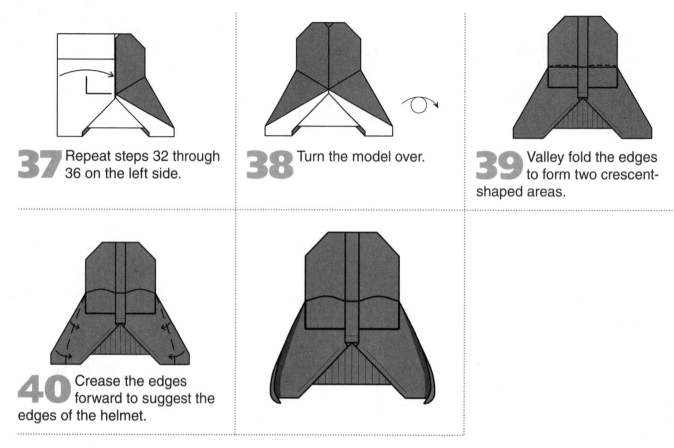

37 Repeat steps 32 through 36 on the left side.

38 Turn the model over.

39 Valley fold the edges to form two crescent-shaped areas.

40 Crease the edges forward to suggest the edges of the helmet.

TEST YOUR STAR WARS IQ:

TRIVIA

1. What color was used for the designation of the Y-wing Squadron at Endor?
A. Yellow
B. Gold
C. Red

2. Who called R2-D2 a "nearsighted scrap pile"?
A. C-3PO
B. Han Solo
C. Lando Calrissian

3. How old was Queen Amidala during the Battle of Endor?
A. twelve
B. thirteen
C. fourteen

4. Who was a Padawan of Count Dooku?
A. Obi-Wan Kenobi
B. Luke Skywalker
C. Qui-Gon Jinn

5. Which of the following was NOT hidden in Jango Fett's armored suit?
A. Throwing knives
B. Dual pistols
C. A snare

6. What was the name of Lando Calrissian's chief administrative aid in Cloud City?
A. Kitster
B. Lobot
C. Dexter

"I'd just as soon kiss a Wookiee."
—PRINCESS LEIA ORGANA

PRINCESS LEIA ORGANA

Princess Leia Organa was adopted at birth by Senator Bail Organa and Queen Breha, Alderaan's ruling family. Beautiful, smart, and outspoken, Leia became a key figure in intergalactic politics and in the rebellion against the Empire. On one such mission, Leia was captured by Darth Vader. In spite of being tortured and forced to watch the complete destruction of Alderaan, she never revealed the rebellion's secrets and was sentenced to death.

While awaiting execution, she was rescued by Luke Skywalker and Han Solo. Leia was later shocked to discover that Darth Vader was her real father, Luke Skywalker was her twin brother, and that she had the potential to become one of the legendary Jedi Knights.

HOW TO FOLD: PRINCESS LEIA ORGANA

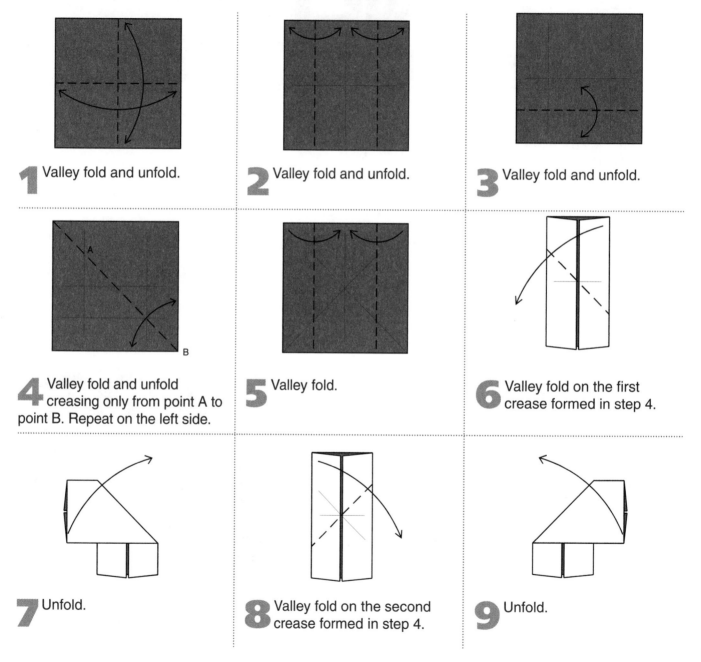

1 Valley fold and unfold.

2 Valley fold and unfold.

3 Valley fold and unfold.

4 Valley fold and unfold creasing only from point A to point B. Repeat on the left side.

5 Valley fold.

6 Valley fold on the first crease formed in step 4.

7 Unfold.

8 Valley fold on the second crease formed in step 4.

9 Unfold.

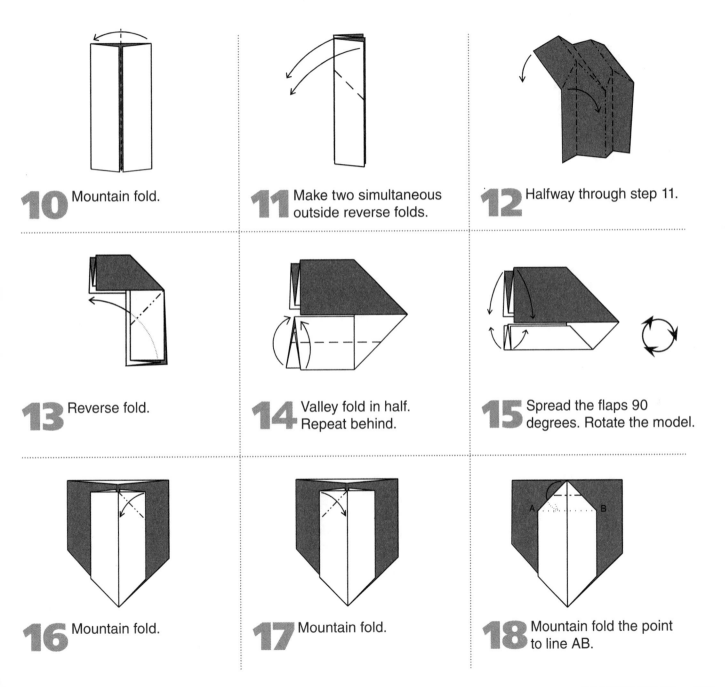

10 Mountain fold.

11 Make two simultaneous outside reverse folds.

12 Halfway through step 11.

13 Reverse fold.

14 Valley fold in half. Repeat behind.

15 Spread the flaps 90 degrees. Rotate the model.

16 Mountain fold.

17 Mountain fold.

18 Mountain fold the point to line AB.

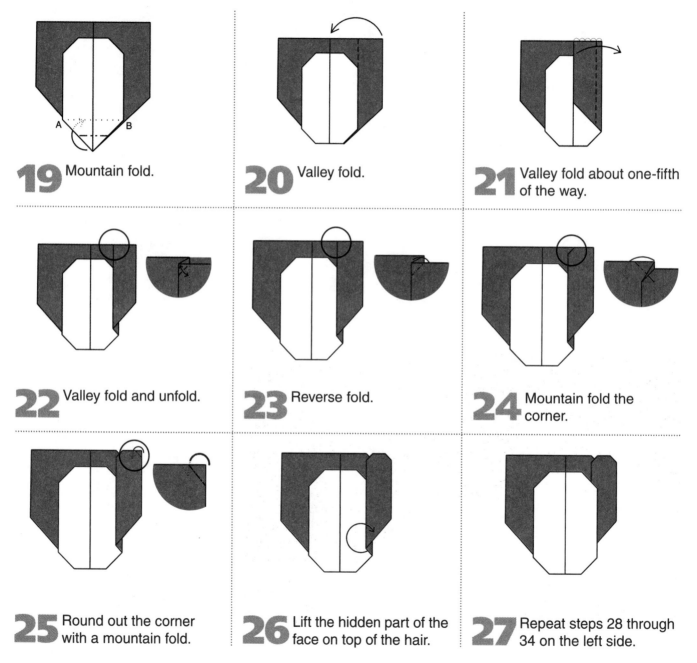

19 Mountain fold.

20 Valley fold.

21 Valley fold about one-fifth of the way.

22 Valley fold and unfold.

23 Reverse fold.

24 Mountain fold the corner.

25 Round out the corner with a mountain fold.

26 Lift the hidden part of the face on top of the hair.

27 Repeat steps 28 through 34 on the left side.

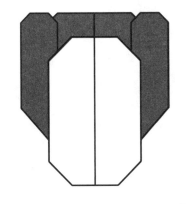

Princess Leia being held captive by Darth Vader.

"I want to learn the ways of the Force and become a Jedi like my father."
—LUKE SKYWALKER

LUKE SKYWALKER

As a young boy on Tatooine dreaming of adventure, Luke Skywalker couldn't know that one day he would be instrumental in bringing about the fall of the Empire. It all began with the purchase of a droid called R2-D2, which contained a hidden plea for help from Princess Leia Organa. Following her rescue, Luke began his Jedi training with Master Yoda on the planet Dagobah. After completing his training, he faced his father, Darth Vader, a second time. Though he was stronger, Luke refused to kill Vader, and in return, Vader saved Luke from the Emperor. Vader was destroyed, and balance returned to the Force.

HOW TO FOLD: LUKE SKYWALKER

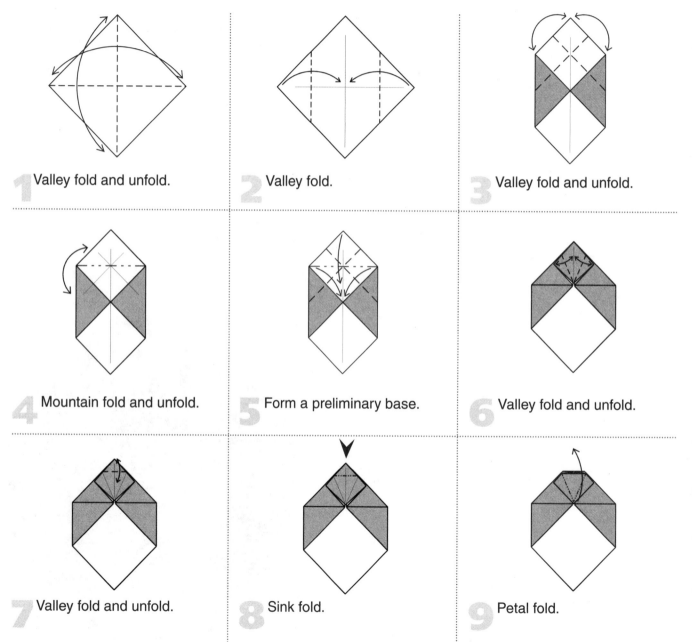

1 Valley fold and unfold.

2 Valley fold.

3 Valley fold and unfold.

4 Mountain fold and unfold.

5 Form a preliminary base.

6 Valley fold and unfold.

7 Valley fold and unfold.

8 Sink fold.

9 Petal fold.

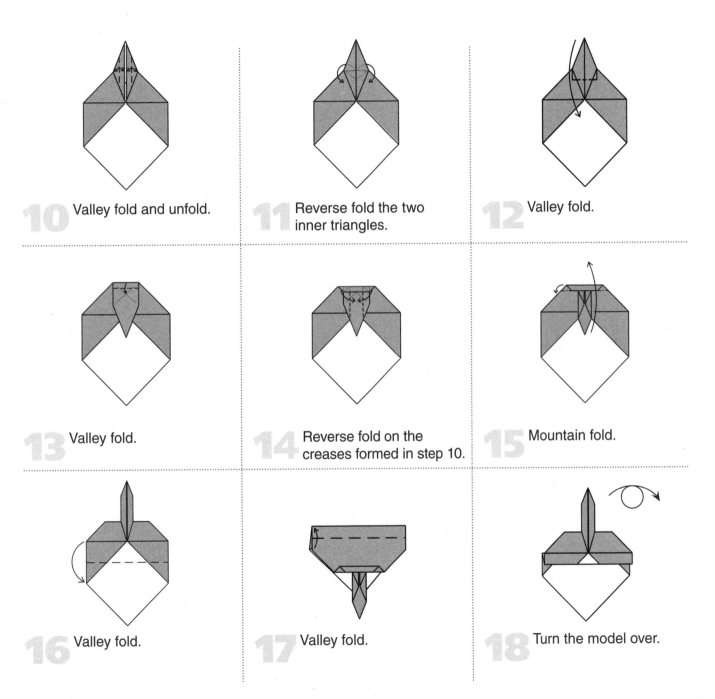

10 Valley fold and unfold.

11 Reverse fold the two inner triangles.

12 Valley fold.

13 Valley fold.

14 Reverse fold on the creases formed in step 10.

15 Mountain fold.

16 Valley fold.

17 Valley fold.

18 Turn the model over.

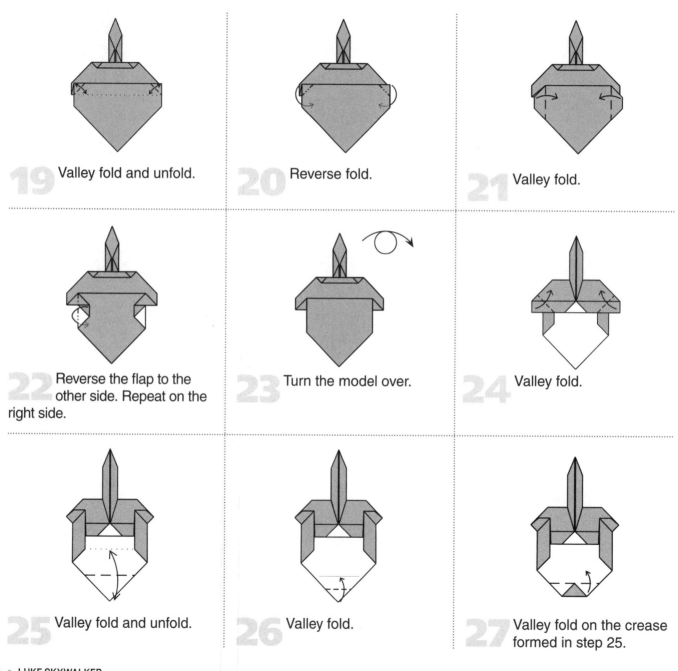

19 Valley fold and unfold.

20 Reverse fold.

21 Valley fold.

22 Reverse the flap to the other side. Repeat on the right side.

23 Turn the model over.

24 Valley fold.

25 Valley fold and unfold.

26 Valley fold.

27 Valley fold on the crease formed in step 25.

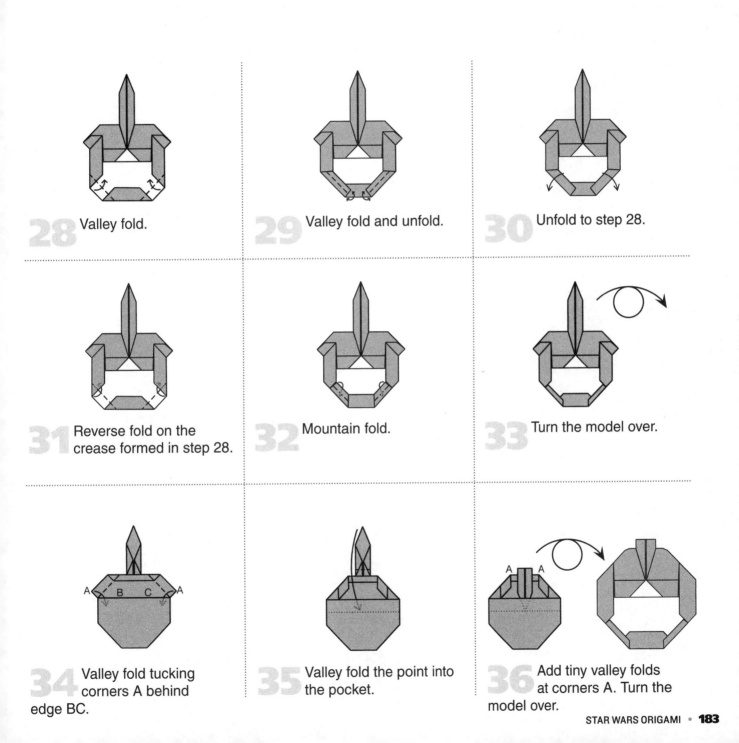

28 Valley fold.

29 Valley fold and unfold.

30 Unfold to step 28.

31 Reverse fold on the crease formed in step 28.

32 Mountain fold.

33 Turn the model over.

34 Valley fold tucking corners A behind edge BC.

35 Valley fold the point into the pocket.

36 Add tiny valley folds at corners A. Turn the model over.

"You know, sometimes I amaze even myself."
—HAN SOLO

HAN SOLO

A smuggler, a scoundrel, and a hero of the Rebel Alliance—Han Solo played all of these roles with equal enthusiasm. As a young man, Han was kicked out of the Imperial Academy for defying orders to kill the Wookiee Chewbacca, an act that sparked a life-long friendship. Han first met Luke Skywalker when Luke needed to hire a good pilot and a fast ship. This was how Han found himself in the middle of the Rebellion that he had no interest in, and in the end turned out to be quite heroic. Not only did he help rescue Princess Leia Organa, he was also instrumental in the destruction of both Death Stars and the eventual collapse of the Empire—even if he did spend some time on Jabba the Hutt's wall, encased in a carbonite block.

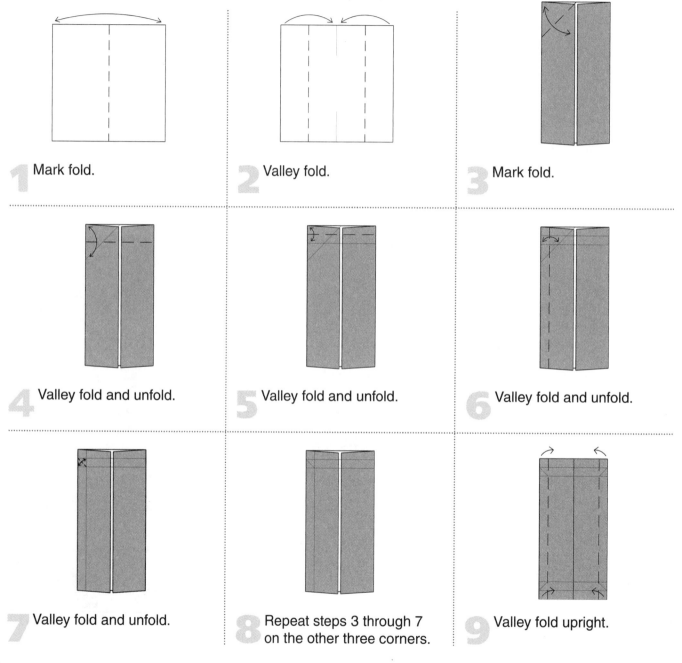

1 Mark fold.

2 Valley fold.

3 Mark fold.

4 Valley fold and unfold.

5 Valley fold and unfold.

6 Valley fold and unfold.

7 Valley fold and unfold.

8 Repeat steps 3 through 7 on the other three corners.

9 Valley fold upright.

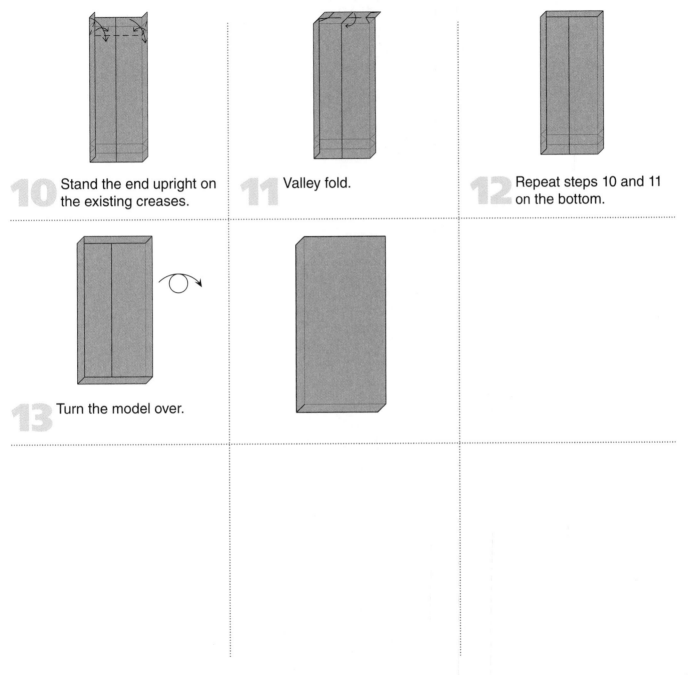

10 Stand the end upright on the existing creases.

11 Valley fold.

12 Repeat steps 10 and 11 on the bottom.

13 Turn the model over.

"I don't know—fly casual."
—HAN SOLO TO CHEWBACCA

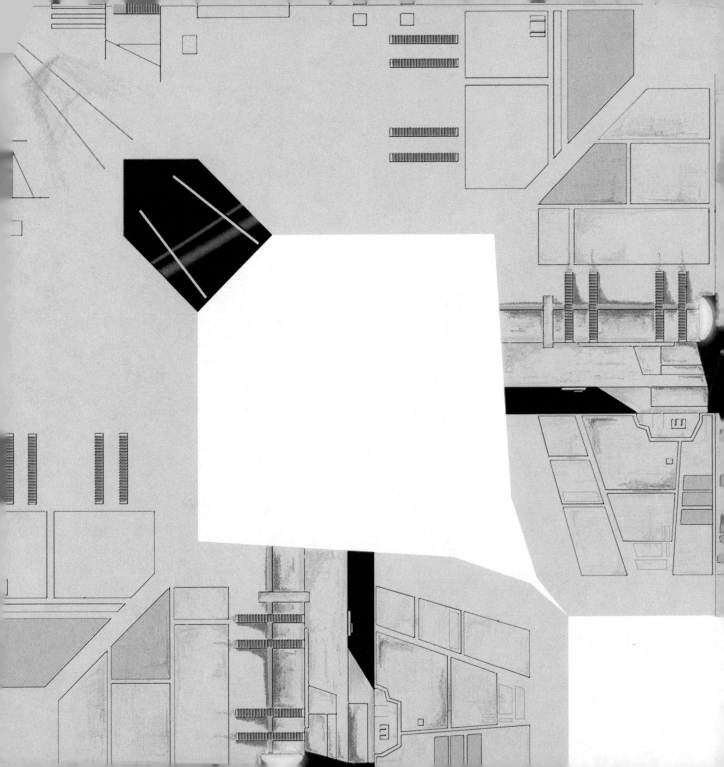

CHEWBACCA

A Wookiee from the planet Kashyyyk, Chewbacca was a hero of the Rebellion from the earliest days. Assigned to Yoda as a bodyguard during the Clone Wars, Chewbacca helped him escape when Chancellor Palpatine called for the death of all Jedi. While on the run from the Imperial forces, Chewbacca was captured by Trandoshan slavers. During this time, Chewbacca met Han Solo, who freed him and saved his life. Chewbacca swore a life-debt to Han and became Han's copilot, and the two grew to be friends. Later, Chewbacca was once again drawn into the Rebellion when he and Han met Luke Skywalker, helped rescue Princess Leia Organa, and together destroyed the Death Star.

NOTE: You need two pieces of paper for this model. Steps 1 through 19 form the lower half. Steps 20 through 51 form the upper half.

HOW TO FOLD: CHEWBACCA

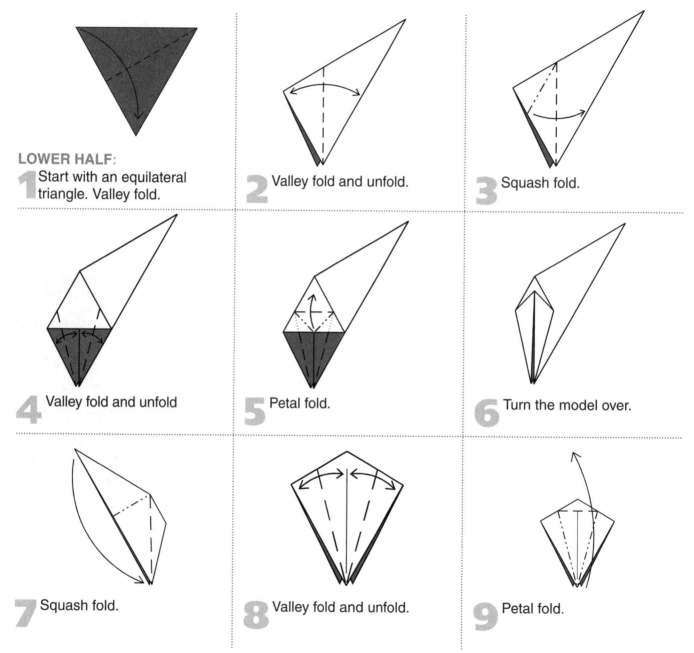

LOWER HALF:

1 Start with an equilateral triangle. Valley fold.

2 Valley fold and unfold.

3 Squash fold.

4 Valley fold and unfold

5 Petal fold.

6 Turn the model over.

7 Squash fold.

8 Valley fold and unfold.

9 Petal fold.

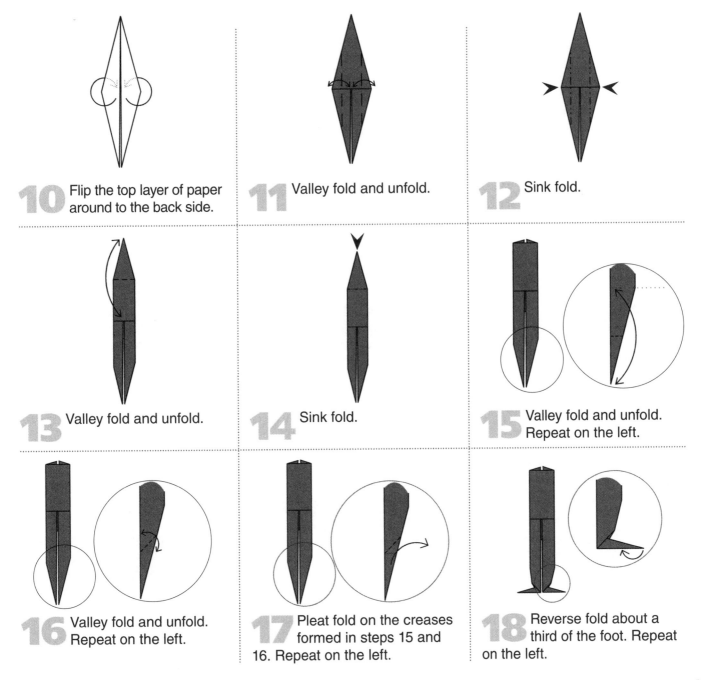

10 Flip the top layer of paper around to the back side.

11 Valley fold and unfold.

12 Sink fold.

13 Valley fold and unfold.

14 Sink fold.

15 Valley fold and unfold. Repeat on the left.

16 Valley fold and unfold. Repeat on the left.

17 Pleat fold on the creases formed in steps 15 and 16. Repeat on the left.

18 Reverse fold about a third of the foot. Repeat on the left.

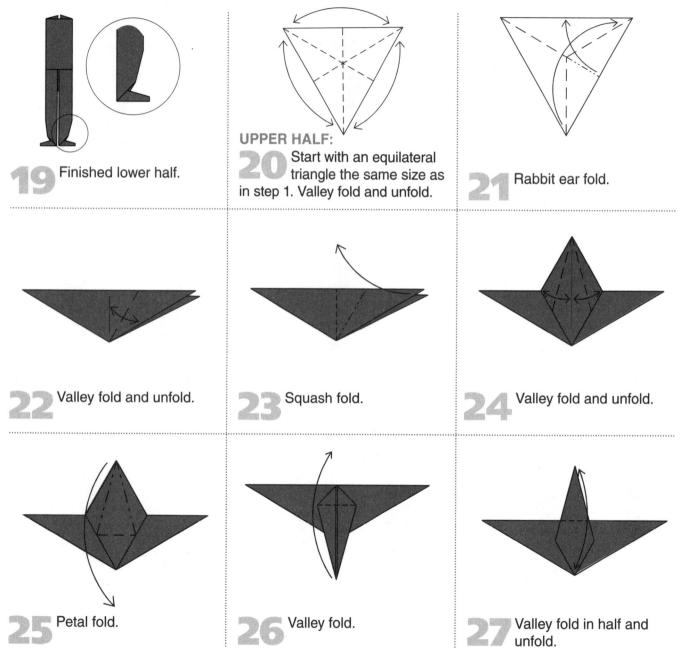

19 Finished lower half.

UPPER HALF:
20 Start with an equilateral triangle the same size as in step 1. Valley fold and unfold.

21 Rabbit ear fold.

22 Valley fold and unfold.

23 Squash fold.

24 Valley fold and unfold.

25 Petal fold.

26 Valley fold.

27 Valley fold in half and unfold.

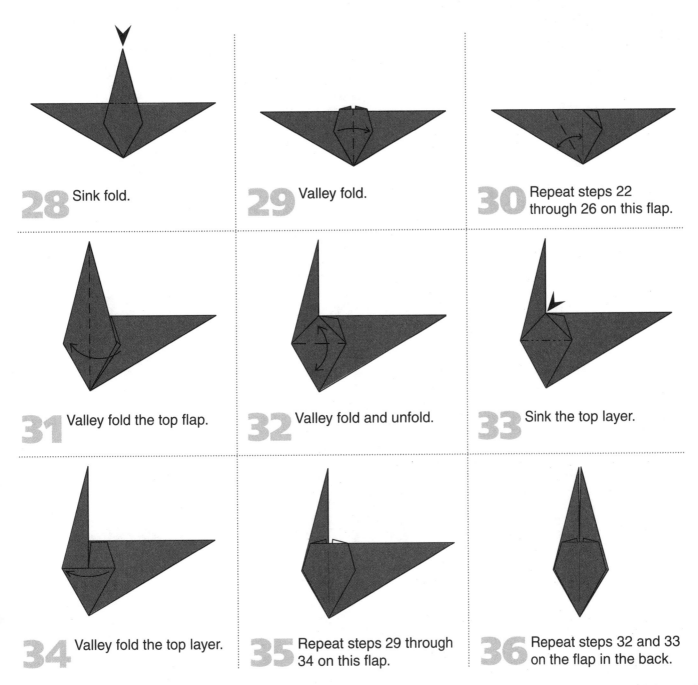

28 Sink fold.

29 Valley fold.

30 Repeat steps 22 through 26 on this flap.

31 Valley fold the top flap.

32 Valley fold and unfold.

33 Sink the top layer.

34 Valley fold the top layer.

35 Repeat steps 29 through 34 on this flap.

36 Repeat steps 32 and 33 on the flap in the back.

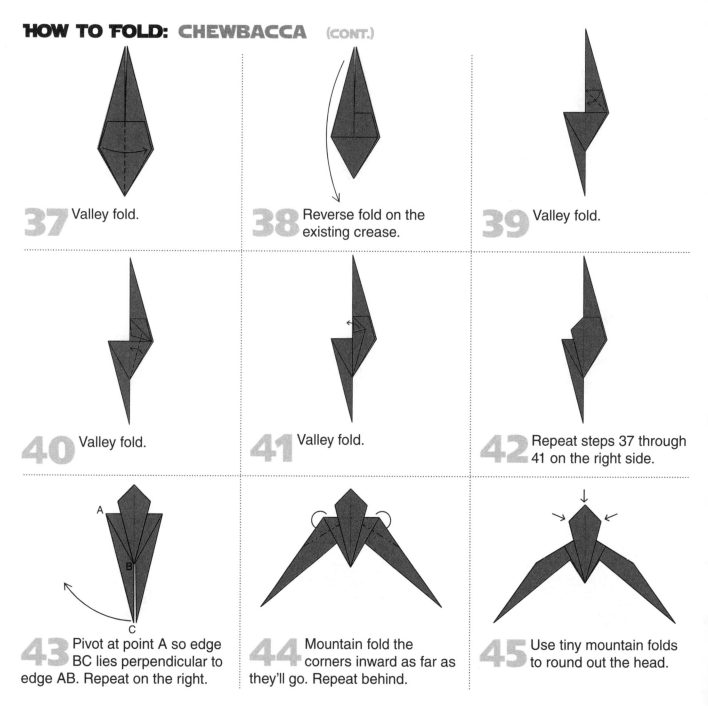

37 Valley fold.

38 Reverse fold on the existing crease.

39 Valley fold.

40 Valley fold.

41 Valley fold.

42 Repeat steps 37 through 41 on the right side.

43 Pivot at point A so edge BC lies perpendicular to edge AB. Repeat on the right.

44 Mountain fold the corners inward as far as they'll go. Repeat behind.

45 Use tiny mountain folds to round out the head.

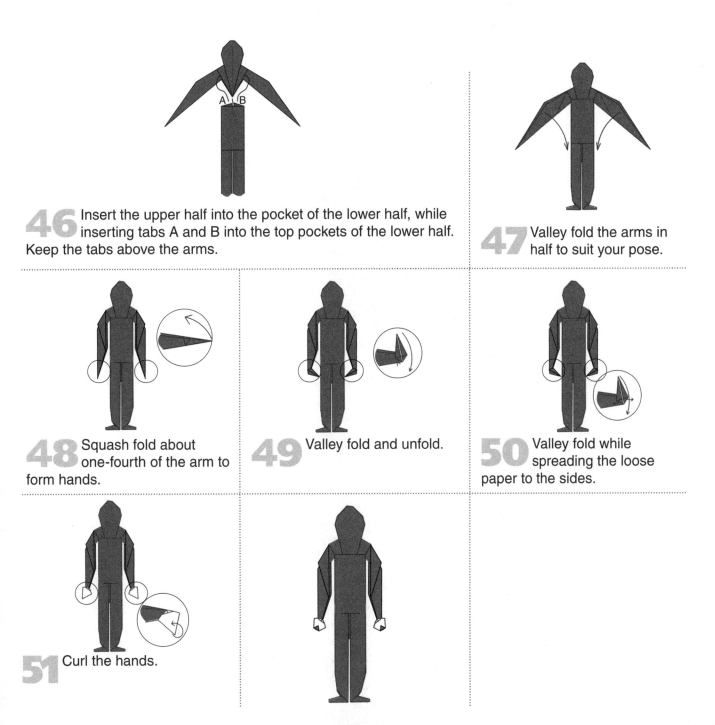

46 Insert the upper half into the pocket of the lower half, while inserting tabs A and B into the top pockets of the lower half. Keep the tabs above the arms.

47 Valley fold the arms in half to suit your pose.

48 Squash fold about one-fourth of the arm to form hands.

49 Valley fold and unfold.

50 Valley fold while spreading the loose paper to the sides.

51 Curl the hands.

"Utinni!"

—JAWAESE FOR "COME HERE!"

JAWA

Jawas were a species of approximately three- to four-foot-tall timid, foul-smelling humanoids native to Tatooine. Always cloaked in long, thick brown robes to protect them from the sun, only their glowing yellow eyes were visible from beneath their large hoods. Their language consisted of a high-pitched chatter that only other Jawas could comprehend, although they could have made themselves understood by others if they had wished to. Most Jawas roamed the desert in huge sandcrawlers searching for discarded machinery, which they patched up and sold. C-3PO was certainly not a fan of the species. After being captured by Jawas, he said, "I can't abide these Jawas. Disgusting creatures."

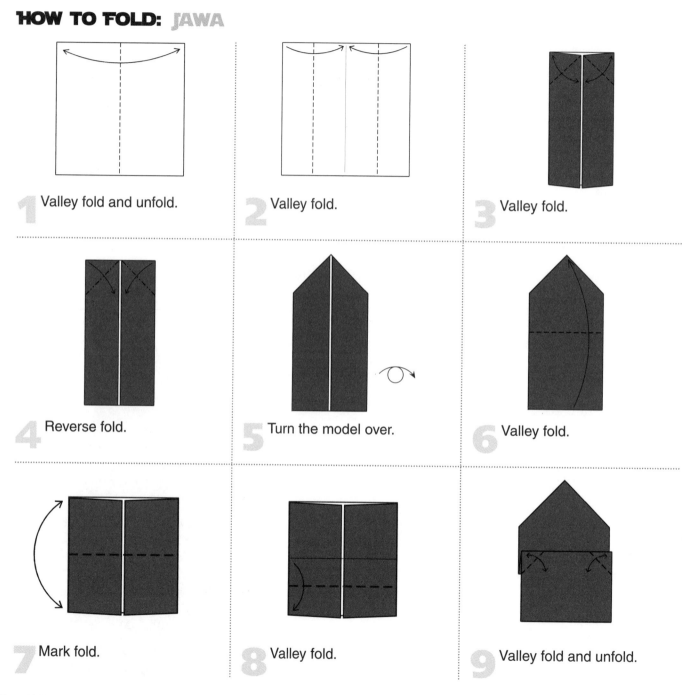

1 Valley fold and unfold.

2 Valley fold.

3 Valley fold.

4 Reverse fold.

5 Turn the model over.

6 Valley fold.

7 Mark fold.

8 Valley fold.

9 Valley fold and unfold.

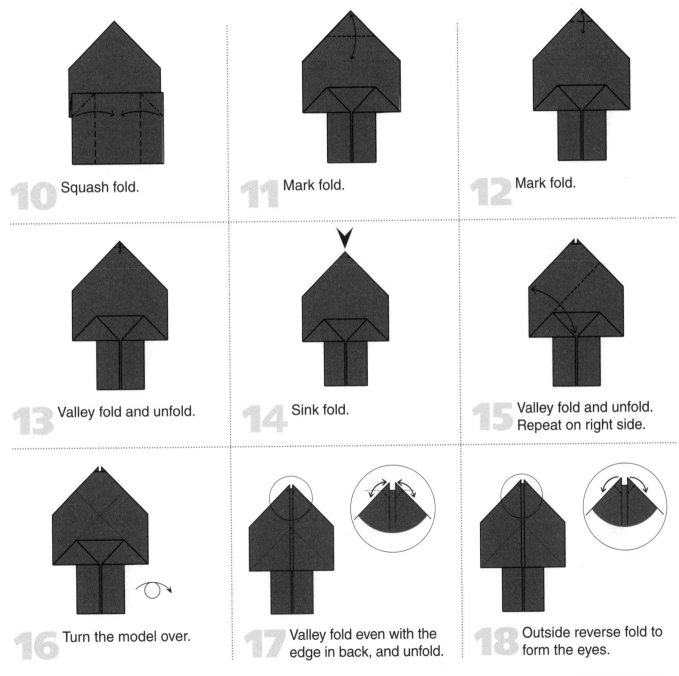

10 Squash fold.

11 Mark fold.

12 Mark fold.

13 Valley fold and unfold.

14 Sink fold.

15 Valley fold and unfold. Repeat on right side.

16 Turn the model over.

17 Valley fold even with the edge in back, and unfold.

18 Outside reverse fold to form the eyes.

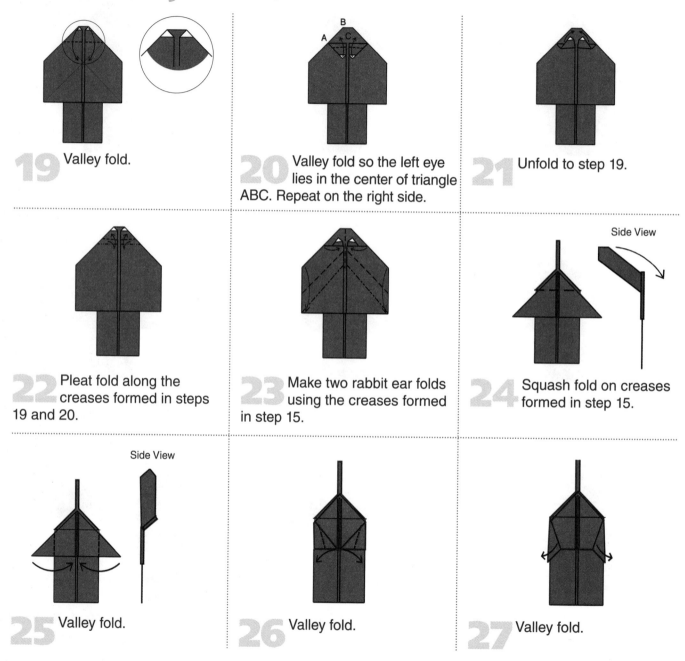

19 Valley fold.

20 Valley fold so the left eye lies in the center of triangle ABC. Repeat on the right side.

21 Unfold to step 19.

22 Pleat fold along the creases formed in steps 19 and 20.

23 Make two rabbit ear folds using the creases formed in step 15.

24 Squash fold on creases formed in step 15.

Side View

25 Valley fold.

26 Valley fold.

27 Valley fold.

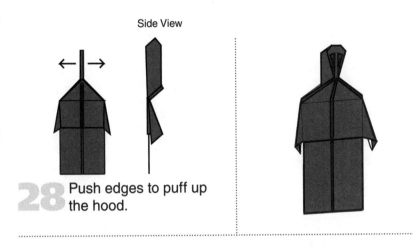

Side View

28 Push edges to puff up the hood.

"What's that? A transport. I'm saved!"

—C-3PO

SANDCRAWLER

Sandcrawlers were massive, multistory vehicles used for shelter, work, and travel by the Jawas on Tatooine. They were about seventy feet tall, could hold three hundred of the diminutive scavengers, and had eight caterpillar treads powered by fusion reactor engines. Jawas roamed the desert in these mobile cities, looking for discarded machinery and junk. This was how R2-D2 and C-3PO were picked up and later sold to Luke Skywalker's uncle.

HOW TO FOLD: SANDCRAWLER

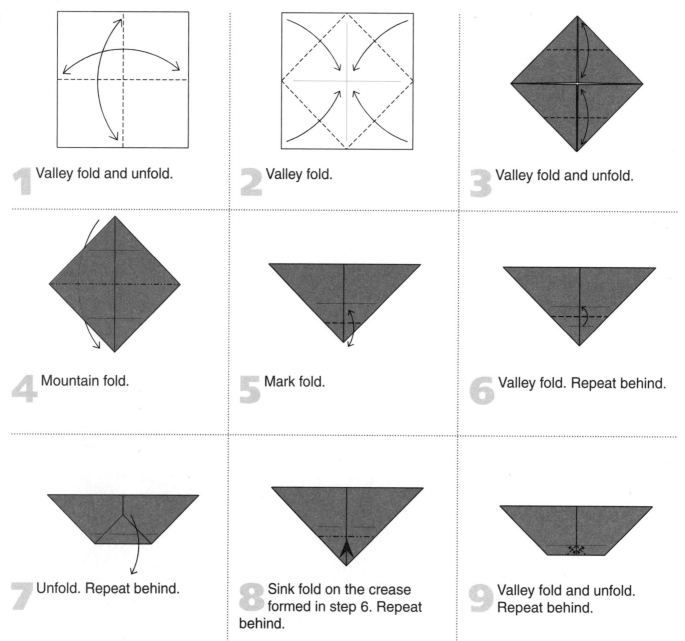

1 Valley fold and unfold.

2 Valley fold.

3 Valley fold and unfold.

4 Mountain fold.

5 Mark fold.

6 Valley fold. Repeat behind.

7 Unfold. Repeat behind.

8 Sink fold on the crease formed in step 6. Repeat behind.

9 Valley fold and unfold. Repeat behind.

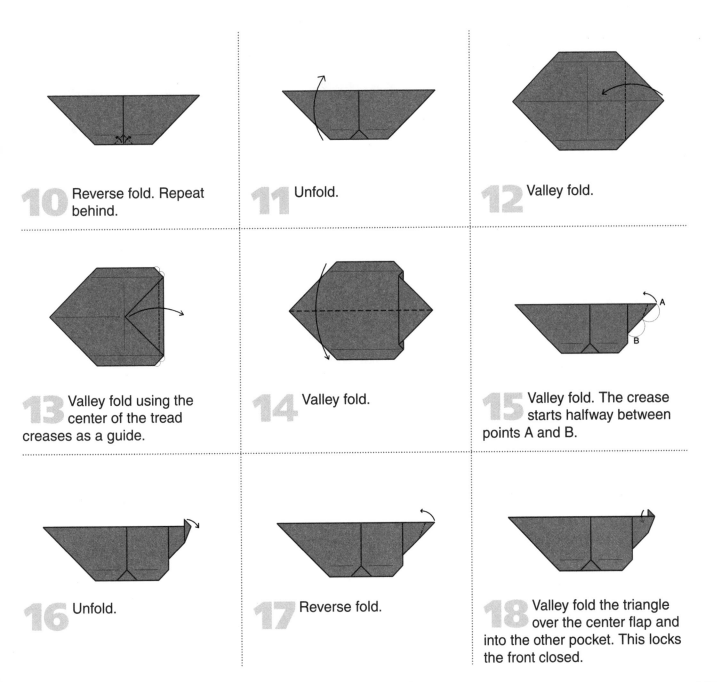

10 Reverse fold. Repeat behind.

11 Unfold.

12 Valley fold.

13 Valley fold using the center of the tread creases as a guide.

14 Valley fold.

15 Valley fold. The crease starts halfway between points A and B.

16 Unfold.

17 Reverse fold.

18 Valley fold the triangle over the center flap and into the other pocket. This locks the front closed.

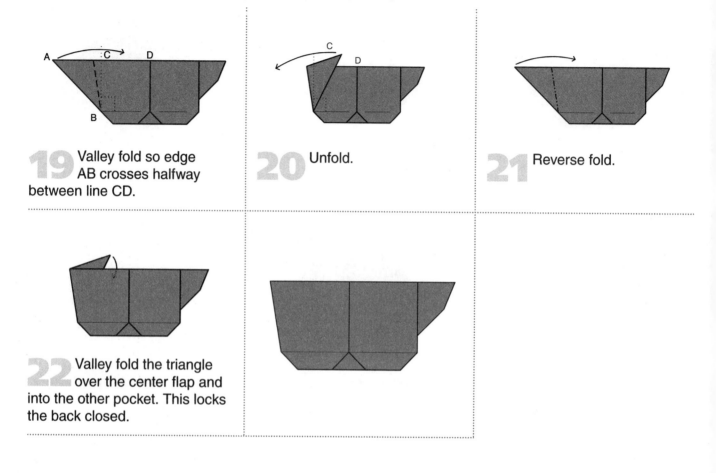

19 Valley fold so edge AB crosses halfway between line CD.

20 Unfold.

21 Reverse fold.

22 Valley fold the triangle over the center flap and into the other pocket. This locks the back closed.

HOW TO SPEAK
JAWAESE

Learn some common words and phrases in the Jawas' language.

PHRASES

Utto nye usabia atoonyoba?
Want to buy a used droid?

A beton nya mombay m'bwa!
This is mine, all mine!

Mombay m'bwa.
That is mine.

Etee uwanna waa.
I want to trade.

Go mob un loo?
How much for this?

M'gasha.
Too much.

Ya e'um pukay.
I won't sell.

Ikeena mee koosa ha speeda.
I would like to rent a speeder.

Ookwass dok pundwa keena?
Where is the nearest fuel station?

Ny shootogawa!
Don't shoot!

WORDS

Ashuna Go

Bopom Kova Mountain

Chikua Them

Dikwass Cliff

Dooka Junk

Gogowa Run

Hunya Enemy

Ibana Yes

Ikee I

Jar k'osa Large

Jubinloo City

Kebee'oto Long ago

Keeza Weapon

Kiizci Cave

Ko lopo Broken

Kurruzza Repair

Lopima Stars

Mambay Okay

M'nuta Hole

M'tuske Steal

M'um m'aloo Greetings, hello

Nyeta No

Okka Up

Ookwass Where

Opakwa Spare parts

Reve Ship

Sabioto Stop

Shootogawa Shoot, blast

Sooga Food

Speeda Speeder

Taa baa Thank you, thanks

Tando Fix

Theek Run

Tomo She

Ton ton Sand

Ubanya Good day, good-bye

Ugama Bantha

Umka Walk

Umpee Empire

Upezzo Market

Utinni Wow, come here (battle cry or alert to other Jawas)

"Ever since the XP-38 came out,
they just aren't in demand."

—LUKE SKYWALKER

LANDSPEEDER

Landspeeders were light transport crafts that could skim above the ground on a repulsor field. They were most commonly used as personal vehicles. Luke Skywalker's X-34 speeder was a two-seater version. The three turbine engines produced excellent speed, and the open cockpit gave it a sporty look. This model was perfect for a "reckless" Tatooine teenager!

HOW TO FOLD: LANDSPEEDER

1 Start with a preliminary base.

2 Valley fold and unfold.

3 Petal fold. Repeat behind.

4 Valley fold the top layer down.

5 Valley fold and unfold.

6 Sink fold.

7 Valley fold and unfold.

8 Sink fold.

9 Valley fold and unfold the back layer.

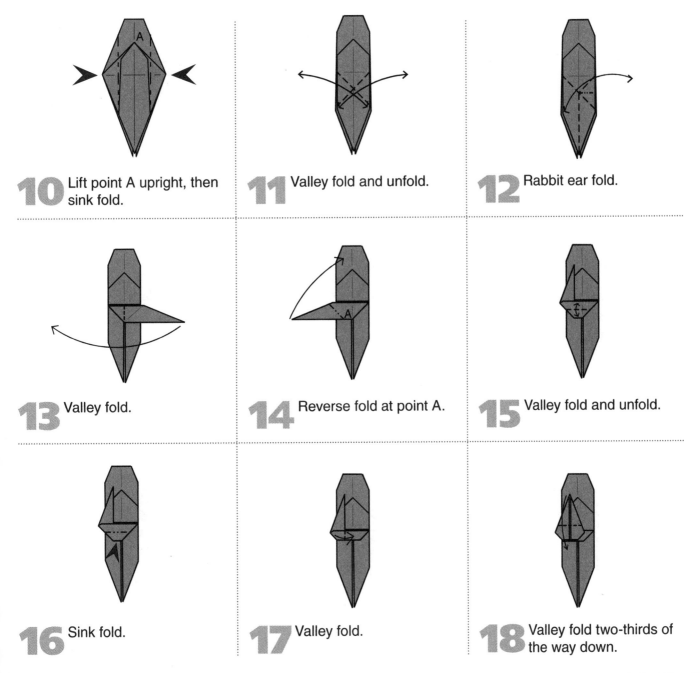

10 Lift point A upright, then sink fold.

11 Valley fold and unfold.

12 Rabbit ear fold.

13 Valley fold.

14 Reverse fold at point A.

15 Valley fold and unfold.

16 Sink fold.

17 Valley fold.

18 Valley fold two-thirds of the way down.

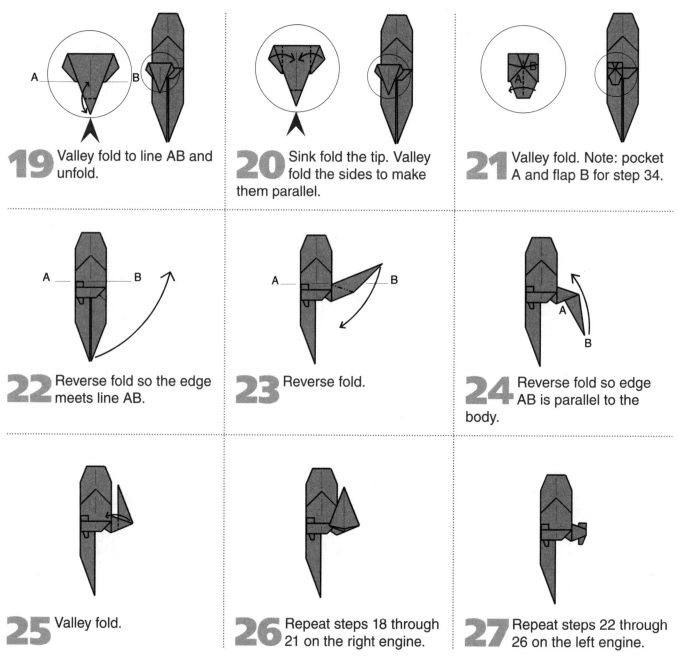

19 Valley fold to line AB and unfold.

20 Sink fold the tip. Valley fold the sides to make them parallel.

21 Valley fold. Note: pocket A and flap B for step 34.

22 Reverse fold so the edge meets line AB.

23 Reverse fold.

24 Reverse fold so edge AB is parallel to the body.

25 Valley fold.

26 Repeat steps 18 through 21 on the right engine.

27 Repeat steps 22 through 26 on the left engine.

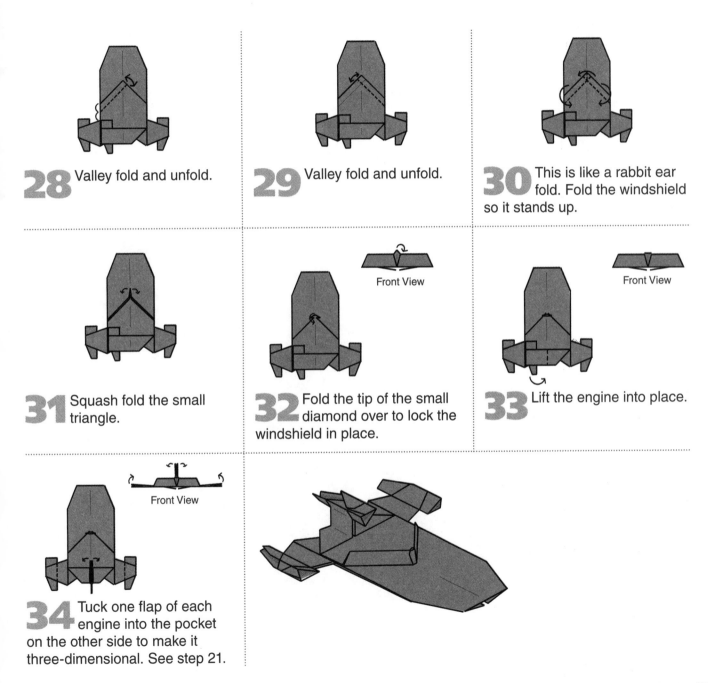

28 Valley fold and unfold.

29 Valley fold and unfold.

30 This is like a rabbit ear fold. Fold the windshield so it stands up.

31 Squash fold the small triangle.

Front View

32 Fold the tip of the small diamond over to lock the windshield in place.

Front View

33 Lift the engine into place.

Front View

34 Tuck one flap of each engine into the pocket on the other side to make it three-dimensional. See step 21.

"Well, there are two banthas
down there. . . . "
—LUKE SKYWALKER

BANTHA

Banthas were giant beasts that roamed the deserts of Tatooine in herds of fifteen or more. Their thick fur coats, long tails, and curved horns enabled them to survive Tatooine's hostile climate and vicious predators. The Sand People, or Tusken Raiders, domesticated the bantha and used them primarily for transportation. On raiding parties, the Sand People rode them single file to hide their numbers.

HOW TO FOLD: BANTHA

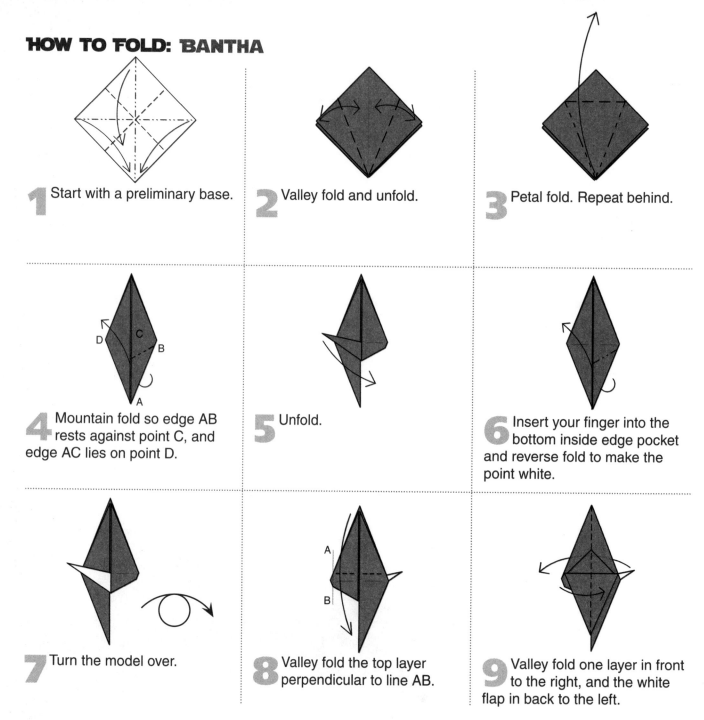

1 Start with a preliminary base.

2 Valley fold and unfold.

3 Petal fold. Repeat behind.

4 Mountain fold so edge AB rests against point C, and edge AC lies on point D.

5 Unfold.

6 Insert your finger into the bottom inside edge pocket and reverse fold to make the point white.

7 Turn the model over.

8 Valley fold the top layer perpendicular to line AB.

9 Valley fold one layer in front to the right, and the white flap in back to the left.

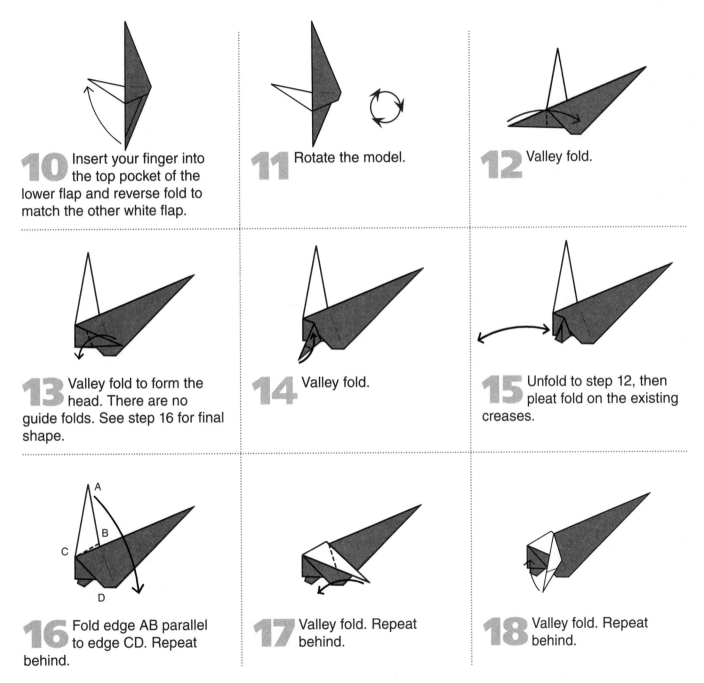

10 Insert your finger into the top pocket of the lower flap and reverse fold to match the other white flap.

11 Rotate the model.

12 Valley fold.

13 Valley fold to form the head. There are no guide folds. See step 16 for final shape.

14 Valley fold.

15 Unfold to step 12, then pleat fold on the existing creases.

16 Fold edge AB parallel to edge CD. Repeat behind.

17 Valley fold. Repeat behind.

18 Valley fold. Repeat behind.

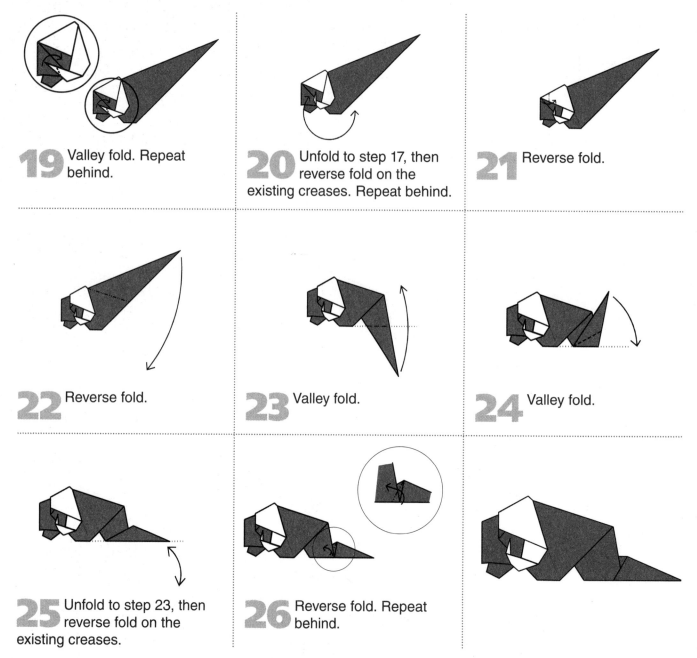

19 Valley fold. Repeat behind.

20 Unfold to step 17, then reverse fold on the existing creases. Repeat behind.

21 Reverse fold.

22 Reverse fold.

23 Valley fold.

24 Valley fold.

25 Unfold to step 23, then reverse fold on the existing creases.

26 Reverse fold. Repeat behind.

TEST YOUR STAR WARS IQ:

MATCHUP

Match the *Star Wars* character to his or her weapon of choice.

1. Anakin Skywalker

2. Darth Vader

3. Princess Leia Organa

4. Mace Windu

5. Han Solo

6. Yoda

7. Boba Fett

A. Red-bladed lightsaber

B. Sporting blaster

C. Blue-bladed lightsaber

D. DL-44 heavy blaster pistol

E. Purple-bladed lightsaber

F. EE-3 blaster rifle

G. Green-bladed lightsaber

"That's no moon.
It's a space station."
—OBI-WAN KENOBI

THE DEATH STAR

The first Death Star was the size of a small moon, was heavily shielded, had 768 tractor beams, seven to nine thousand TIE fighters, a crew of more than a million, and fire power greater than half the Imperial starfleet. Such a weapon would have enabled the Emperor to maintain total control over the galaxy had Luke Skywalker not destroyed the first Death Star after a small flaw in its design was discovered by the Rebels. The second Death Star was bigger and more dangerous than the first. It, too, was destroyed after a coordinated planetary and space assault.

HOW TO FOLD: THE DEATH STAR

1 Valley fold and unfold.

2 Valley fold and unfold. Steps 2 through 8 give the Death Star texture. Do not crease them too sharply.

3 Valley fold in half and unfold.

4 Valley fold in fourths and unfold.

5 Valley fold in eighths and unfold.

6 Valley fold in sixteenths and unfold.

7 Repeat steps 3 through 6 on the right side.

8 Repeat steps 3 through 6 on the top and bottom.

9 Turn the paper over.

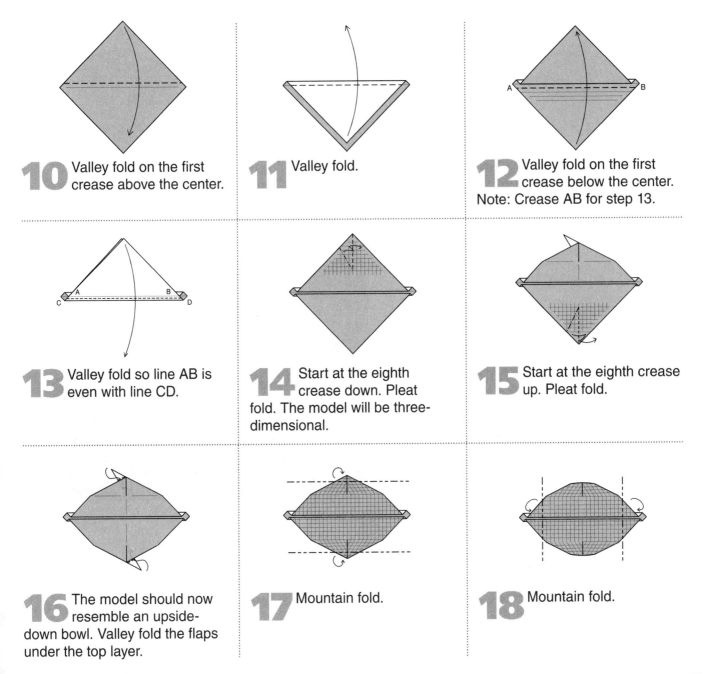

10 Valley fold on the first crease above the center.

11 Valley fold.

12 Valley fold on the first crease below the center. Note: Crease AB for step 13.

13 Valley fold so line AB is even with line CD.

14 Start at the eighth crease down. Pleat fold. The model will be three-dimensional.

15 Start at the eighth crease up. Pleat fold.

16 The model should now resemble an upside-down bowl. Valley fold the flaps under the top layer.

17 Mountain fold.

18 Mountain fold.

HOW TO FOLD: THE DEATH STAR (CONT.)

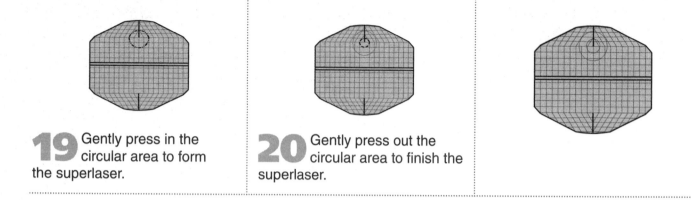

19 Gently press in the circular area to form the superlaser.

20 Gently press out the circular area to finish the superlaser.

A TIE fighter flying toward the Death Star.

TEST YOUR STAR WARS IQ:

TRIVIA

1. How man suns did the planet Tatooine have?

2. Which Jedi helped Anakin Skywalker win his freedom from Watto?

3. What four-armed chef ran the diner on the planet Coruscant?

4. In an arena on what planet did Obi-Wan Kenobi, Anakin Skywalker, and Padmé Amidala nearly die?

5. Which Imperial officer was put in charge of the first Death Star?

6. Was Endor a moon, a planet, or a sun?

ANSWERS: 1. Two. 2. Qui-Gon Jinn. 3. Dexter Jettster. 4. Geonosis. 5. Grand Moff Wilhuff Tarkin. 6. A moon (one of nine orbiting a giant gas planet in the Outer Rim)

"You came in that thing?
You're braver than I thought!"
—LEIA ORGANA TO HAN SOLO

MILLENNIUM FALCON

D escribed as "a piece of junk," a "bucket of bolts," and "the fastest hunk of junk in the galaxy," the *Millennium Falcon* constantly broke down at the most inconvenient times, but always, somehow, came through in the end. Han Solo boasted that she was capable of point five past lightspeed, made the Kessel Run in less than twelve parsecs, and outran Imperial starships. She also escaped Imperial blockades, dodged through asteroid fields, and played a prominent role in the destruction of two Death Stars. In the words of her captain, Han Solo, "She may not look like much, but she's got it where it counts."

HOW TO FOLD: MILLENNIUM FALCON

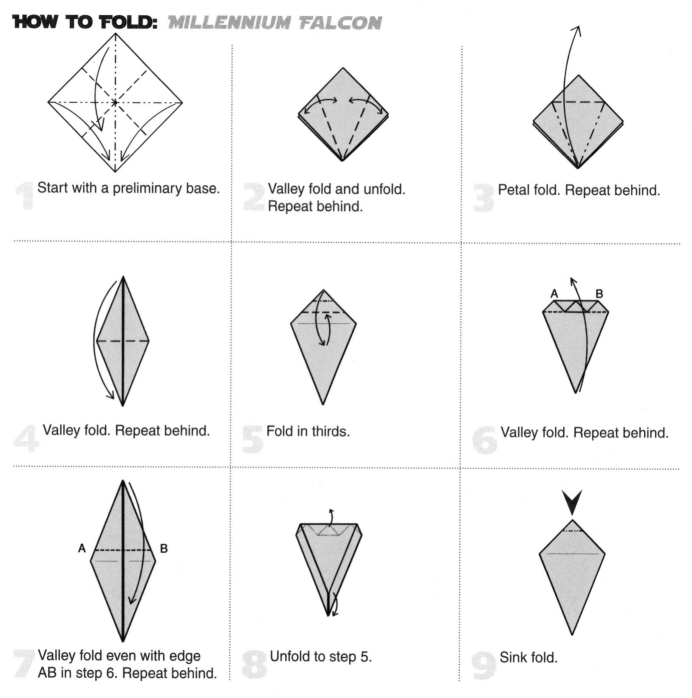

1 Start with a preliminary base.

2 Valley fold and unfold. Repeat behind.

3 Petal fold. Repeat behind.

4 Valley fold. Repeat behind.

5 Fold in thirds.

6 Valley fold. Repeat behind.

7 Valley fold even with edge AB in step 6. Repeat behind.

8 Unfold to step 5.

9 Sink fold.

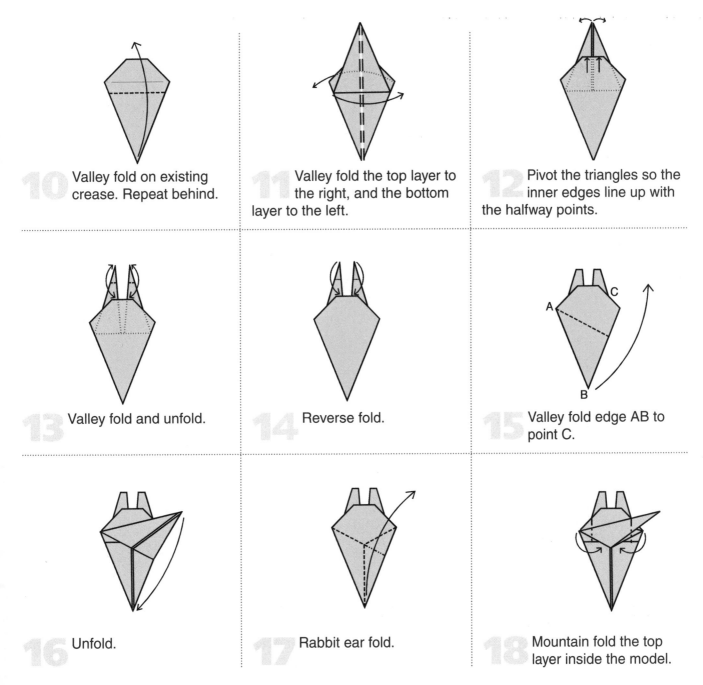

10 Valley fold on existing crease. Repeat behind.

11 Valley fold the top layer to the right, and the bottom layer to the left.

12 Pivot the triangles so the inner edges line up with the halfway points.

13 Valley fold and unfold.

14 Reverse fold.

15 Valley fold edge AB to point C.

16 Unfold.

17 Rabbit ear fold.

18 Mountain fold the top layer inside the model.

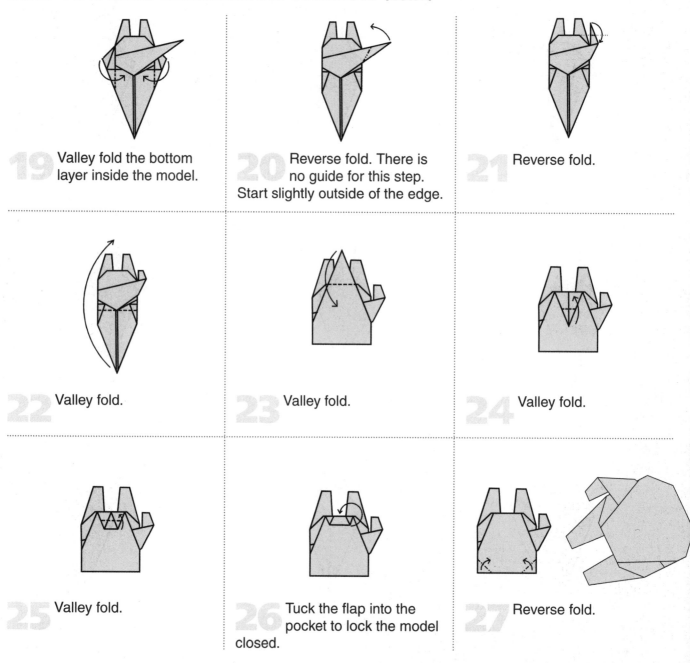

19 Valley fold the bottom layer inside the model.

20 Reverse fold. There is no guide for this step. Start slightly outside of the edge.

21 Reverse fold.

22 Valley fold.

23 Valley fold.

24 Valley fold.

25 Valley fold.

26 Tuck the flap into the pocket to lock the model closed.

27 Reverse fold.

TEST YOUR STAR WARS IQ:

WHO SAID IT?

Match the quote to the correct *Star Wars* character.

1. "I will become a Jedi and I will come back and free you."

2. "I'm a Toydarian—mind tricks don't work on me. Only money."

3. "Use the Force, Luke."

4. "Governor Tarkin, I should have expected to find you holding Vader's leash."

5. "Wonderful girl. Either I'm going to kill her or I'm beginning to like her."

6. "No. I am your father."

A. Obi-Wan Kenobi

B. Han Solo

C. Princess Leia Organa

D. Anakin Skywalker

E. Watto

F. Darth Vader

ANSWERS: 1. D Anakin Skywalker to his mother, 2. E Watto to Qui-Gon Jinn, 3. A Obi-Wan Kenobi, 4. C Princess Leia Organa, 5. B Han Solo, about Princess Leia, 6. F Darth Vader to Luke Skywalker

231

"We'll have to destroy them
ship-to-ship. Get the crews to their fighters."
—DARTH VADER

TIE FIGHTER

I f the Star Destroyer was the backbone of the Imperial Navy, the TIE fighter was the fist. The TIE was named for its twin ion engines and was powered by two large solar panels. TIEs were armed with two powerful laser cannons but had no shields, life-support systems, or hyperdrive. The lack of this extra equipment made the ship extremely maneuverable, and its small profile made it very hard to hit. During the battle of Yavin, TIEs destroyed nearly all of the attacking starfighters. At the end of the battle just four Rebel fighters remained.

NOTE: You need three pieces of paper for this model. Steps 1 through 8 form one wing. You will need to make two wings. Steps 9 through 24 form the cockpit.

HOW TO FOLD: TIE FIGHTER

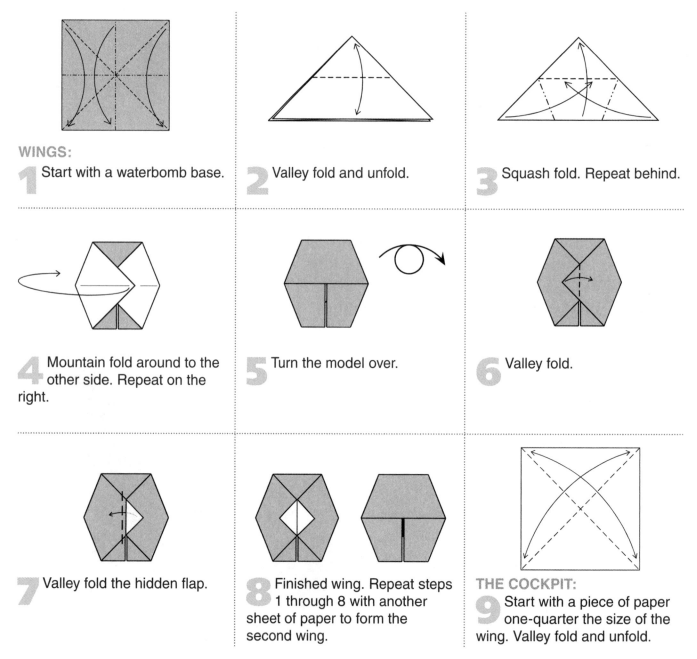

WINGS:

1 Start with a waterbomb base.

2 Valley fold and unfold.

3 Squash fold. Repeat behind.

4 Mountain fold around to the other side. Repeat on the right.

5 Turn the model over.

6 Valley fold.

7 Valley fold the hidden flap.

8 Finished wing. Repeat steps 1 through 8 with another sheet of paper to form the second wing.

THE COCKPIT:

9 Start with a piece of paper one-quarter the size of the wing. Valley fold and unfold.

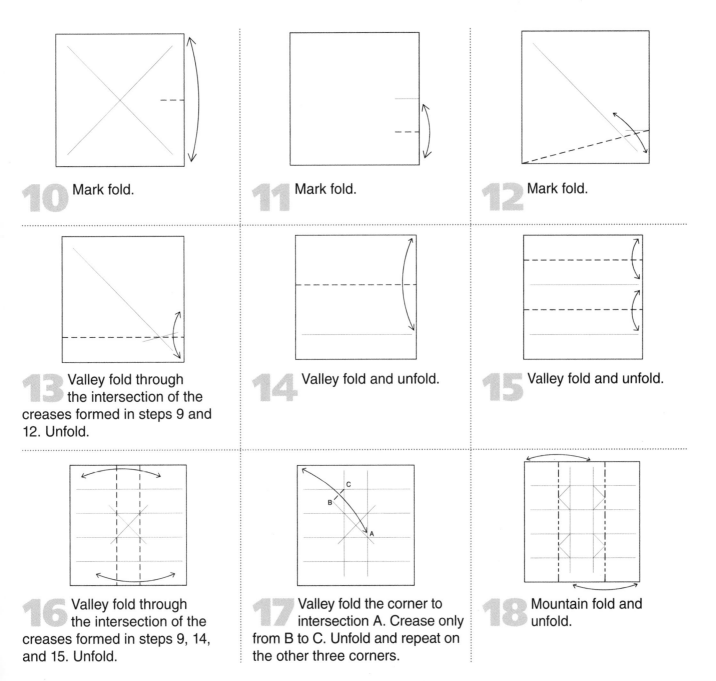

10 Mark fold.

11 Mark fold.

12 Mark fold.

13 Valley fold through the intersection of the creases formed in steps 9 and 12. Unfold.

14 Valley fold and unfold.

15 Valley fold and unfold.

16 Valley fold through the intersection of the creases formed in steps 9, 14, and 15. Unfold.

17 Valley fold the corner to intersection A. Crease only from B to C. Unfold and repeat on the other three corners.

18 Mountain fold and unfold.

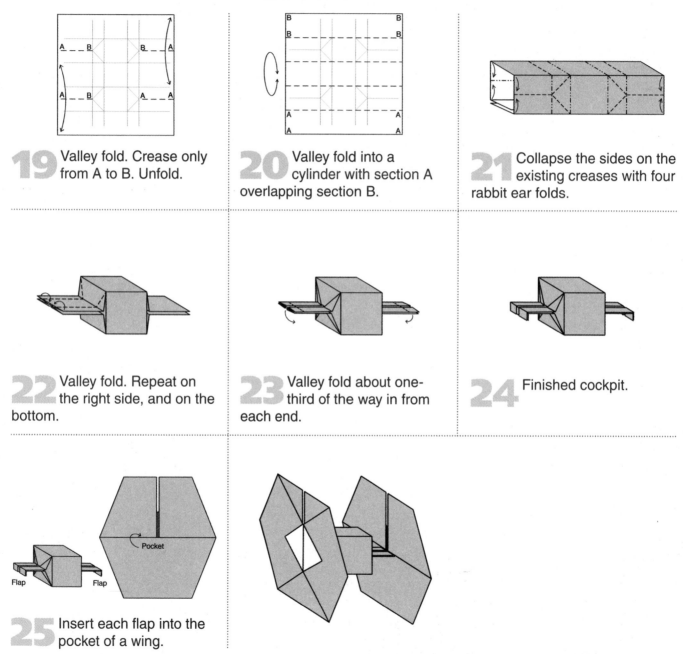

19 Valley fold. Crease only from A to B. Unfold.

20 Valley fold into a cylinder with section A overlapping section B.

21 Collapse the sides on the existing creases with four rabbit ear folds.

22 Valley fold. Repeat on the right side, and on the bottom.

23 Valley fold about one-third of the way in from each end.

24 Finished cockpit.

25 Insert each flap into the pocket of a wing.

Pocket

Flap   Flap

TRIVIA

1. What color are the markings on an X-wing starfighter?
  A. Pink
  B. Red
  C. Silver

2. Who erased C-3PO's memory after the fall of the Old Republic?
  A. Padmé Amidala
  B. Bail Organa
  C. Princess Leia Organa

3. Who defeated Darth Maul on Naboo?
  A. Obi-Wan Kenobi
  B. Qui-Gon Jinn
  C. Anakin Skywalker

4. What was the main purpose of Darth Vader's black armor?
  A. Style
  B. Intimidation
  C. Life support

5. How was Cloud City held in the air?
  A. Repulsorlifts in its frame
  B. Helium platforms
  C. Special gravitational pull

6. What monstrous creature was unable to digest Boba Fett's armor, thus saving his life?
  A. Sarlacc
  B. Glitterstim
  C. Carkoon

"We count thirty Rebel ships, Lord Vader, but they're so small they're evading our turbolasers."

—LIEUTENANT TANBRIS

X-WING STARFIGHTER

The Rebellion's most advanced starfighter, the X-wing, was a truly versatile ship. It was armed with four high-powered laser cannons and two torpedo launchers, and had strong shields for protection. It could assault ground emplacements, space platforms, starships, and, of course, Death Stars. This was the ship Luke Skywalker was flying in the battle of Yavin when he fired two torpedoes into a small thermal exhaust port, destroying the first Death Star.

HOW TO FOLD: X-WING STARFIGHTER

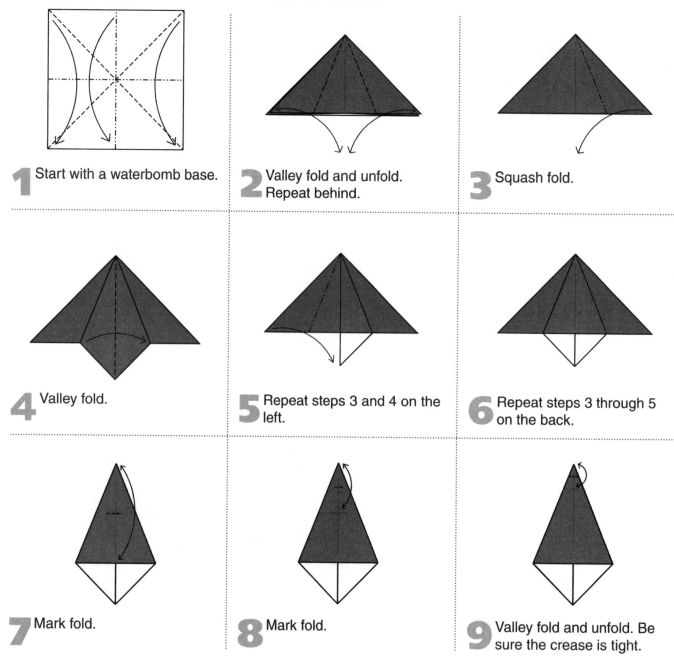

1 Start with a waterbomb base.

2 Valley fold and unfold. Repeat behind.

3 Squash fold.

4 Valley fold.

5 Repeat steps 3 and 4 on the left.

6 Repeat steps 3 through 5 on the back.

7 Mark fold.

8 Mark fold.

9 Valley fold and unfold. Be sure the crease is tight.

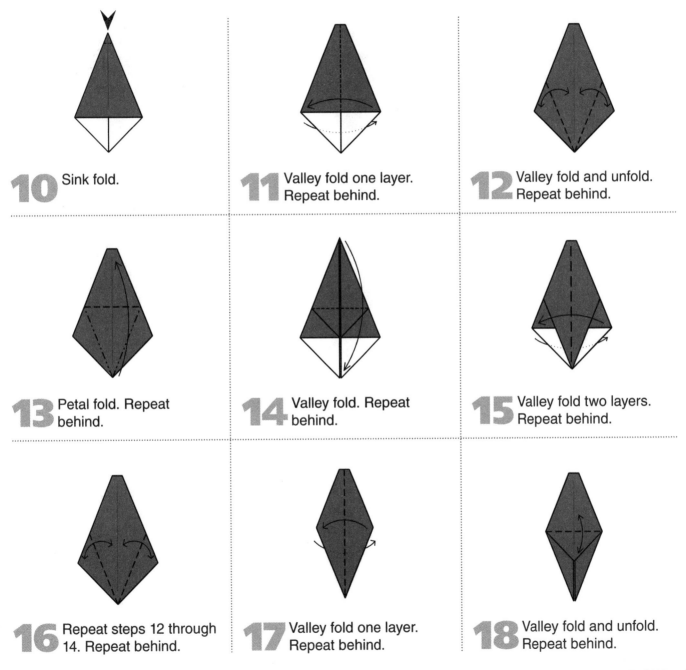

10 Sink fold.

11 Valley fold one layer. Repeat behind.

12 Valley fold and unfold. Repeat behind.

13 Petal fold. Repeat behind.

14 Valley fold. Repeat behind.

15 Valley fold two layers. Repeat behind.

16 Repeat steps 12 through 14. Repeat behind.

17 Valley fold one layer. Repeat behind.

18 Valley fold and unfold. Repeat behind.

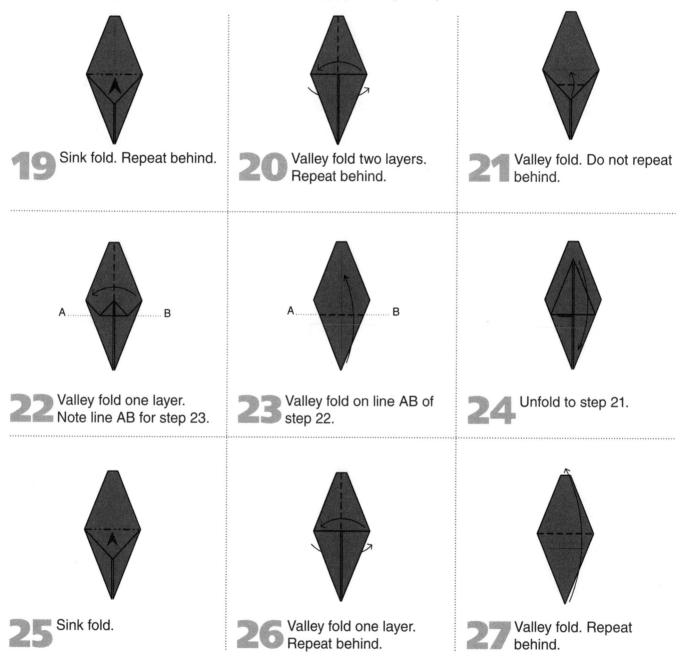

19 Sink fold. Repeat behind.

20 Valley fold two layers. Repeat behind.

21 Valley fold. Do not repeat behind.

22 Valley fold one layer. Note line AB for step 23.

23 Valley fold on line AB of step 22.

24 Unfold to step 21.

25 Sink fold.

26 Valley fold one layer. Repeat behind.

27 Valley fold. Repeat behind.

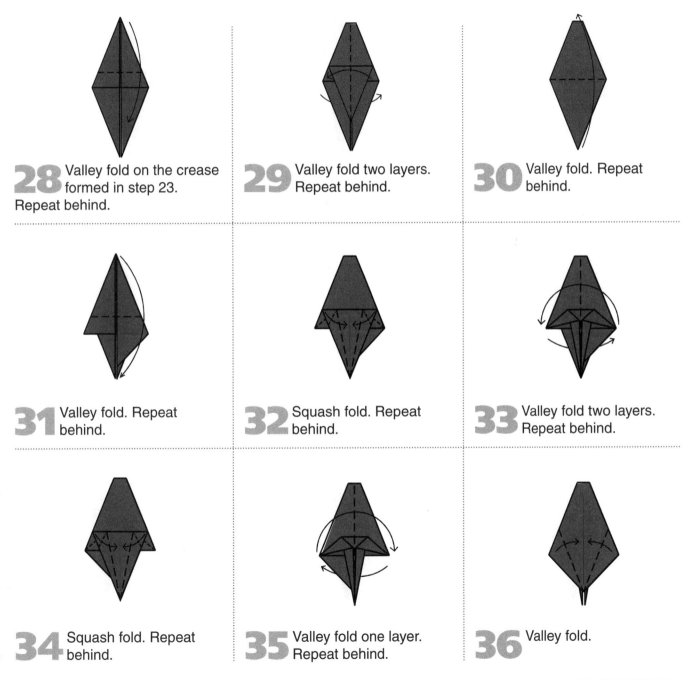

28 Valley fold on the crease formed in step 23. Repeat behind.

29 Valley fold two layers. Repeat behind.

30 Valley fold. Repeat behind.

31 Valley fold. Repeat behind.

32 Squash fold. Repeat behind.

33 Valley fold two layers. Repeat behind.

34 Squash fold. Repeat behind.

35 Valley fold one layer. Repeat behind.

36 Valley fold.

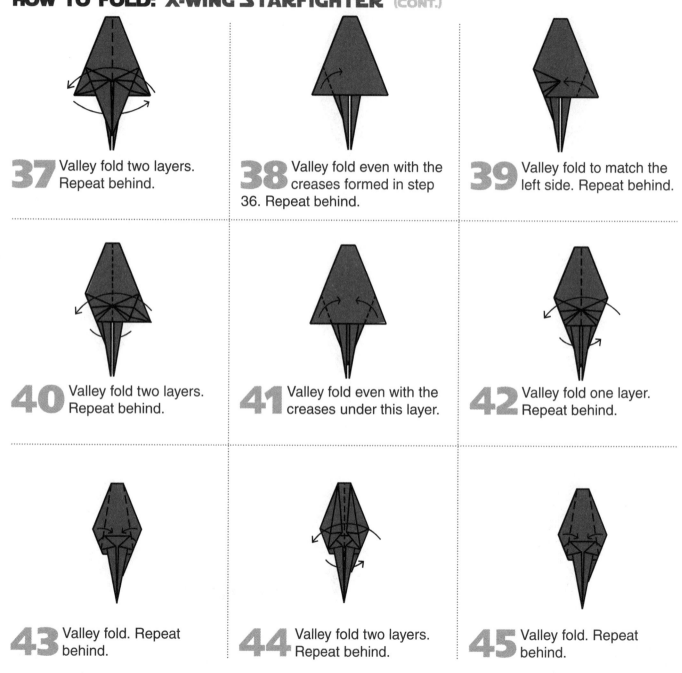

37 Valley fold two layers. Repeat behind.

38 Valley fold even with the creases formed in step 36. Repeat behind.

39 Valley fold to match the left side. Repeat behind.

40 Valley fold two layers. Repeat behind.

41 Valley fold even with the creases under this layer.

42 Valley fold one layer. Repeat behind.

43 Valley fold. Repeat behind.

44 Valley fold two layers. Repeat behind.

45 Valley fold. Repeat behind.

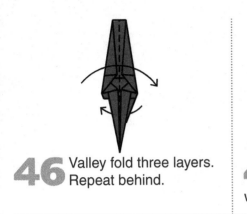

46 Valley fold three layers. Repeat behind.

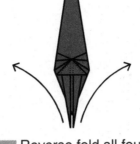

47 Reverse fold all four wings as far as they will go.

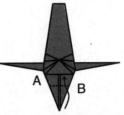

A B

48 To lock the model closed, insert the triangular flap into the top pocket. Make sure it is in snugly, then crease folds A and B sharply.

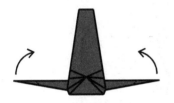

49 Outside reverse fold all four laser cannons at the halfway point.

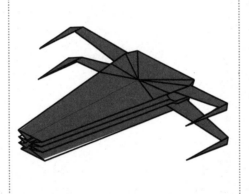

"I'll take them myself. Cover me."
—DARTH VADER

DARTH VADER'S TIE ADVANCED FIGHTER X1

This TIE was the prototype for the next generation of TIE fighter. Flown by Darth Vader, Dark Lord of the Sith, it had four engines instead of two, hyperdrive capability, and angled solar panels that made it more maneuverable than the standard TIE. While flying this ship, Darth Vader destroyed several rebel starfighters over the Death Star during the battle of Yavin.

HOW TO FOLD: DARTH VADER'S TIE ADVANCED FIGHTER X1

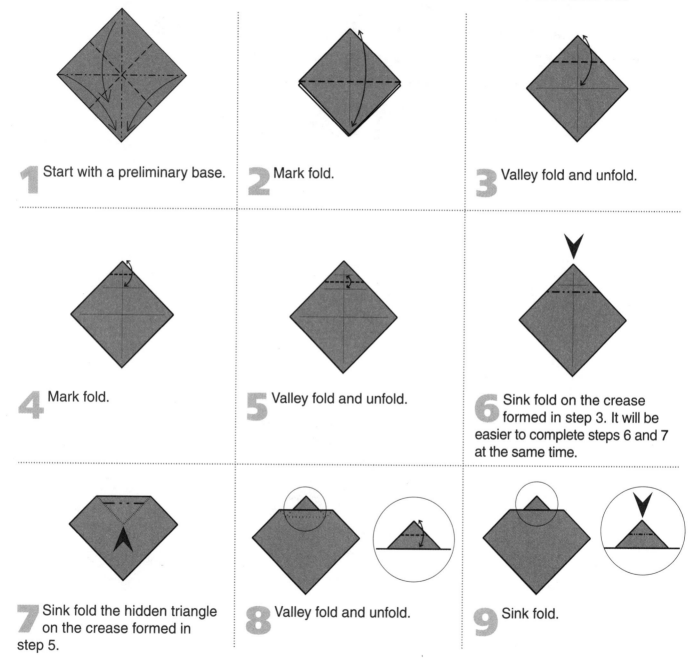

1 Start with a preliminary base.

2 Mark fold.

3 Valley fold and unfold.

4 Mark fold.

5 Valley fold and unfold.

6 Sink fold on the crease formed in step 3. It will be easier to complete steps 6 and 7 at the same time.

7 Sink fold the hidden triangle on the crease formed in step 5.

8 Valley fold and unfold.

9 Sink fold.

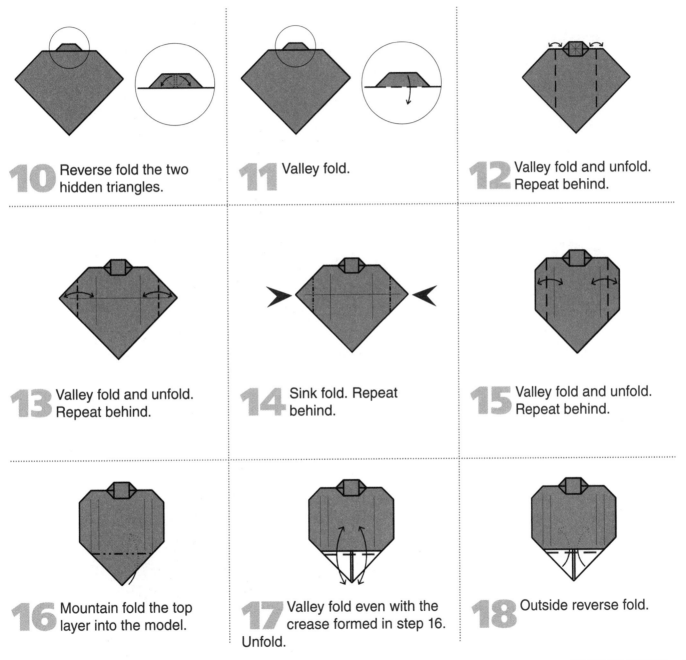

10 Reverse fold the two hidden triangles.

11 Valley fold.

12 Valley fold and unfold. Repeat behind.

13 Valley fold and unfold. Repeat behind.

14 Sink fold. Repeat behind.

15 Valley fold and unfold. Repeat behind.

16 Mountain fold the top layer into the model.

17 Valley fold even with the crease formed in step 16. Unfold.

18 Outside reverse fold.

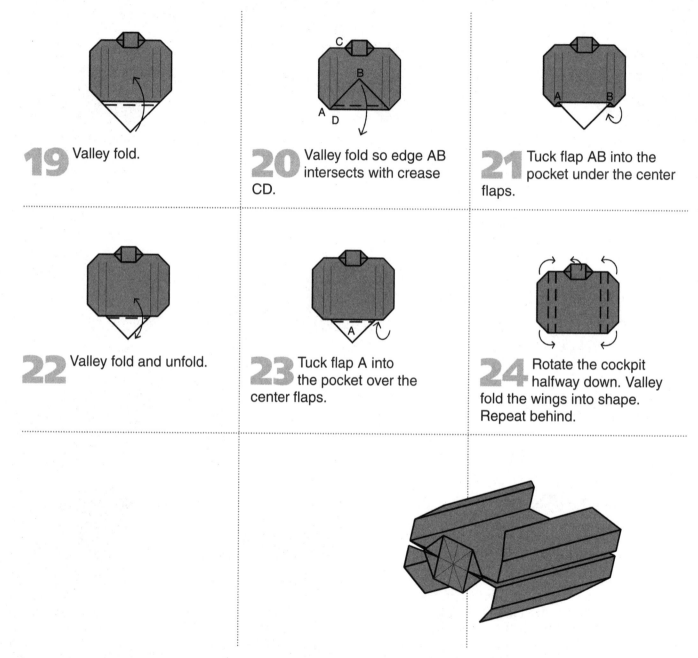

19 Valley fold.

20 Valley fold so edge AB intersects with crease CD.

21 Tuck flap AB into the pocket under the center flaps.

22 Valley fold and unfold.

23 Tuck flap A into the pocket over the center flaps.

24 Rotate the cockpit halfway down. Valley fold the wings into shape. Repeat behind.

TEST YOUR STAR WARS IQ:

WHO SAID IT?

Match the quote to the correct *Star Wars* character.

1. "I'm afraid our furry companion has gone and done something rather rash."

2. "You know, sometimes I amaze even myself."

3. "Our worst fear has been realized."

4. "There are too few of us, Your Highness. We have no army."

5. "You can't win, Darth. If you strike me down, I shall become more powerful than you can possibly imagine."

6. "Try not. Do, or do not. There is no try."

A. Mace Windu

B. Obi-Wan Kenobi

C. Yoda

D. C-3PO

E. Han Solo

F. Captain Panaka

ANSWERS: 1. D C-3PO, on the Ewok Paploo. 2. E Han Solo. 3. A Mace Windu, on the realization that the Sith exist. 4. F Captain Panaka. 5. B Obi-Wan Kenobi. 6. C Yoda to Luke Skywalker

251

"Let's see what this piece of junk can do."
—HAN SOLO

IMPERIAL SHUTTLE

The *Lambda*-class shuttle was the Empire's multipurpose transport craft. It was hyperspace-capable and could carry twenty passengers or several tons of cargo. The two side wings swung down to stabilize it while in flight, and when landing, they swung up to save room in docking bays. As a defense, it had eight forward- and two rear-facing laser cannons.

The Rebel Alliance stole one of these ships, the *Tydirium,* and used it to sneak past the Imperial Starfleet. Their cover was a routine shipment of parts and technical crews. In reality, it carried a squad of rebel commandos tasked with landing on Endor and destroying the shield generator that protected the second Death Star.

HOW TO FOLD: IMPERIAL SHUTTLE

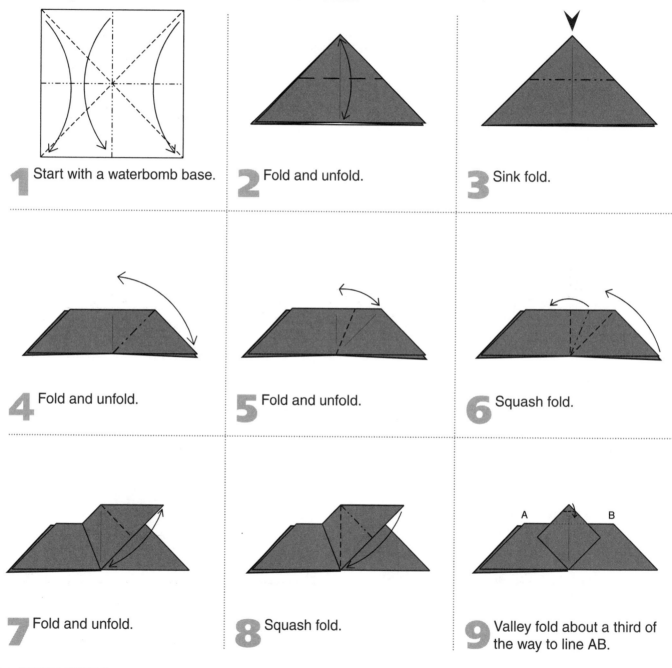

1 Start with a waterbomb base.

2 Fold and unfold.

3 Sink fold.

4 Fold and unfold.

5 Fold and unfold.

6 Squash fold.

7 Fold and unfold.

8 Squash fold.

9 Valley fold about a third of the way to line AB.

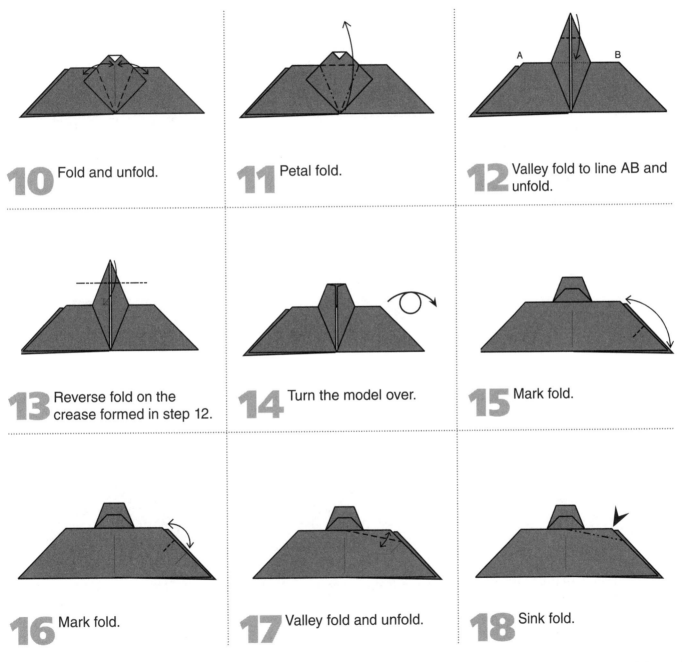

10 Fold and unfold.

11 Petal fold.

12 Valley fold to line AB and unfold.

13 Reverse fold on the crease formed in step 12.

14 Turn the model over.

15 Mark fold.

16 Mark fold.

17 Valley fold and unfold.

18 Sink fold.

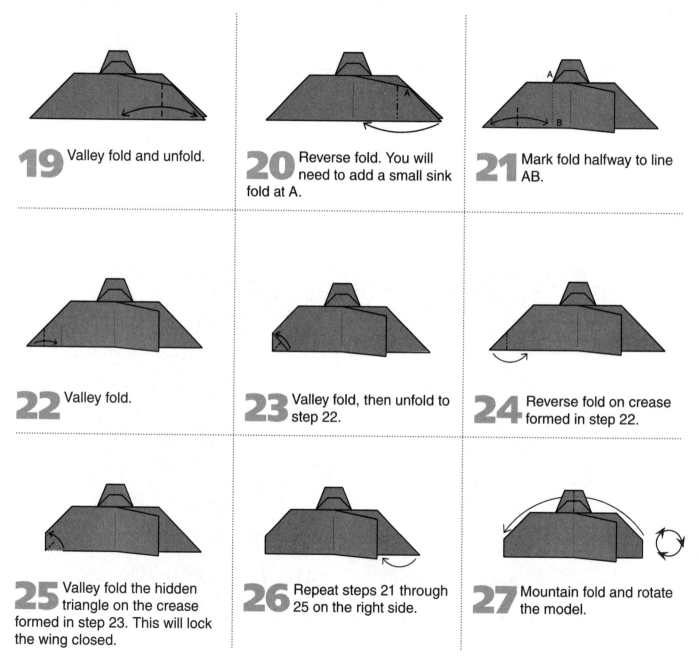

19 Valley fold and unfold.

20 Reverse fold. You will need to add a small sink fold at A.

21 Mark fold halfway to line AB.

22 Valley fold.

23 Valley fold, then unfold to step 22.

24 Reverse fold on crease formed in step 22.

25 Valley fold the hidden triangle on the crease formed in step 23. This will lock the wing closed.

26 Repeat steps 21 through 25 on the right side.

27 Mountain fold and rotate the model.

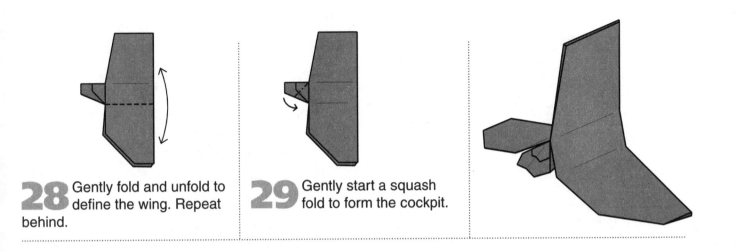

28 Gently fold and unfold to define the wing. Repeat behind.

29 Gently start a squash fold to form the cockpit.

Inside the Imperial shuttle.

INDEX

PROJECTS BY LEVEL OF DIFFICULTY

Some of the models in this book are easier to fold than others, and they are grouped into four levels of difficulty: Youngling (easy), Padawan (medium), Jedi Knight (difficult), and Jedi Master (very tricky!). Unless you're already an origami guru, you might want to start with the Youngling or Padawan models first.

JEDI MASTER (VERY TRICKY!)

ALPHABETICAL LIST OF PROJECTS

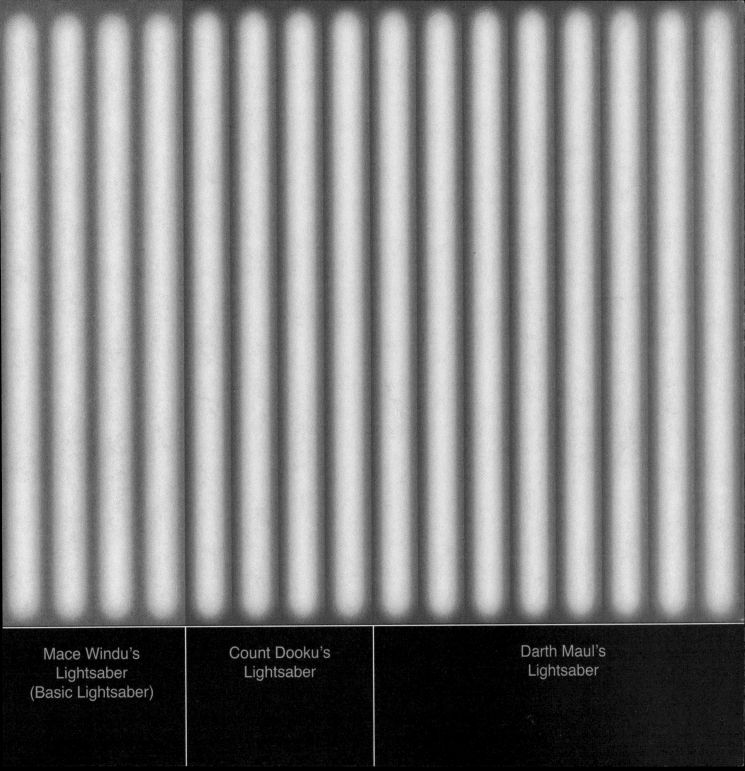

Mace Windu's
Lightsaber
(Basic Lightsaber)

Count Dooku's
Lightsaber

Darth Maul's
Lightsaber

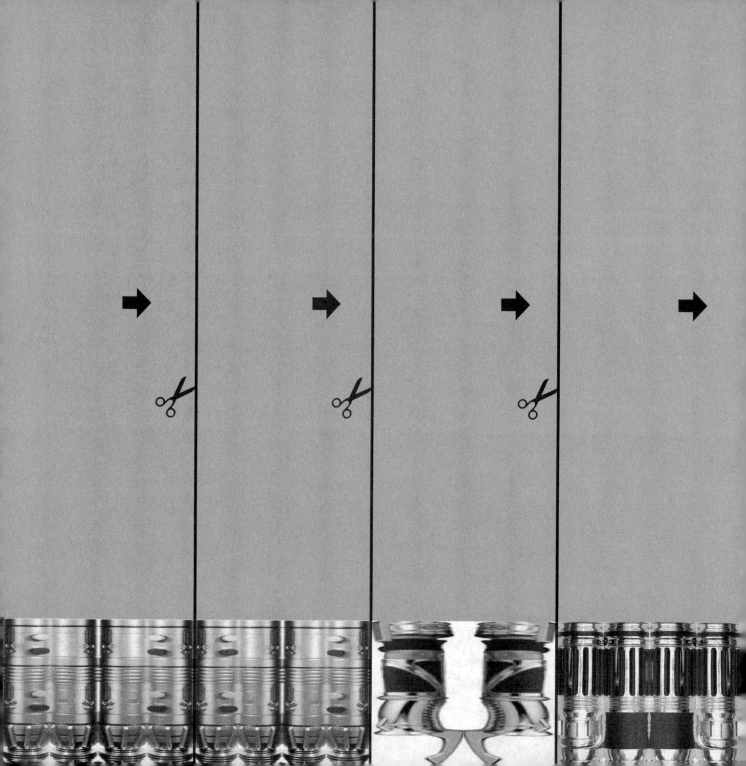

Luke's
Lightsaber
(Basic Lightsaber)

Obi Wan's
Lightsaber
(Basic Lightsaber)

Yoda's
Lightsaber
(Basic Lightsaber)

Darth Vader's
Lightsaber
(Basic Lightsaber)

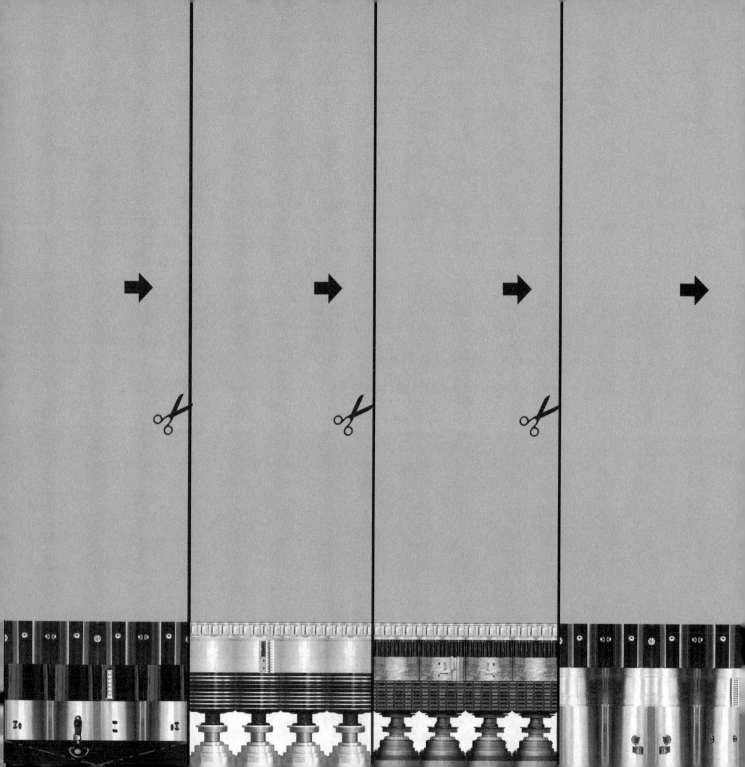

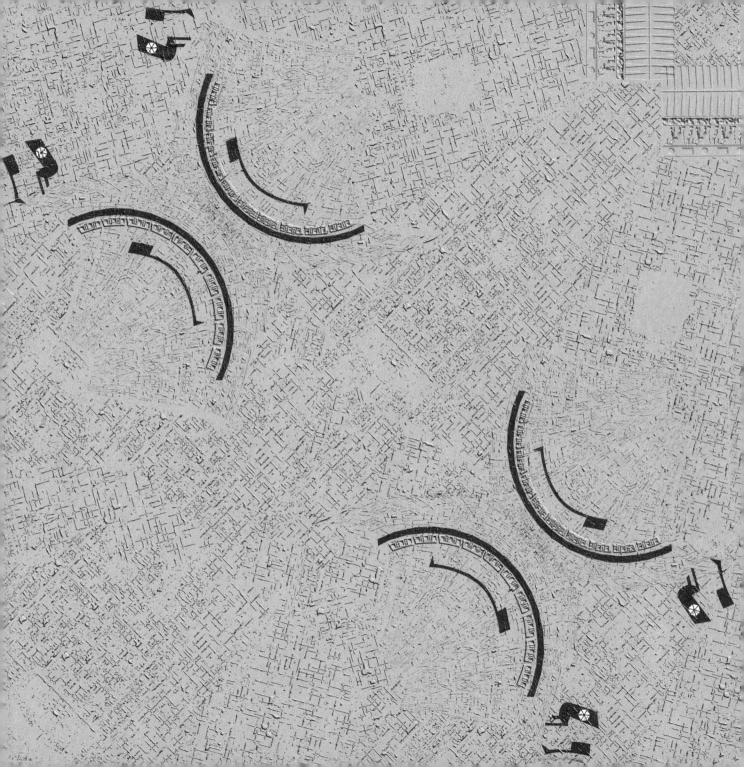

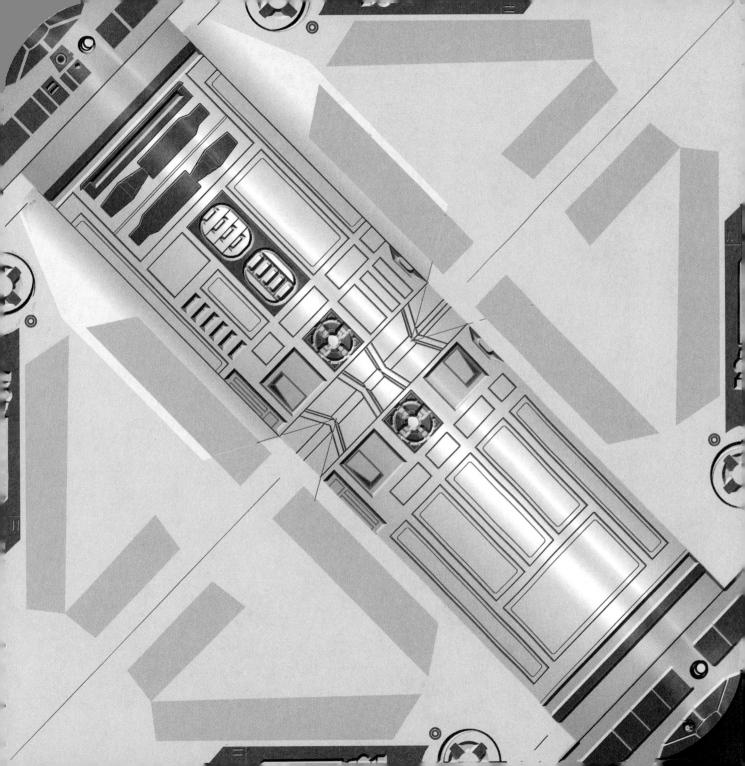

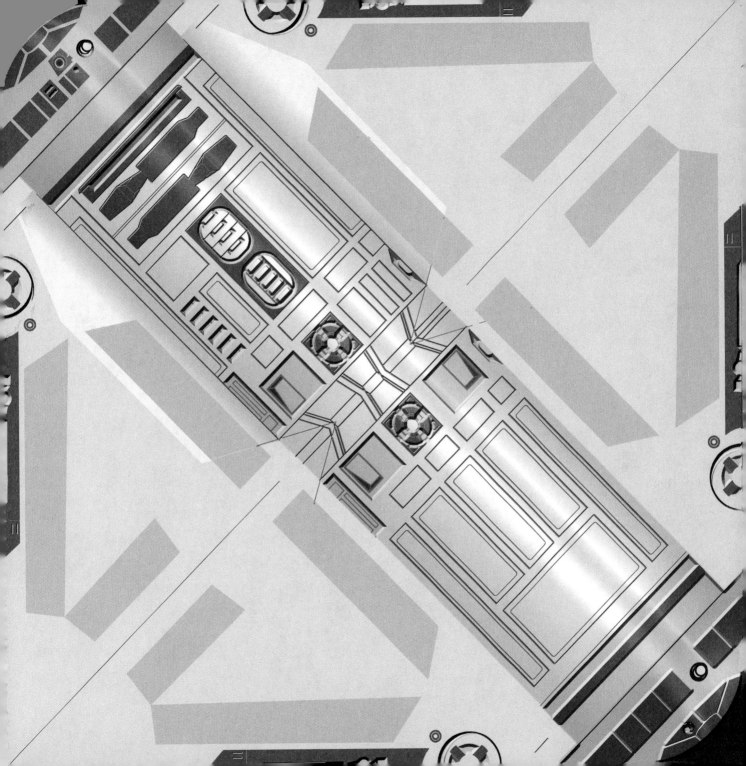

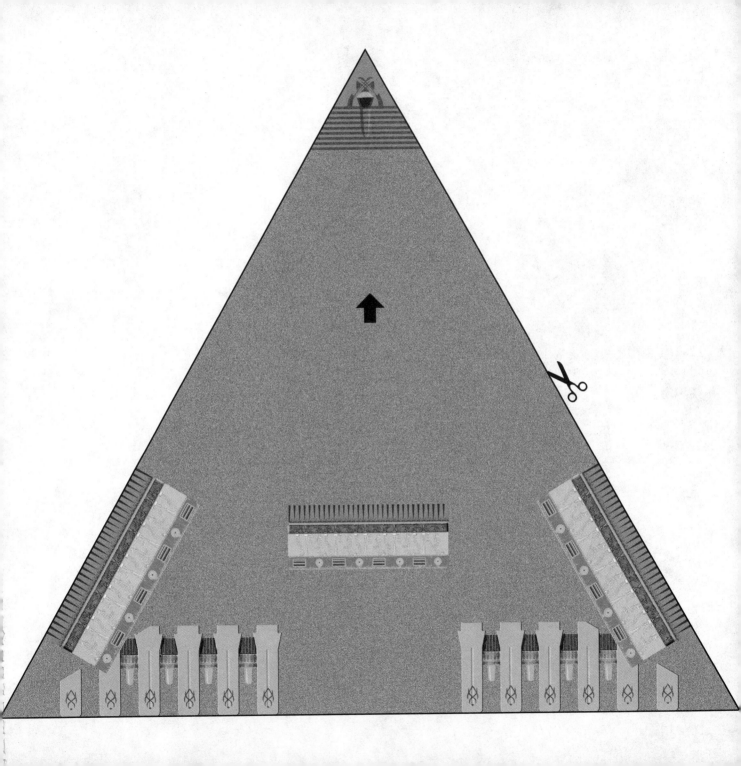

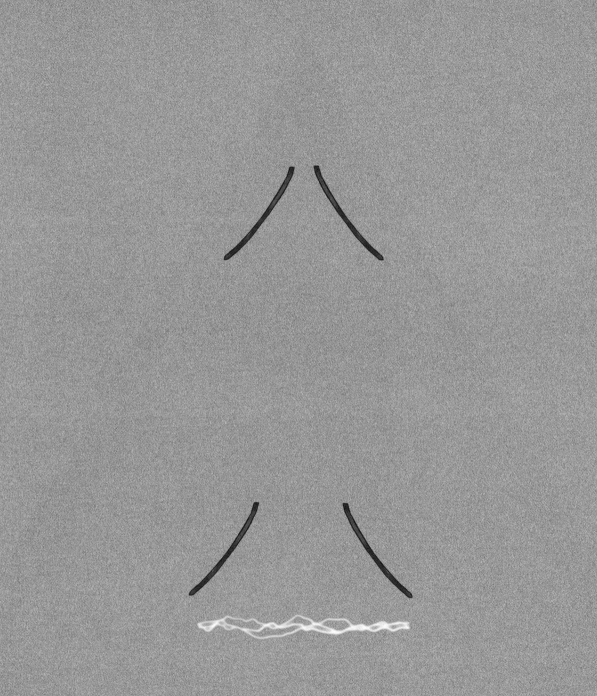

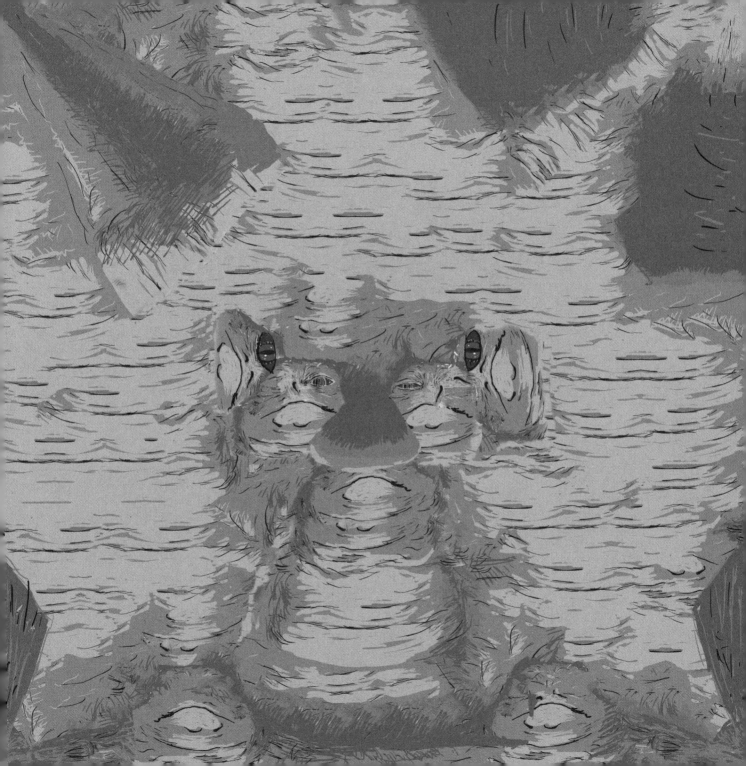

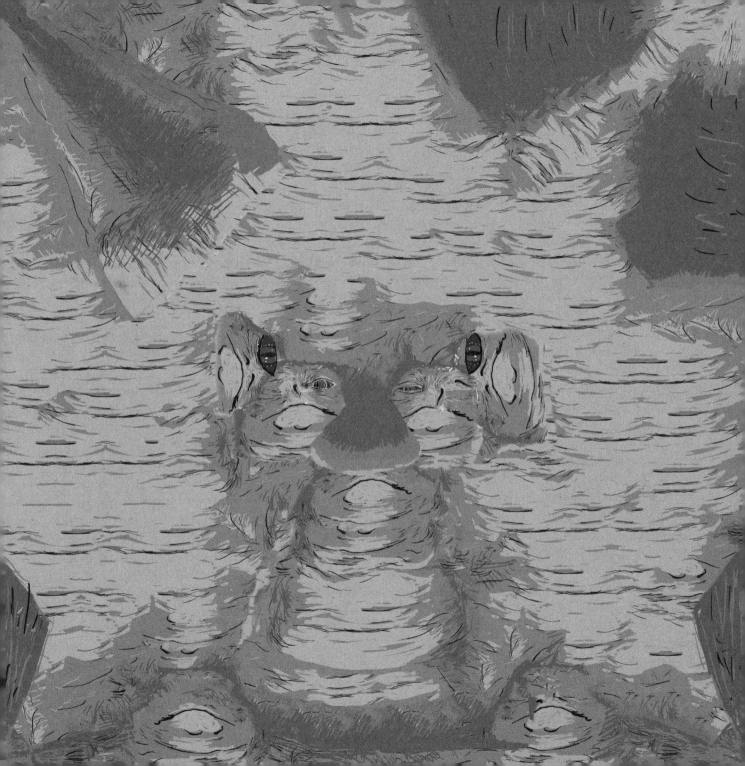

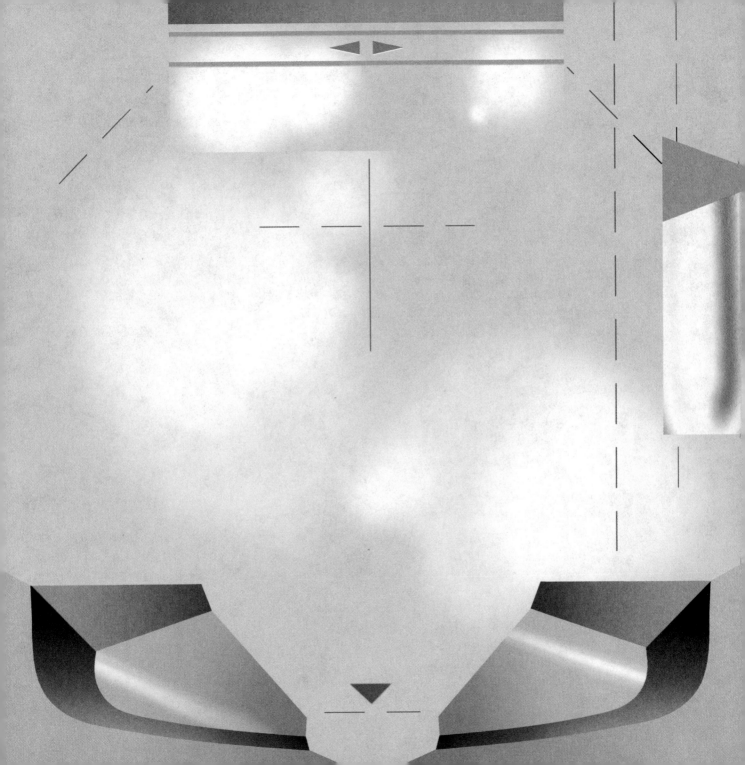

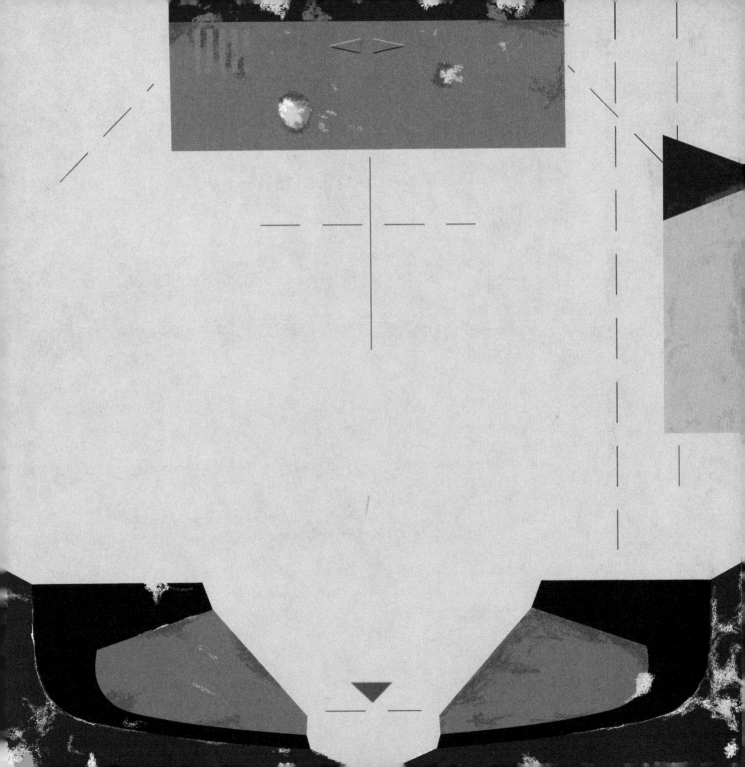

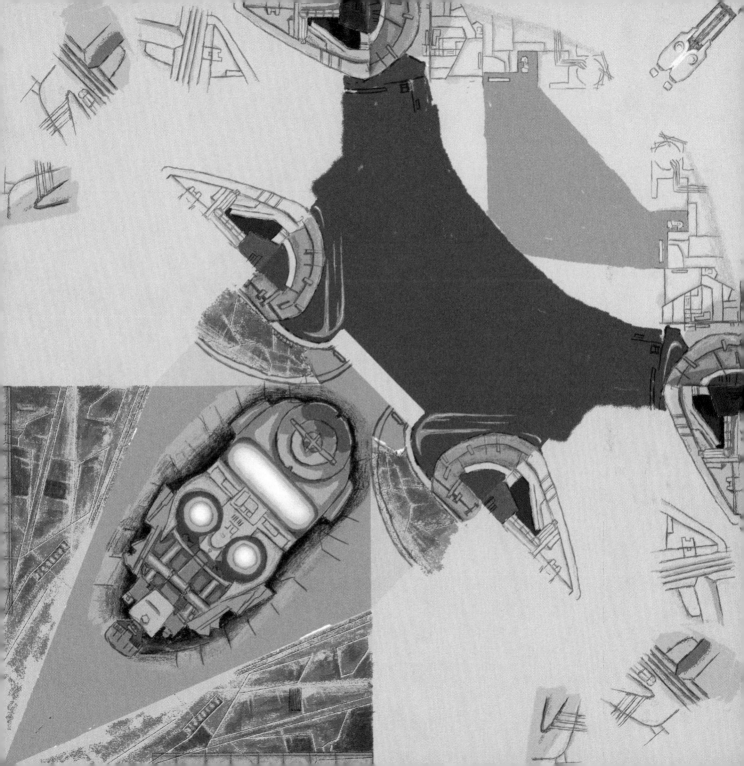

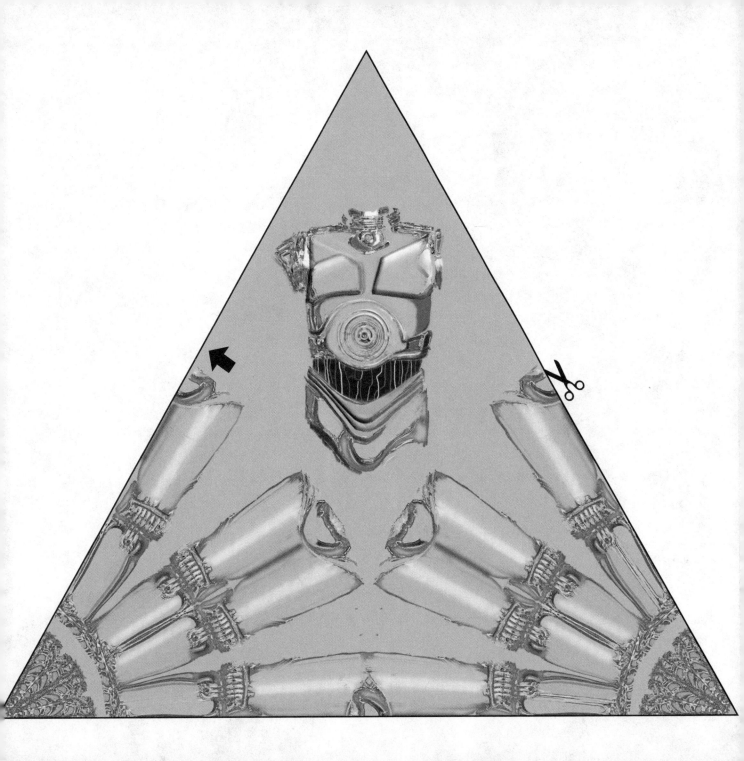

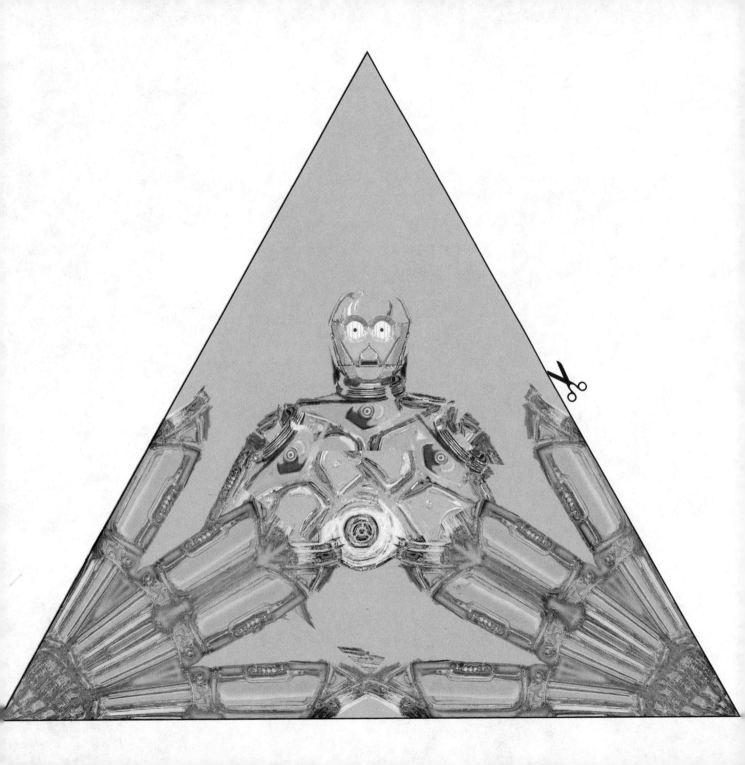

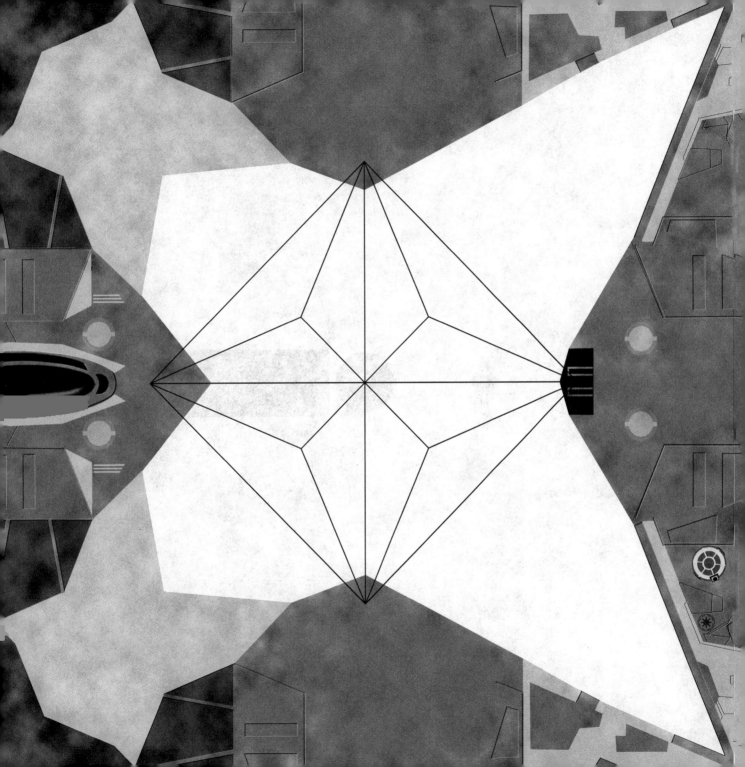

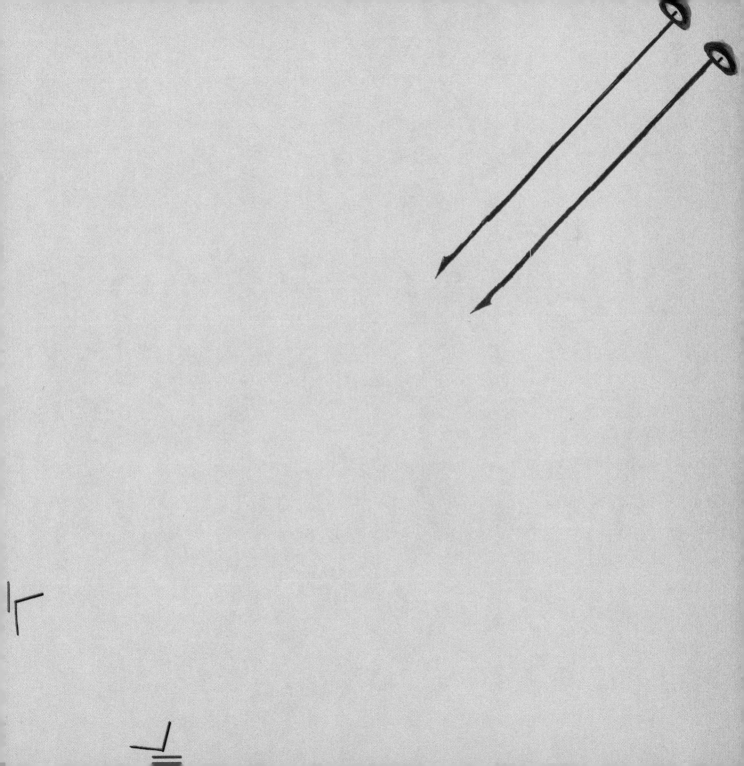

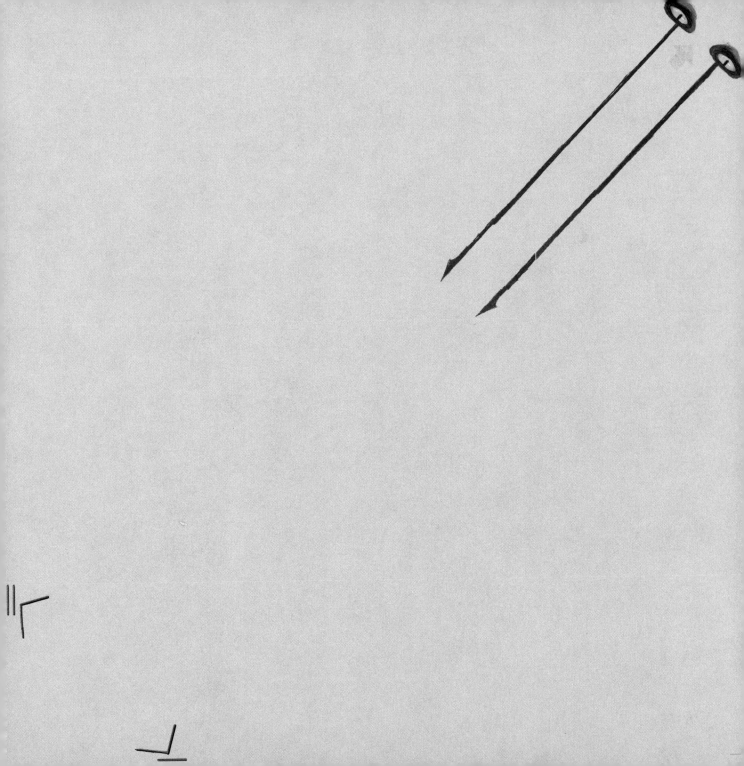

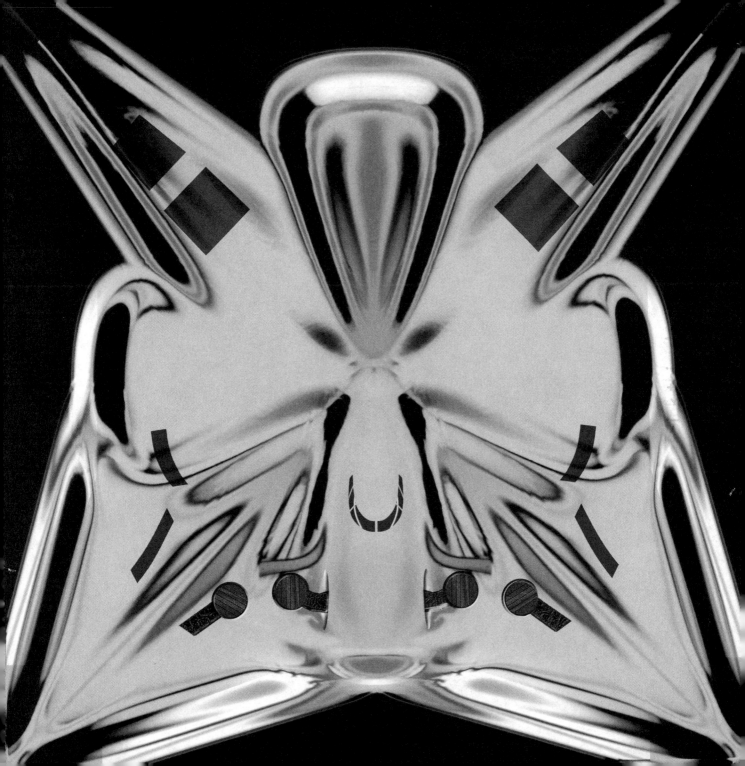

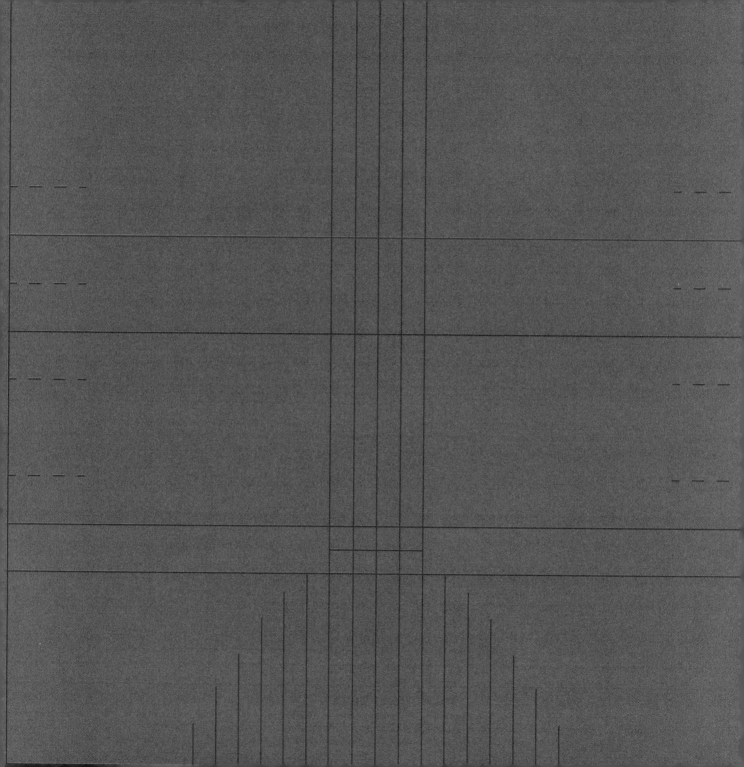

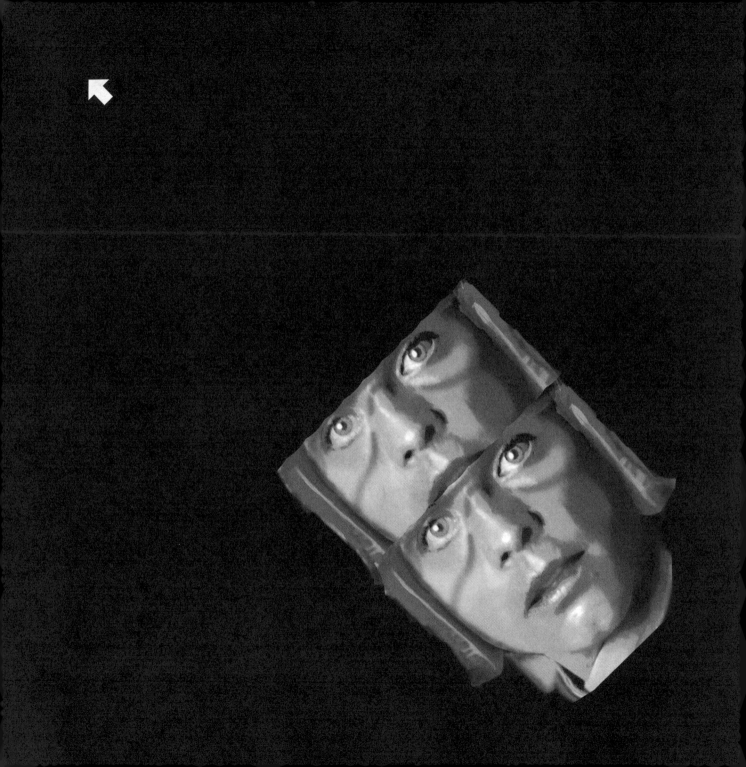

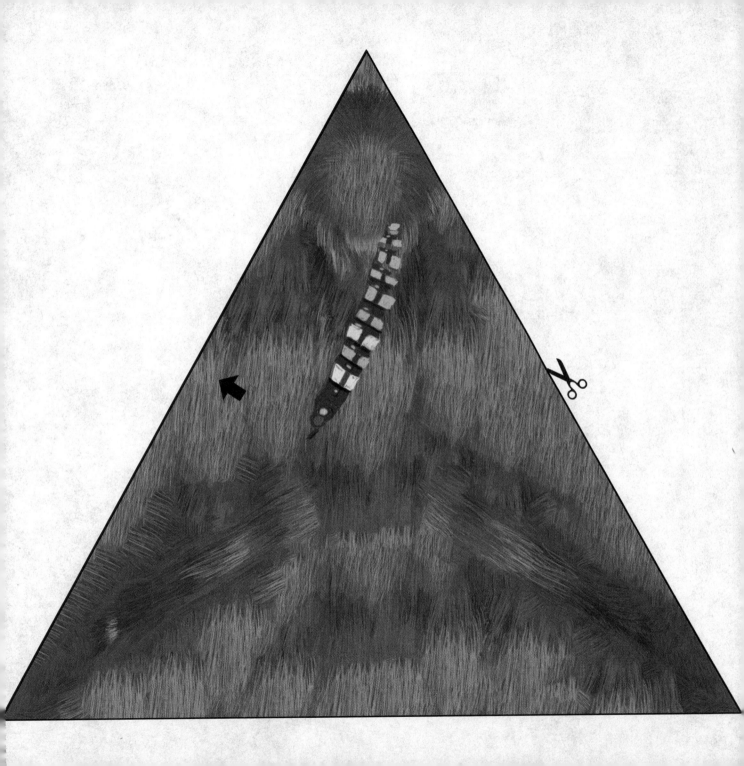

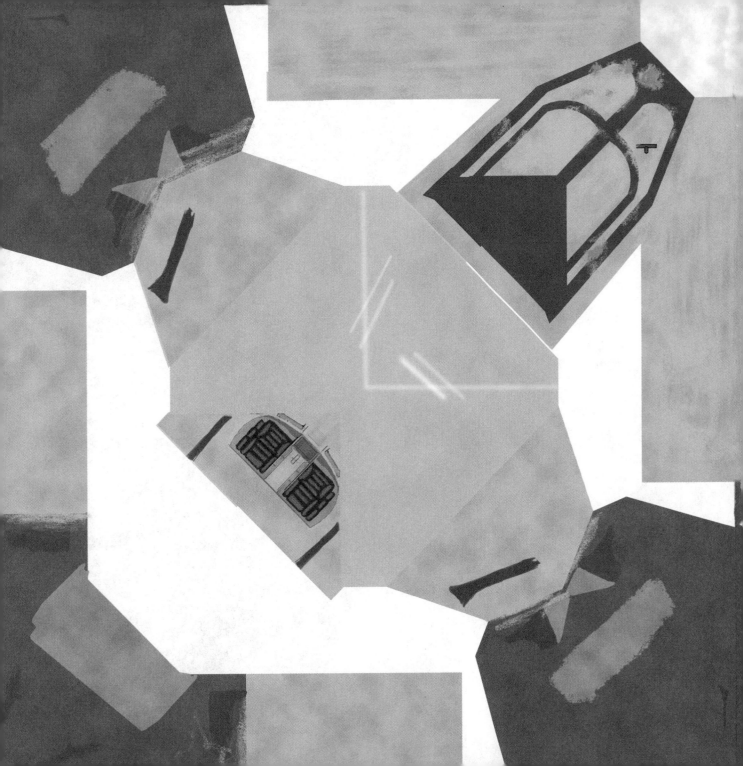

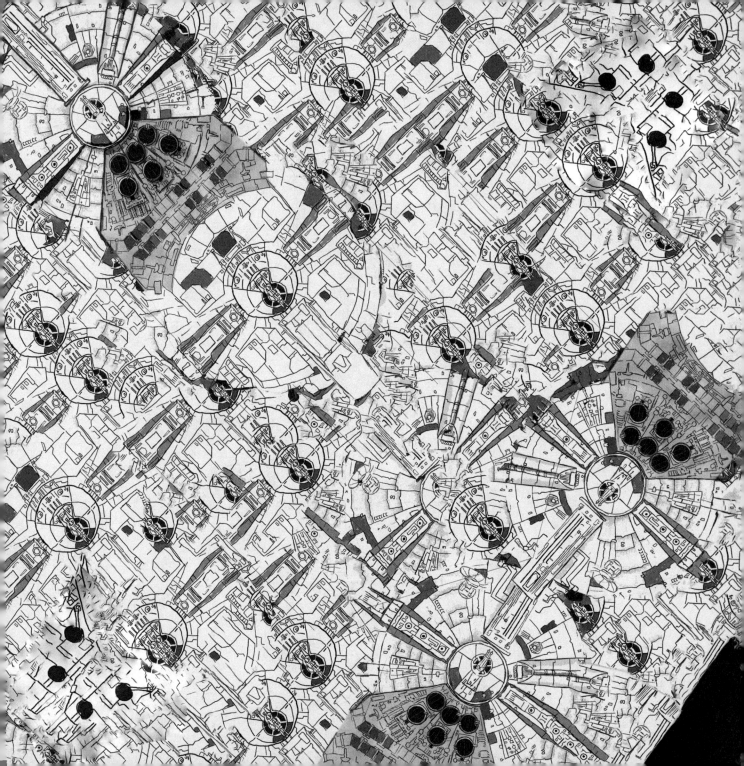

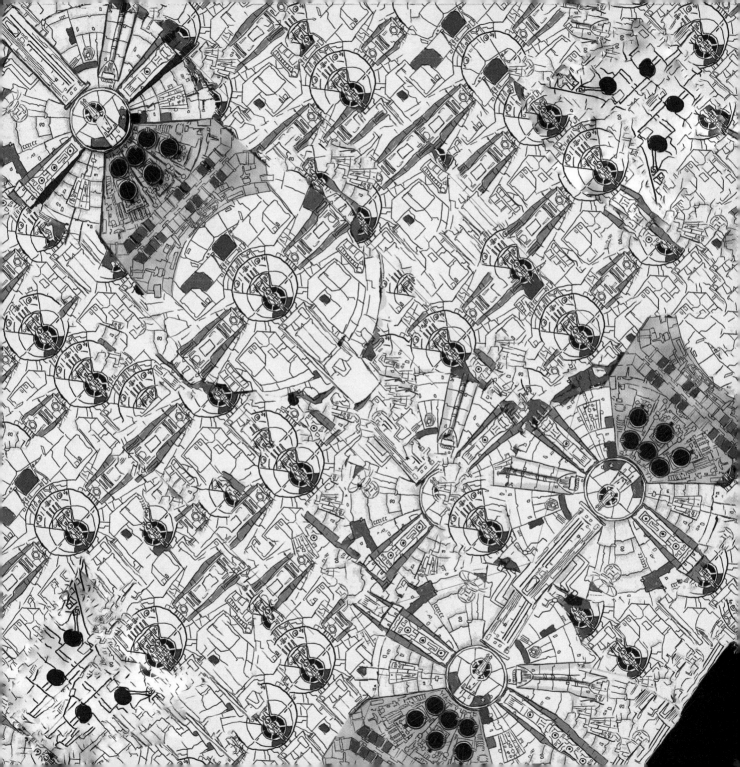

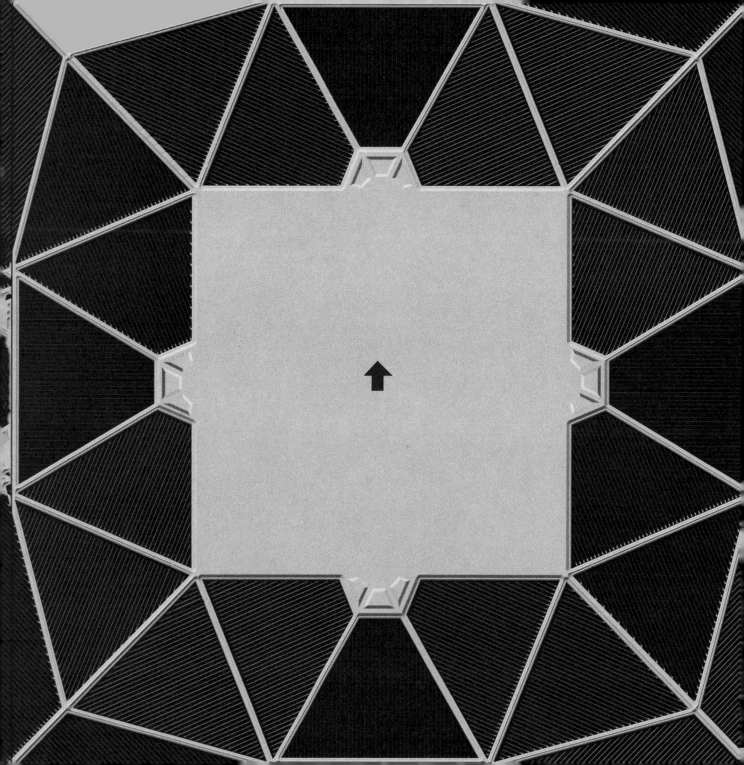

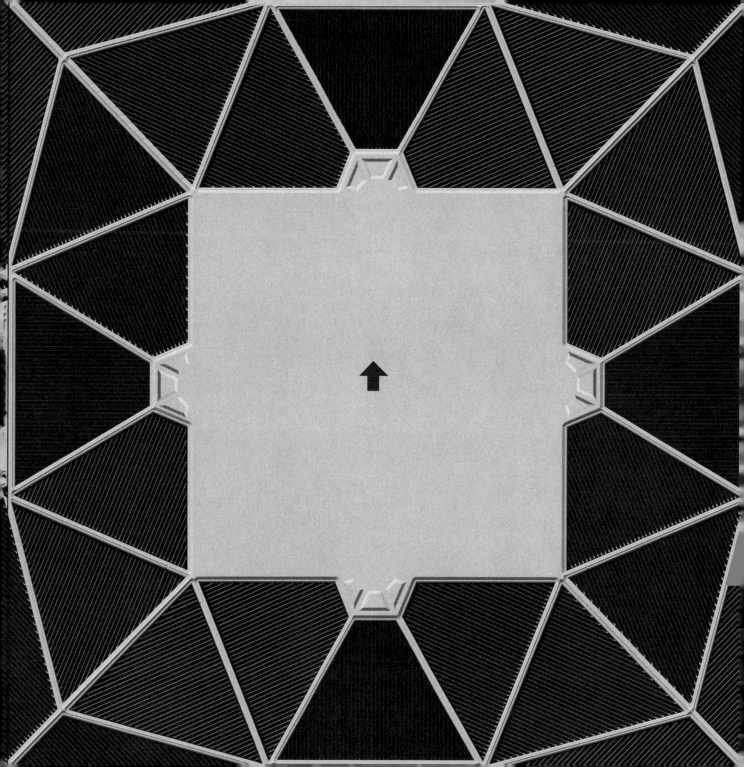

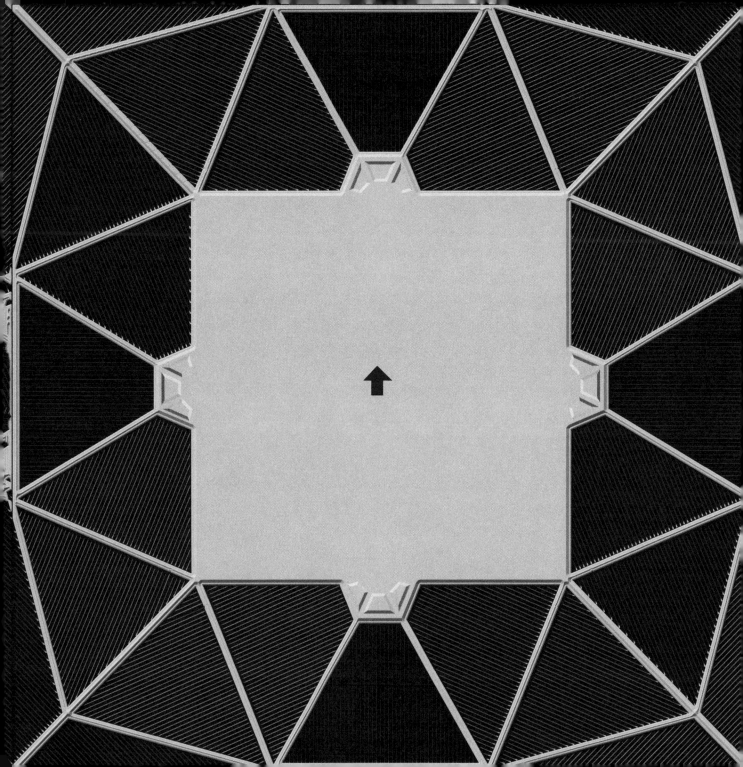

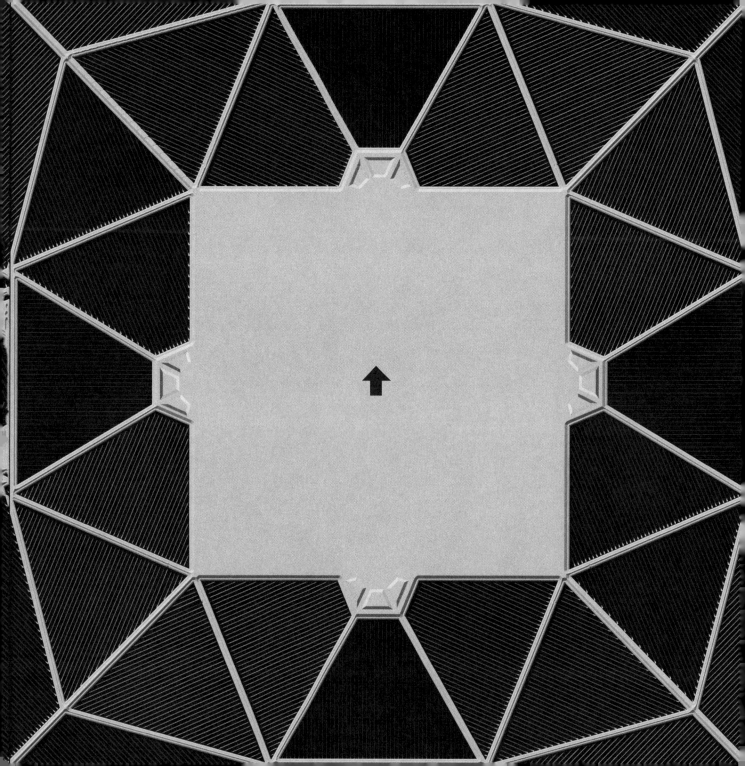

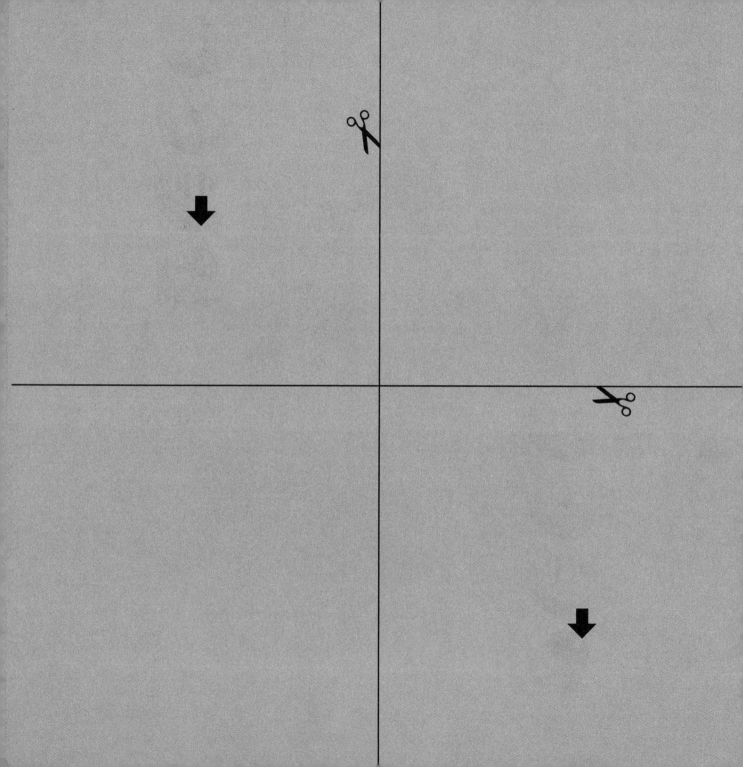

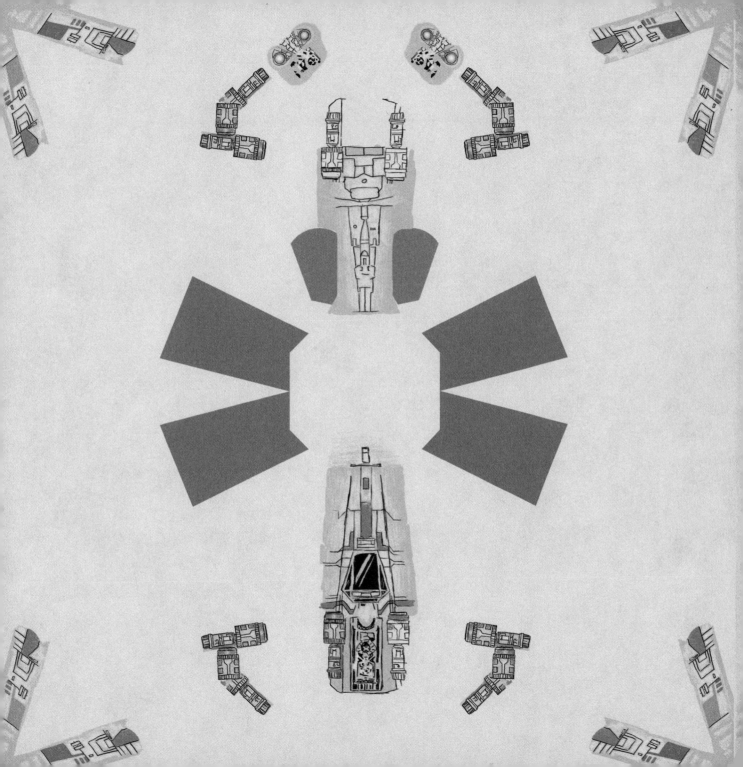

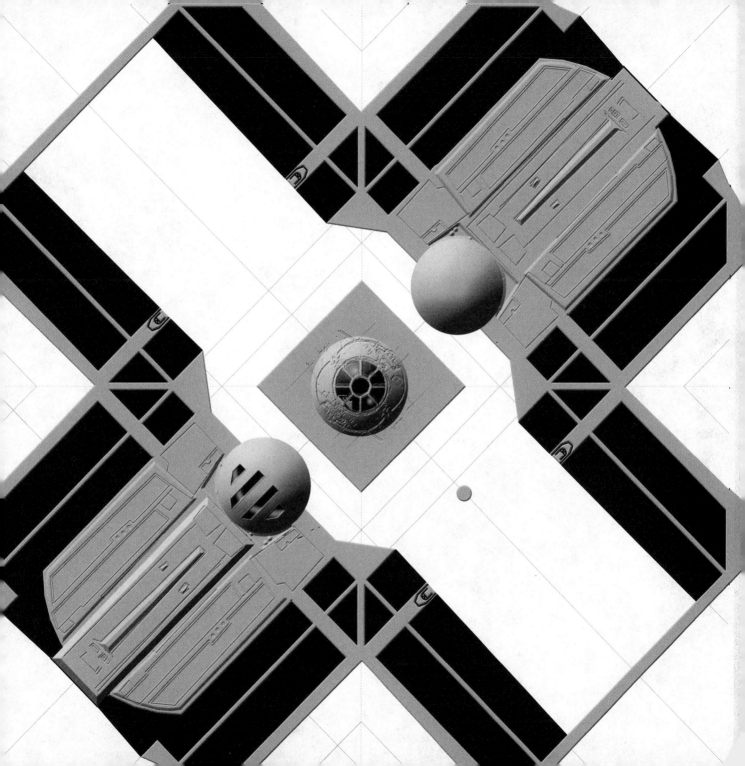